D1259651

An urgent collection of essays by first- and second-generation immigrants, exploring what it's like to be othered in an increasingly divided America

From Trump's proposed border wall and travel ban to the marching of white supremacists in Charlottesville, America is consumed by tensions over immigration and the question of which bodies are welcome. In this much-anticipated follow-up to the bestselling UK edition, hailed by Zadie Smith as 'lively and vital', editors Nikesh Shukla and Chimene Suleyman hand the microphone to an incredible range of writers whose humanity and right to be in the USA is under attack.

Chigozie Obioma unpacks an Igbo proverb that helped him navigate his journey to America from Nigeria. Jenny Zhang analyses cultural appropriation in 90s fashion, recalling her own pain and confusion as a teenager trying to fit in. Fatimah Asghar describes the flood of memory and emotion triggered by an encounter with an Uber driver from Kashmir. Alexander Chee writes of a visit to Korea that changed his relationship to his heritage. These writers, and the many others in this singular collection, share powerful personal stories of living between cultures and languages while struggling to figure out who they are and where they belong.

By turns heartbreaking and hilarious, troubling and uplifting, the essays in *The Good Immigrant USA* come together to create a provocative, conversation-sparking, multivocal portrait of America now.

THE
GOOD
IMMIGRANT
USA

THE
GOOD
IMMIGRANT
USA

26 Writers Reflect on America

EDITED BY
NIKESH SHUKLA and
CHIMENE SULEYMAN

dialogue
books

DIALOGUE BOOKS

First published in the United States in 2019 by Little, Brown and Company
First published in Great Britain in 2019 by Dialogue Books

10 9 8 7 6 5 4 3 2 1

A CIP catalogue record for this book is available from the British Library.

ISBN 978-0-349-70036-6

Printed and bound in Great Britain by CPI Group (UK) Ltd, Croydon CR0 4YY

Papers used by Dialogue Books are from well-managed forests and other responsible sources.

Dialogue Books
An imprint of
Little, Brown Book Group
Carmelite House
50 Victoria Embankment
London EC4Y 0DZ

An Hachette UK Company
www.hachette.co.uk

www.littlebrown.co.uk

Contents

For Jitu Shukla and Şehit Süleyman Recep.
For Coco and Sunnie and Mya.

Editors' Note

In 2016 we put out *The Good Immigrant,* a collection of essays by twenty-one British writers of color who spoke about race and immigration. Actor Riz Ahmed talked about performing as a brown Muslim man, not only in auditions but every time he goes through airport security. Journalist Bim Adewunmi broke down what we mean when we talk about "tokenism." Actor and playwright Daniel York Loh spoke sadly of discovering that his only East Asian hero, a masked wrestler called Kendo Nagasaki, was actually a white guy. Each piece was bright and rich and necessary.

When we conceived of the project, it was about trying to diversify publishing. When we talked about the need for better representation in UK publishing, people would ask, "But where are the writers?" Nikesh's answer to that (patronizing, incurious) question was *The Good Immigrant.* Here are some of them, all together in one book, doing what they do best.

The title was a response to the narrative that immigrants are "bad" by default until they prove themselves otherwise. They are job stealers, benefit scroungers, girlfriend thieves, and criminals. Only when they win an Olympic medal, treat you at your local hospital, or rescue a child from the side of a building do they become *good.* We wanted to humanize immigrants, let them tell their own stories and finally be in charge of their own narrative.

What we didn't know at the time was that Brexit was just around the corner, that the immigration debate was about to become truly toxic, and that the far right would use this as their moment to retake center stage in our domestic political conversations. The book inadvertently became a political tool. And a bestseller. And an award winner. And a comfort for people of color in the UK wanting to see themselves reflected somewhere, anywhere, in the culture.

Meanwhile, we looked across the Atlantic and watched a similar resurgence of far-right and white-supremacist rhetoric overtake the United States. By then, Chimene, who was a contributor to the original book, was living in the States and having frequent conversations with writers and artists about the precariousness of being a person from an immigrant background here, in this country of immigrants.

So we decided to talk to some of our favorite writers, actors, comedians, directors, and artists based in America, all with experiences of being first- or second-generation immigrants. We thought it was vital that each of them have an opportunity to express their experiences, as varied and as nuanced and as messy and as precarious as the immigrant experience is all over the world.

Their voices came together to create this book, the US edition of *The Good Immigrant,* in which twenty-six writers reflect on America as they have known it. In doing so, they engage with the most vital question we now face: What do we want America to be? They cannot speak for all immigrants, but their stories illuminate a whole world of experience that is too often hidden from view. The time has come to reclaim the narrative.

Chimene Suleyman and Nikesh Shukla
Summer 2018

THE
GOOD
IMMIGRANT
USA

How to Write Iranian-America, or The Last Essay

Porochista Khakpour

1.

Begin by writing about anything else. Go to the public library in your Los Angeles suburb and ask for *all the great books people in New York City read, please.* Wonder if the reference librarian knows a living writer, and ask her what would a living writer read—*and an American one, please.* When she realizes you are still in the single digits and asks, *Where are your parents, young lady?* don't answer, and demand Shakespeare and take that big book home and cry because you can't understand it. Tomorrow, go back to reading the dictionary a letter at a time and cry because you can't learn the words. (Ask your father if you will cry daily for the rest of your life, and remember his answer decades later: *When you are older you will care less about things.*) Pray to a god you still believe in that you will once more avoid ESL with all its teachers who look to you with the shine of love but the stench of pity: *refugee, resident alien, political asylum, immigrant, foreigner*—the only words you know that you don't want to know.

Write because it's something to do, something your parents will let you do because it looks like homework. Write because one place to live is in your head and it's not broken yet; write because it's something to drown out the sound of their fighting deep into every night. When the second-grade teacher—the teacher your father calls an alcoholic—tells you that you will be an author one day and suggests *The Market Guide for Young Writers,* step right up and call yourself a Young Writer. Decide to really write, and write about anything but Iranian-America. *Ghosts. Victorian girls, maybe ones with tough names. Easter bunnies that are homicidal* (you might have ripped off *Bunnicula*). *Candy. White girls. More white girls.* (Even then you understood sales.) Worry about the fact that your family won't be able to afford a computer and worry about how your fingers get stuck in between the keys of a yellow typewriter your father brought back from Iran, and learn that the only way for your brain not to spiral in worry is to write.

Worry about how you, Young Writer, will ever get to New York City, until you do. Get a scholarship to a fancy college with writers and *writing workshops,* a thing you've heard of, full of other students told they'd be an author one day. Ignore the dorm politics and the suitemates who tell you their dad paid for you to be there, and write, write about anything else. *Los Angeles. The devil. Literary theory. Art. The East Village. White men. And more white men.* Become known as a writer there, a writer who doesn't write about that, in a time when everyone is talking identity. No identity for you, you tell yourself, you tell them. Wear black and big glasses and smoke cigarettes, because you are a New York Young Writer, and that can be anyone. When your favorite professor, senior year, fails your paper on modernism that you worked on for weeks, when she tells you that she can tell English is your second language, when she tells you that maybe writing is not for you, that maybe you need to go into a field like those new *Iranian studies fields*—you keep imagining these *fields* like the villages of your homeland they label third world—go to your dorm and expect to cry but don't. Chain-smoke a pack of cigarettes and never forget her words and commit yourself to writing more, writing more about anything else.

Years later, attend another prestigious college for grad school, and spend long hours with a famous writer as your professor and advisor who tells you to forget that other professor, that you are a writer, that you can do this. Hold on to her words and almost miss it when she says, *But why don't you write what you know?* Thank her as you always do and hope she doesn't see your tears—*Writing what I know was never my thing,* you whisper. Keep turning in stories about anything else. *Math. Chaos theory. Rape.* (The time you were raped but in a sci-fi premise; the time you were raped in a fantasy premise; the time you were raped in something they call metafiction.) *Dogs. Suicidal people. Suicidal people with dogs. 9/11,* which gets a little too close to writing what you know, but keep reminding them it was because you are a New Yorker, not because you are a Middle Easterner, that you felt the trauma; keep reminding them the hijackers were not Iranian. When they tell you they don't know what you are anyway, don't say a word, just keep working harder than they ever will and tell yourself you will beat the ones who hurt you most for that fellowship for another year. Get the fellowship and avoid all their eyes.

When your advisor suggests you work on a novel—that you are, after all, a novelist—hear *novel* like a curse: an arranged marriage and a death sentence, all that unknown potential for devotion to writing anything else.

2.

Until suddenly you can't write about anything else. Sit in your first apartment without a roommate and realize you have nothing else to write about for the span of a novel. Hate yourself and it and then go ahead and write it, your Iranian-America, because no one else will see it. This is your first real novel, and what do you know? You are a fellow at the most famous university in Baltimore, which doesn't pay you enough to teach, so you add on being a hostess at a bistro where the parents of your students go, sometimes with the tenured professors of your department, who pretend they don't see you as they kiss and hug the owner, who sexually harasses you every day. Why would a word you write matter?

Quit smoking, start smoking, quit again, start again.

And watch it come out, more and more in every draft: anger with your parents, frustration with your blood, anxieties surrounding the somehow still-new land—all that is Iranian-America. Let your truth come out hard and fast and untranslatable because no one else will see it anyway.

3.

Until they do. Four years later, after all sorts of troubles, it is your first novel and it is published and you are *Miss Literary Iranian-America*, a friend jokes. *First Iranian-American novelist,* a journalist mistakenly writes, while another calls your debut novel the first work that is entirely Iranian-American, all diaspora with no Iran setting, which gets closer to the truth but you want to think still not close enough. Who can even tally who they ignored before you? When they ask you to represent the Iranian diaspora in Los Angeles, start by explaining you grew up a half hour and many realities away from Tehrangeles, that your family could never afford those areas, that you were raised in a tiny apartment in the low-income district of a small suburb, with no Iranian people.

When they ask you to do it anyway, go through with it. Regret quitting smoking. Try to speak of other things. *But about Iranian-Americans,* they always go, and a friend who is tired of your sighs tells you, *Look, you did that to yourself. It's all in your novel.* Say, *Fair enough,* and start smoking again.

Around Persian New Year, months after your first novel comes out, start to run out of money again. Old problem but maybe now a new solution, you think. Ask friends if they know someone at the most respected newspaper in the country—the venerable paper where they gave you a very good review of your debut novel. Pitch a piece on Iranians celebrating Persian New Year that 2008. Your angle: being Iranian in a bad time to be Iranian. Think, *When was there ever a good time to be Iranian here?* and pitch it anyway. Hear nothing back and tell yourself you and your Iranian-America are not yet worthy of that newspaper.

Be more shocked than gracious a few months later when, out of nowhere, an editor of another section of that very paper writes you and mentions he is a fan of your work and would you like to contribute an essay to this author series on summer? You can't believe it—this editor has acknowledged your novel and yet is not asking you to write a particular thing about Iranian-America. But when you sit down to write, you surprise yourself: It's about your mother and you, and so it's about Iranian-America. Feel slightly defeated—*Writing what I know was never my thing,* you know you used to whisper—but a part of you anticipates they will want this, and they do.

Behold the awe of everyone around you, behold your own awe: You are in your dream paper, an essayist suddenly. Editors who never heard of you or your novel start asking for your essays of Iranian-America. Soon you are back in that same paper with another essay about, of all things, Barbie's fiftieth anniversary, and somehow you make it also about Iranian-America. You've learned to interview your parents and dig up whatever they will give you from their past and add that to messy memories of your childhood and glue it all to-gether: an essay on Iranian-America! Be amazed at how your formula sometimes helps you work out some things, be amazed at how it sometimes seems to help others. Remind yourself this can't last. Iranian-Americans from all over the country write you and thank you, and you tell everyone this was a nice run—you did your part—and now you will go back to what you were meant to write: anything else.

4.

Except you don't. They ask and you keep writing it. Tell yourself this is your new life every time an essay comes out in that venerable paper of yours—you start to call it *yours* because three-figure checks must mean love if two-figure checks mean like, or so you tell yourself. Oc-casionally try to remind them you were a journalist before all this, a writer who wrote about music and art and fashion and books, but no one remembers or cares anymore. Editors start asking for a collection of essays, but you think, *I've just begun.* Tell them in 2009 you're just entering your thirties—what do you know?

Know you're an essayist and know you can't back out now. During an interview someone asks you why essays, and you remind them you write fiction, and they ask again why essays, and you joke about them finding you, and they ask again why essays, and you stumble on another answer: *Service.* That somehow your people are not visible, these three decades of being in the US, and people have needed you, and while you can't speak for everyone, you can speak some part of this truth. *Service? Service.* Afterward, bum the few cigarettes the interviewer offers and smoke through a silence you did your best to create.

Start to wish other Iranian-Americans would write essays; even try to introduce the few who seem interested to editors, but the editors always ask for more essays from you. How many essays can you write, you wonder, but every time one comes out, you start to see how they see it, and you see more. Step back from yourself and spin absolutely everything from the lens of Iranian-Americana. An Iranian-American sensibility, an Iranian-American outfit, an Iranian-American state of mind, Iranian-American flora and fauna, an Iranian-American bowl of goddamn fruit. Watch yourself pitch the editor at the venerable publication an essay on the hit TV show *Thirtysomething,* a show you loved, and because in 2009 it's a big deal that it's out on DVD, and it seems like something to watch in your thirties now. Hear the editor in your head long before your real editor asks you if you can include your Iranian-American family in it, and catch yourself saying, *Yes, of course,* and do it, and never imagine years later you will teach that essay of yours as a mistake. Consider later that maybe you knew and didn't care, you knew the *service* and moreover you knew your function: you were not just writing Iranian-America, maybe you were helping them create it.

Write the Persian New Year piece you once wanted to, though it's no reported piece but a personal essay—that's what they want and that's what you deliver. By this point your parents know why you are asking when you call; they have gotten used to the fact that you will write about them and anything else Iranian-America. When friends and family begin to marvel at all this, Miss Literary Iranian-America, don't you deny it—smile and be grateful and lie that this is exactly what you dreamed of one day.

When another section editor of that same paper emails you (a section that pays a lot more—if three is love, four figures must mean marriage), accept their request for a new essay, knowing you can write an essay on absolutely anything for these people, provided it's about Iranian-America—which it will be. Muslim reality TV the first time, Iranian reality TV the second time, *But we're big fans of your essays, so can you make it an essay, not a review?* They want feelings, not facts; you know this by now. Write the first and write the second and duck all the love hurling itself at you, a love you can't feel, a love you might fear.

Writing Iranian-America turns out to have some downsides, but you think you know how to handle them. When Iranians write you and say you are not Iranian enough for them, thank them, and when others say you are too Iranian for them, thank them too. Too pro-IRI and too Royalist, too anti-Iranian and too nationalistic, too relatable and not relatable enough, maybe neocon and maybe communist—and where is your name from? Are you really Iranian? Why are you not married? Are both your parents really Iranian? Why do you say Iranian and not Persian? Why are you embarrassing us? Why are you not writing happy things? Why are there so many jokes? What do you think of us? Are we good or bad? Are you good or bad? Why do you call us brown? Why are we not brown to them? Why do you not look more white? Why do you look so white? What god is your god? Why can't you write in a way I can understand? Why do you write at all? Why don't you stop writing? Why don't you stop smoking? When you get those messages, learn to let the senders say what they need to say. Occasionally engage, and often don't. *Service.*

Learn to live with hating yourself. Learn to live with hating Iranian-America. Imagine the hell of dying in America while your parents envision the beauty of dying in Iran, and you wonder if there was ever anything in between for you.

5.

When your editors leave the section where they first published you and when the paper experiences horrible layoffs, think this is it, what you've been waiting for—your run is over. Tell everyone you know it's been great, four years as an essayist of Iranian-America! Imagine all the topics you were supposed to write about, but you can't quite remember what they were. Try to remember and fail. *Hip-hop? White girls? Bars? Wars?* Try to remember and fail.

When, a few years later, new editors are back in that old first section of the venerable paper that made you Young Essayist, pause at the first line of their email to you. A pitch in the greeting, a story you know: an Iranian band in Brooklyn has been the victim of a murder-suicide. For days you've considered reporting on this, thinking of the right venue, but now here is the op-ed section again wanting a personal essay. *It seems to me like there might be something interesting to say, about the Iranian expat community, the American Dream betrayed, or something along those lines.* Think about the editor's take for a moment, and think about how you can't: how this story has nothing to do with assimilation but is about a deranged person from your part of the world who shot some people from your part of the world but is much more about gun control and America and its dream not betrayed at all. Ask her if you can face America here, not just Iranian-America, in the only piece you can write; pitch this to her and know the answer.

Remind yourself that you have been chronically ill for many years and buying cigarettes is no longer an option.

Write for other sections of that paper—the Book Review, where you sometimes wonder why they don't give you topics related to Iranian-America—until once again, in 2017, another editor from that section writes you, this time with a name that is definitely of Iranian-America. When she says she wants a Persian New Year piece, a sweet nostalgia piece, remind her that four years ago, many editors ago, you wrote one. Tell her you have nothing happy to write this year and you weren't going to write this and tell her your idea of a New Year in the time of the Trump administration's Muslim ban. Remember your first Persian New Year pitch to this paper: being Iranian in a bad time to be Iranian, and now, a decade later, witness that same silence with awe. When she writes, *We're not looking for something excessively political and angry for our token Nowruz piece,* know that you will take this piece elsewhere and it will live. Try to put away any disappointment you have in her, your fellow Iranian-American, because ultimately both you and she are microscopic cogs in the venerable paper's unfathomable machinery. Both you and she have come this far, both you and she might never know exactly why.

Observe others writing about Iranian-America. Encourage and amplify the many voices and viewpoints of your people, now nearly four decades as a minority in this America, finally with their own stories surfacing too. Enjoy reading their accounts, until readers warn you against your own enthusiasm. *I feel like they're ripping you off,* go messages from the concerned, and you don't know what to make of them. Against your better judgment, read more closely. Decide you will pretend not to notice. Pretend you are better than this competitive game they have set up for all of you to destroy yourselves in. Pretend so hard that you wonder if you ever even knew how that game works anyway.

Pretend to chain-smoke a couple of packs of cigarettes, killing hours in bottomless depression—pretend you're all smoke and ashes, let it burn right through you—and pretend Iranian-America is all theirs, whoever wants this wreckage.

6.

Tell yourself this is The Last Essay, but remind yourself of all the other Last Essays. Wonder how much more of this you can take. Count that out of seventy pieces of nonfiction you've written since your first book came out in 2007, forty-eight have had to do with Iranian-America. Ask yourself if it's too much or too little, given where America is at, still at. Watch the news and marvel at how your entire life they have obsessed over your country of origin, and continue to. Wonder if you and your family will end up in Muslim Camp after all. When people look at you with the pity and the regret again—*refugee, resident alien, political asylum, immigrant, foreigner*—let them have it, and let yourself take it. What has changed but nothing at all?

Write about it and make sure you keep writing about it. Plan out three more books, and call it the end; each and every one is about Iranian-America. Write all the secrets like every essay is a suicide note. One reveals your Zoroastrian name is a fraud and you are a Muslim, and watch everyone applaud it, from all sorts of people online to your own father, who gave you your name. Wonder if anyone is reading properly. Put *Iranian-American refugee* in your Twitter profile, the way all the other refugees are doing. Question if this is empowering. Imagine you've been throwing yourself off a cliff every time you've been writing, but it's hard to know if you are killing yourself or trying to fly. Wonder if a cliché like that is all you've got. Wonder if the death you've been imagining is just you becoming a bad writer.

Watch yourself making posts on Facebook and Twitter more than ever in 2017. Watch Americans at first dive into it and then, over time, walk away from it, until you start to find yourself asking white people to repost or echo the same sentiment so your ideas can get heard. Watch white Americans listen to one another but suddenly they are not so sure about your words. Remind them that you know Iranian-America and that they seemed to love reading you—quote your own pieces, send them the links, remind them they knew you—but watch them slowly back away. Watch other friends tell you that you are reading into this, that it's not happening. Watch yourself worry about every word. Watch yourself apologize for things no one understands. Watch yourself think only in Farsi, like this—America—never happened. Watch yourself burn out on the worry, and remind yourself of where this essay started: begin by writing about anything else. *End by thinking about anything yourself,* you tell yourself, but look at how you're all out of jokes about smoking.

7.

Be a little astonished that there is still one more section of The Last Essay that is not The Last Essay, you and your editor and whoever is still here must know by now. Notice you've learned a few things about essays in this decade, like the ones you must write will write themselves for you. Remind yourself that when the performance is honest two things happen: the essay will feel like it's killing you and the ending will not be what you thought it might be. Learn to respect more than resent those parallel planes of living and the rendering of living.

Note that you're not thinking about this when you read and then reread an email you receive late one night a few weeks after this first Persian New Year of the Trump administration, from an Iranian-American aspiring writer who tells you your work has saved her life, a woman twenty years your junior who asks if you have any words of advice. You thank her and feel embarrassed by your discomfort in reading her praise, and you try to channel her joy and enthusiasm and you fail, and you draft an email where you tell her to run, but don't say which way. *One word: Run. Run with everything you've got, dear reader.*

Delete the email and start over, and watch weeks and weeks go by. One day open the draft and see the word *love.* Try to delete it, but it won't go away. Tell yourself your delete key is broken and get it fixed and still try. *Love.* Tell yourself it was sent to you for a reason—laugh at the audacity, the idiocy, the cliché—and one day, many years into a version of a future you might get, go as far as to grow into it again.

Thank you, the young woman writes. *I think I know what to do.*

You wait for more, but that's it.

Swimmer

Nicole Dennis-Benn

I wanted more.

Shortly after I declared this fact, my father left me at the entrance of my dormitory, perhaps thinking that the college with ivy running up and down red-brick buildings was like a five-star hotel. That there would be sheets and pillows and comforters, and robes, and toiletries arranged just-so on a bathroom counter inside a spacious room. The only things he left me with were his words: "Know yuh place, keep quiet, an' work hard." I stood in my place with my one suitcase and watched him leave in his work van, which had all the tools he used to fix rich people's pools in Long Island when he wasn't driving his taxi. The van stood out on campus next to the Volvos, Lexuses, and BMWs. As the first in my immediate family to go to college, I already knew, or had given myself some reason to believe, that I was no longer my father's problem. I looked around, almost bewildered that I was by myself—far away from my father's apartment in Hempstead and definitely far away from home in Jamaica with my siblings, my mother, and my grandmother. I must have been terrified, because I remember standing there outside the dorm building for a very long time. I had a hundred dollars in my pocket, a suitcase, ambition, and no clue.

I could not fault my father for leaving me so abruptly. I was the smart one, the responsible one, the eldest who was going to be a doctor, after all. But as I looked around my new environment, this place where doctors were made, dread, the taste of seawater, set in. "Jus' hol' yuh breath an' kick," he said to me once, during an attempt to teach me how to swim. This was long before he left us to go to America. I was about three years old. He used to take us to the beach and help us float above sea and sand. I remember watching his face as I kicked—a face that remains the same in flashes of memory, bright like the sun, a face that had aged by the time I came to live with him in America at the age of seventeen. I had left home for more or less the same reasons he did—the ability to thrive, the desire for upward mobility—and though unlike him I didn't have children to support, I knew deep down that I'd want them with a woman.

Now here I was by myself on a college campus where I was expected to ride the waves. The swimming lessons returned to me then, as I stood on the steps of my dormitory. Somehow I remembered the day I mistakenly opened my mouth to catch my breath and swallowed a gulp of seawater—a terrifying moment, which still nauseates me to this day. And though I cannot swim today, I've managed to remember the lessons.

The campus was beautiful in the sunlight (although, I would later learn that the sky turns dove gray in October and remains that way until May). Parents were helping their children move into their dorms. Fathers were carrying heavy boxes, bean-bag chairs, shelves; mothers cradled special lamps, pillows, fleece comforters, and bags of snacks; siblings lagged behind, their eyes wandering around the manicured campus where they might end up, and where their parents had probably met. Once inside, I looked back at my quiet, empty room with my one suitcase.

The rest of that first semester on campus was a blur. My roommate never showed up, so it was just me in my room. I spent the financial aid money that was supposed to be for books on sheets, comforters, toiletries, and other things I needed for my dorm. I drank soda and ate pizza until I stopped eating altogether. I found a spot in the library where I could scribble poems about home inside my biology textbooks. I began to miss home, my family, my real friends. And though I was feeling this way, I could never tell anyone. For how could one be sad in America? How could one complain about an opportunity to go away to college knowing they'd come out with a degree from an Ivy League, which would forever establish them in their new country?

I began to miss the community college where I'd started in Long Island, the place my father had thought would help me to acculturate. There I sat in classes with other immigrants who had already settled in America. They were pursuing dreams of careers in nursing, physical therapy, radiology, teaching, as the head sales associate at a department store—sensible jobs that could allow them to send money back home or help them to afford rent in homes where they lived with other family members in Queens or the Long Island suburbs. If they had other passions, they never mentioned them. It was common sense not to. I learned very early that to be an immigrant in this country meant I didn't have the luxury of choosing what I wanted, only what was necessary. Following this rule, many of my classmates at the community college strove to complete their two-year degree, accepting that it might take four years given that most worked two jobs or more. They knew, too, they couldn't afford for their ambitions to be bigger than their pockets unless their ambitions would prove to be lucrative; and they knew their American Dream was really about independence. And so, I chose medicine.

I read books to cope with my new country. I stayed in the library until late at night. Later, I applied for a job at the school library so I could stay even longer, running my hands along the spines of books as though they were visas in my passport. I yearned for what was in those books—a freedom to go anywhere I pleased without feeling lost, alien. Back in Long Island, it was my writing that had set me free. My stepmother must have resented the idea of me coming to live with them, had found my journal and read about my romantic feelings for women. "Is it true?" my father asked me when she told him. I denied it, but I immediately sought out a college advisor at the community college and told her I wanted to go away. The woman's eyebrows knitted at the center. Very rarely did she come across a student who wanted to go beyond nearby Hofstra University or Adelphi, maybe City College in Manhattan. She was a black American woman with a penchant for elephants. They were all over her office. She gave me a few college brochures, and my index finger landed on one. I had learned about the school from a representative a year before in my high school back home. I was able to afford college prep and SAT classes with the money my father made in America driving a taxi and building pools. So by the time I sat before this woman in her office full of tiny elephants, I was ready to transfer to the place that stood like a castle on a hill far, far away. I was bound to be happy in a place that looked like a fairy tale.

"How far is Ithaca from here?" I asked the advisor.

"About six hours?" she replied. "Five if the roads are clear."

That was all I needed to hear.

I worked extra hard that year, using school as an excuse to stay away from home as much as possible. My stepmother seemed furious that I was allowed to stay. Then she became vocal. She knew—as women *must* know—that she didn't have my father's heart. And she knew—as mothers *must* know—that her real issue had nothing to do with me. There were times I could not return to my father's apartment. He hated confrontation and told me to be the bigger person. "Jus' ignore har." He didn't want to acknowledge what he already suspected to be true about my sexuality, and neither did he want to upset my stepmother any more with my presence. This broke my heart, the fact that my father failed in that moment to stand up for me. I depended on him. And yet as soon as I got my college acceptance, he whisked me off to campus and left me there like a sack of clothes at Goodwill.

My first Thanksgiving away was spent in the home of a literature professor, a regal middle-aged black American woman who wore elaborate shawls, had a shaved head, collected African art, spoke of her trips to West Africa—where she had adopted her beautiful daughter—and reminisced about James Baldwin like she had known him well. I was taken by her, her books, her art, and how she looked me steadily in the eyes with intensity and knowing—the first time anyone had looked at me that way in America—when she said, "You never truly left home. Home is here with you in your memories, which, like the imagination, only belongs to you." Years later I would finally come to understand what she meant. That Thanksgiving break, in the depths of my homesickness and loneliness, she strode up out of the sea and saved me.

I made friends with the other pre-med students, most of whom were Caribbean and African immigrants with aspirations as big as mine. One day at lunch they said I "seemed not to be a part of things," as if my mind was elsewhere. When I looked at them askance, they recounted times when we huddled in the library to study in groups, and how I would stare at them, as though setting myself apart. Little did they know that I stared because I envied them. I envied them because I wished I still wanted what they wanted; I wished I was not carrying this personal burden of making it in America all by myself; I wished I could desire something simply because I was told to desire it. I knew my friends would eventually find out that I was an impostor. "I'm thinking of changing my major," I later blurted to the small group of three, thinking of the books I had seen on the professor's bookshelf and the way I had felt after purging my homesickness with words.

"To what?" Yasmine, a girl from Guyana, asked.

"English," I replied. "With a creative writing minor."

They fell silent. They looked at me as if I was to be pitied. It was obvious from their eyes that they expected me to burst out laughing and say I was joking. Their expressions reminded me of the time not long before when I came out as a lesbian to my friend in high school back home. It was a gutsy move, I knew, but I felt if I kept it inside it would combust and I would be blown to pieces.

My new friends looked at each other, then down at the biology cheat sheets as though the sheets were food that had gone to waste. Chi-Chi, the Nigerian in the group, made a clucking noise and said, "You can't be serious. If you want English, then what you doing here?" She emphasized "here" to remind me that I was taking my opportunity for granted, that we were students at one of the most competitive schools for pre-med in the country, that any first-generation immigrant with the weight of her family on her back would kill to take my spot. This was no joke. This was life or death. After a pause, my friends chuckled softly and shook their heads. The fact that I had revealed this to them was significant. It meant I was beginning to value their friendship and thought they'd understand. It did not take me long to discover that we were all absolutely and mercilessly united by our ambitions to stay afloat on our parents' dreams—the American Dream. We were, after all, the good immigrants. I lowered my head and continued to study, the memory of the ocean rising in my gut. I threw up in the restroom after lunch.

I moved to Ann Arbor, Michigan, for graduate school—the bravest thing a Jamaican immigrant could do, being that it was in the middle of nowhere. Jamaicans tend to like coasts—places where they can slip in and out of the country if need be and be around other Jamaican immigrants. But for me, Ann Arbor was an escape. At the time, I was dating a woman. I thought she was good for me because she was Jamaican. I had never dated a Jamaican woman before then. I thought she was a miracle, the fact that she existed as a Jamaican woman who loved women. We were a miracle together. Never mind that she found it necessary each time we loved to tell me she was straight, never mind that our relationship was a secret, never mind that she spoke extensively about marrying a man someday, never mind that she was the reason I was forced to come out to my mother, who heard me sobbing over one of our many breakups when I visited home. "Two women don't g'waan like dat wid each other. Is she really jus' yuh friend?" she asked. Tired of denying, I told the truth, and sure enough, I was no longer welcomed home.

But that was near the end. In the beginning, I was full of want. I threw myself deeper into the relationship because she was the only thing I had left of home. There weren't many women I could share histories with—a culture, a whole country. She probably chose me for the same reason. "We can't afford to be dis way," she would tell me. I wanted to tell her that we were free to be whatever we wanted in

America. But her mind was already made up. She was also studying to be a doctor, so it was understandable. I had considered this fate too—the expectation to pass as straight in order to be successful. At the time, there were no visible examples of black lesbians, much less Jamaican lesbians, doing well professionally back home or abroad. She wanted to move back home to make a difference in our country. "It's our responsibility!" she would argue. And I wouldn't argue back. I just listened to her talk. It was as though she was convincing herself. She was already deemed a darling back home anyway—one of those overachieving young Jamaicans sent abroad, having been groomed from a young age to be leaders, the ones who diligently rehearsed their roles as replicas of the older generation that still clung to a colonial mindset. For we were supposed to be little ambassadors in training. We were supposed to make our country proud. Be good immigrants. Be great. I knew I couldn't stop her—that I wasn't enough to make her live a lie in her beloved country, which would condemn her truth.

Yet I stayed, because every time she wrapped her arms around me, I disappeared. Pressed against her softness, I rode the undulating waves and opened my mouth, swallowing everything she gave: love, anger, resentment, hate. I wanted her to carry me home, bury me there, inside her. I didn't have the strength to leave. I felt as though I was being physically dragged by one leg in a rip current. In a desperate attempt to save myself from plunging to the bottom of the ocean floor, I latched on to the one thing I had: my ability to write good lies. I had been accepted into graduate school for something I didn't care much for. By the time I managed to crawl out from under the weight of that relationship, I was emotionally bruised, living in the middle of America, alone, where ice sheathed the Great Lakes, where trees seemed barren save for the blackbirds on their branches,

and I bit my tongue and nearly swallowed my own truths, where I
remained frozen.

A year later, I moved to New York City. There was something about
the chaos that calmed me. I was working and living in the basement
of a Brooklyn brownstone with two other women. We were all hustling to make it in our respective careers: Karen as a deejay, Bridgette
in modeling, and me in—well—the closest I could get to medicine,
which was public health. My first job was teaching new mothers in
Brooklyn how to breastfeed. I was horrible at it for obvious reasons—
I didn't have children and have never breastfed. I watched mothers
watching me, wondering how I got the job and what had happened
to the busty no-nonsense middle-aged woman one might imagine
as more qualified for it. They kept looking around for her to walk
through the door, trailing behind me—a shy, skinny twentysome-
thing with baby dreadlocks and a nose ring. My refusal to meet their
gaze confirmed their suspicion. Yet in great weariness (or maybe
pity), they allowed me to demonstrate with the fake breast I carried
around in a book bag what they ought to be doing and how they
ought to be doing it. I pretended to ignore the quiet sniffles of mothers who could not do it. I wish I had known it then, but now I
realize that the closed faces and down-turned mouths were responses
to judgment. I was not the one judging these women—mostly low-
income blacks and Latinas, many of them immigrants—but a society
that deemed them inept mothers. My rent was being paid by the state
based on this fact—at the inexpressible expense of other women's
dignity.

Cornered in my dilemma, I turned to writing. I wrote often,
mostly at night while I could hear the voices of my roommates and

their friends and lovers muffled through my door. All I had were my words. I was desperate for release. Once, I used my lunch hour to write and never returned to my cubicle that day. I knew then what I wanted to do, but I had no idea how to pursue it. Whenever I met anyone, I'd tell them I was a writer and then wish I hadn't when they asked what I'd published. One day I said this to someone who stared at me with the same intensity and knowing as the literature professor years before. No one had stared at me like that in a long time. Or perhaps if they had, I had been too distracted to notice. To be examined that way—not as a foreigner, a piece of ass, or a trophy, but as a whole person—was exactly what I needed. "If you're a writer, then write." Abruptly, my head was lifted out of water, and the sky above me came into focus. Four years later, I married her—this woman who encouraged me to go after my dream as a writer. We married in a courthouse in Brooklyn and then had a private wedding celebration in Jamaica, where I was finally able to return. Though Jamaica is highly homophobic, it meant a lot to me to be able to exchange vows with the woman I love in the country of my birth—as I was able to do in hers.

"You're living the American Dream now," a friend said to me exactly fifteen years after my father left me on the steps of my dorm. I had just published my first book to much acclaim. Suddenly, I was on everyone's radar, including my college friends, now all doctors. One evening they invited me out for drinks. "Let's celebrate you in your success!" They seemed the same at first, barely aged since I last saw them, except for the glistening diamond-encrusted wedding bands. They shyly scooted over to give me a seat at the table, smiling down at their half-empty glasses. I remembered how they had welcomed me and accepted me during our college days. I had changed, but they were the same girls who huddled in the campus library, chasing mapped-out dreams. They still spoke of old classmates, what they were doing, who they'd married. They still believed in being good immigrants, avoiding any mention of me being married to a woman, focusing only on how I'd made a name for myself in America. They asked me about my travels, and as I told them, I could see in that moment their guarded respect and admiration. "You've made it! We're so proud of you!"

I began to claim this American Dream, which my friends insisted I had achieved. Until one day it struck me—I was nowhere near it. A few months after the 2016 election I was at a restaurant with my wife and a few writer friends. Everyone at the table had been born American except me; all were white, except me and my wife. We were talking about writing and living in America in the time of Trump. I had been reluctant to share my thoughts. My writer friends, speaking in low tones by candlelight over wine, began to discuss the possibility of moving to another country. "Black Americans have always struggled here and we stayed," my wife countered. It was as though they were all speaking a different language as Americans. I began to painfully discern that their America was different from the America I looked to for my freedom. I had never been a part of the history they were individually reacting to. And though they all came from different backgrounds as Americans, they were responding to the potential loss of an empire—their empire. I felt like that newly arrived seventeen-year-old foreigner again. It was strange to find myself in this country of my sojourn, listening to the natives—white Americans—speak of leaving in the same way working-class Jamaicans felt the need to leave the island. I pushed away my wine, which had suddenly gone bitter, and looked on in mild bewilderment at the strangers at the table, strangers who had significance in my life in this foreign land, strangers who had embraced me.

"What do you think, Nicole?" They all turned to me.

Perhaps they had noticed me drifting, the way my college friends had noticed over the biology cheat sheets. Would I ever want to leave? They wanted to know. Although I opened my mouth to speak, nothing came out. I had been treading in the deep end of the ocean all along. I had learned to accept the terror and the loneliness of surviving on my own in a new country, the dangerous depths stretching below me. And though I'm weary from all the proverbial strikes against me, I learned long ago, under the warmth of another sun, never to swim against a rip current, but to float, to conserve energy, to remain as calm as possible, drifting on the high seas of uncertainty. Yes, I had struggled in America, but I had also learned the most valuable lessons about myself, and I had fallen in love. I realized right then, sitting at the table, that the measure of my success is not the American Dream but my ability to swim out of the current, parallel to shore, and trust that the waves would carry me. "Jus' hol' yuh breath an' kick," came an echo from far, far away.

Sidra (in 12 Movements)

Rahawa Haile

I.

Before she is born, the Good Immigrant delivers his daughter from
the probability of bondage. He comes to America for a life of ordinary
disappointments. But not war, not famine. At thirty-six, the Good Immigrant has spent his every breath under foreign occupation. Italy, the
UK, Ethiopia. The Good Immigrant knows nothing of black living in
America and yet too much of black life under white conquest all at
once. White-sanctioned conquest too. At least now he will see their
faces, nescient eyes weighing the merit and threat of him by the lilt of
an accent they cannot place. Their soft relief: black but other. There
but only just. African. Guilt Black, not Hate Black (not usually). As in,
"Man! There are people starving back in ____." As in, "Thank God.
For a minute there I thought you were a nigger."

II.

In Miami, the heat is inescapable. Have you been? You will see that
even the trees sweat at night, clear tendrils snaking down their brows,
past their chins, zigzagging in the limp breeze toward the salmon-

colored walkway below. They tell wailing children it is good luck when a tree sweats on your head at night, but it isn't just the trees. In Miami, even the heat sweats at night, and that is where humidity comes from. Thermodynamic self-loathing. Forget what they taught you. Imagine what it means to be so sick of yourself you cry and that crying makes things worse for everyone around you. Now you know how the heat feels. The Good Immigrant understands too much about the water cycle to believe any of this but has taken to wearing a light cap all the same. At the grocery, he places a small carton of orange juice in his shopping cart and slides his change into his pocket, enough for a cafecito, too little for a proper breakfast. Half a guava-and-cheese pastelito, if that. The Good Immigrant is versed in many types of hunger. Could count more of them than he'd care to if pressed. He files tonight's away where it belongs, not quite desperate—he'd passed the rice aisle earlier, after all—but somewhere between heartache and home. How do you feed a heart with $1.40? Trick question. You learn to feed something else.

III.

Every morning, before he gets dressed, the Good Immigrant shaves, sits before the daily paper, and splits his body in half lengthwise, searching. He finds it easier to work this way. Each half its own despair. He misses whistling, on occasion, but finds he can leave the rest, which eventually he does. His wardrobe follows suit. A nearby tailor alters his shirts to more easily be buttoned with one hand. The Good Immigrant upgrades from sneakers to loafers, downgrades from loafers to flip-flops. Why not? His halves spend their waking hours frantic, worried—on top of everything else—what the other may have found. This is how the Good Immigrant comes to give himself completely to the Immigrant's Lament—an endless fight on two fronts: here and Home, where here is home now and Home is hope, until it consumes him. Until his heart and all its beating have nowhere left to yearn. Here, in this land, America, where his daughter might, could, and would someday, even if it kills him.

IV.

What did you think would be left of you, Baba? What were we to do with air?

V.

Despite reading widely before his departure—yes, the Good African read widely; what did you expect?—he had never lived in the pure vulnerability of his skin, a thing until now either alive or dead, transmuted into a liminal namelessness against the blood-white canvas of the United States. The Good Immigrant spends days staring at himself in the mirror. At the swiftness with which a person can become less than without changing a thing at all. The same could have happened elsewhere, he knows. Paris, without question. Milan, for sure. The Good Immigrant chafes at a theft of dignity for which no quantity of books could have prepared him. When he startles awake one night shouting from a bad dream, it is not in English or Tigrinya or Amharic or Italian but in Vigilance, a new tongue that will crowd out the others for his remaining days. This alloy-organ rests heavily in his mouth. His lunchtime curry goat tastes of copper (his) and steel (its). He cannot remember the last time he licked his lips and counted his blessings. When the Good Immigrant finally sees a dentist, he tenses. He opens wide and expects her to wince at the blade of him. Instead, nothing happens. One of his molars has a cavity. The Good Immigrant, it turns out, is not a Good Flosser. He tries asking about his tongue, but the words come out wrong. A receptionist slides him a scraper and bids him farewell.

Years pass. A daughter is born. At the hospital, the Good Immigrant tries and fails to say "I love you" without making it sound like a warning. What comes out is a forecast: "I love you today."

VI.

The Good Immigrant's wife has asked for a divorce. While the Good Immigrant has been many things, a great husband is not one of them. He spends the day at the beach with his daughter, now seven. They've packed towels, fried chicken, a fist of napkins. A hard cooler filled with sliced mangoes and Coca-Cola doubles as a small table. The Good Daughter carries a float longer than her body under each arm and marches toward the water, cawing at the gulls. The Good Family floats. They paddle back ashore. The Good Immigrant and his child watch men with serious expressions perform aerial tricks with V-shaped stunt kites designed to look like sharks.

He lunges after her. She is chasing the kites barefoot, indifferent to the dead jellyfish on the shore. The Good Immigrant yells out, "They can still sting you!" but it sounds like this: "Run fast enough to fly and nothing can hurt you." One of the shark kites dives at an alarming speed near the Good Daughter and nearly crashes. Later, they learn that this is also a stunt kite maneuver. The Good Immigrant carries his daughter back to their towels and watches her sleep. When she awakens, he is upright, his gaze locked on the surf as though he could stop it in its tracks. The Good Immigrant is many feet away from her and motionless. The swash runs over his legs hungrily, again and again, the sand reaching halfway up his shins as though the sinking was the point.

When he returns, the Good Immigrant sits beside his daughter with his arms propped on his knees. He says the sand feels nothing like the salt of his childhood, bahri, the Red Sea, but at least it is sand. Smooth and familiar beneath a sagging Florida sun. He says this in English, and when the Good Daughter fails to remember the word for "sand" in Tigrinya, her first language, she says the word "rock," imni, un-yielding and familiar, linking it to baba, "father," and bahri, "the sea." She smiles and begins to pack. It will be twenty-five years before the Good Daughter learns that the word "imni," as in English, can also mean "fool."

VII.

At present, the Good Immigrant and the Other Daughter have not spoken in twenty-five years.

Oh yes.

There is another daughter. A first. A Good Daughter too, though the Good Immigrant will never understand. It is complicated except for this: he is dead to her, whereas she is only half dead to him, a memory that carries itself still alive in the real world. She has done well for herself. The Good Immigrant seems pleased his memory is still alive but only half listens when he asks the Good Daughter about it. The Good Daughter initially thinks this a form of self-protection and only later sees it clearly as self-harm. She is disturbed by how quickly the Good Immigrant can lose blood, walk away from it like a self-healing gunshot wound. It is the only way he knows to keep a memory a preference instead of a warm, breathing reckoning.

The Good Daughter considers what else her father has given his heart to and kept his heart from, the causes and regrets. How foolish he'd been to think either a choice. The Good Daughter concludes you can't build a life with what the heart alone wants. You have to pause, weigh options, stay open, close shut. There are times when the cruelest thing a person can do is love you back.

She wonders how long the Other Daughter has known this to be true and hopes for even longer.

VIII.

In 2018, the Good Immigrant is missing or perhaps has chosen to be gone. He does this sometimes. Calls it quits. The Good Daughter has seen it before with others. She swallows and remembers a recent dream. In one future, death moved into her throat and waited. Two sparrows fell out of a tree and lay still when they overheard her singing. Hours later, she answered the phone and killed a friend. When the Dream Daughter screamed, every tenant in her building leapt out of their windows in unison as though pulled by strings. In another dream, death laid eggs in her ear. They itched and obscured her senses. The world blinked in and out, in and out, or sometimes cascaded, streaming gray down and dull. When they hatched, the baby deaths poured out of her. Each stole one memory of the twenty-nine still keeping her alive, while the last death stayed inside, her body now its.

The Good Daughter tries not to dwell on what it all means. She thinks about her name, her grandmother's gift. The Good Daughter used to say its proper pronunciation was reserved for family alone. A small thing that could be hers and her people's. Yet the Good Daughter is beginning to realize how dangerous this can be, how easy it is to find herself disappearing in the absence of those tongues. How lonely, when surrounded by so many mouths intentionally misled.

IX.

Who did you want to be, Baba? And what did you want to do with who you'd made?

X.

The Good Daughter sits at her computer. "Some children are born to fathers," she types. "Others, to mysteries." She'd had the luck and occasional misfortune of encountering both in the same man, one who loved her fiercely when he wasn't receding from view. The Good Daughter will spend the rest of her life believing in ghosts because she has met her father and knows he wasn't entirely man, that a part of the Good Immigrant was always slipping away. She wonders what will happen if she marries. If all the vanishings, half gones, and pasts will assemble to wish her well. Perhaps this wondering is it.

The Good Daughter takes a break from writing to catch up on the news. The Italian government has closed its ports to rescue ships. She watches a video from one such ship of African refugees thrashing in the Mediterranean. The film is dark. The African vessel sank at night. The Good Daughter keeps an ear out for the high note of her language, finds it, and breaks. Recently, a man from her country (Eritrea) killed himself after being denied asylum by her country (America). The Good Daughter slips an arm through one of her father's former half shirts and searches for a name.

At a gathering that evening, the Good Daughter tries to have a good time. She does not know how to tell her friends it is a daily struggle to love them as more than the half dead. How she was raised to love the almost missing deeply and to a fault.

XI.

The Good Immigrant does not know where he is. If he is alive or dead. Only that he never said goodbye.

XII.

Goodbye, Baba. Kinirahebina.

On the Blackness of the Panther

Teju Cole

I began to become African a little more than twenty-five years ago. That was when I left Nigeria and moved to the US. I had been born in the US in the summer of 1975 and had been taken to Nigeria in the fall of the same year. For the next seventeen years, Nigeria was home. But I also knew I was American, that the US was a kind of home too, because I had been born there. But was I African? I didn't feel it. What I felt was that I was a Lagos boy, a speaker of Yoruba, a citizen of Nigeria. The Africans were those other people, some of whom I read about in books, or had seen wearing tribal costumes in magazines, or encountered in weird fictional form in movies.

In the summer of 1992, that began to change. The US provided a contrast to my latent Africanness. "What are you?" "I'm Nigerian." "Where are you from, man?" "Lagos." "Leggo my Eggo?" No one had heard of Lagos. I was African—that was the kind of "other" I was. It was news to me, but I didn't fight back for long. I fell in with others who were in a similar predicament, and began to learn African.

I sometimes feel in my body a paradoxical loss: the loss of forgetting. I find myself longing for an earlier time when what I knew was contingent and always sheltered by what I didn't know. Knowledge, in the days before instantaneous electronic recall, was full of potential energy. It was attended by a guesswork that fostered a different way of knowing, one that allowed for ranges rather than insisting on points.

Here is an attempt to struggle to remember: I know, or knew, a few things about the big cats. Lions are found on the Serengeti; tigers, in South Asia. Both are enormous. Cheetahs are the fastest, obviously; leopards, good climbers, dragging their prey up a tree. Both are African (animals can be African, but only people can be *Africans*). The scientific names of big cats contain *"Panthera,"* though I can't be sure. *Panthera leo.* That's lions, I think. Jaguars look like leopards but are of a stockier and more compact build. They're South American. This is where it gets cloudier. Are panthers jaguars? Or are they their own thing? If panthers are monochrome jaguars, then they can't be African, because jaguars are South American. Is a black panther the same thing as a black leopard? And what the fuck is a puma? What are mountain lions? I think they're the same as pumas: aren't they the North American ones? Wait. What about cougars?

I was into the big cats as a kid. Knew my cats back then, and also freelanced in birds of prey (eagles, hawks, falcons, ospreys), which had a similarly complex family structure. Dabbled in dinosaurs too, but not seriously. I don't mind that I have now lost much of my taxonomic memory of these peak predators. What's sad is that, in the blink of an eye, I can look it all up.

On the morning of October 11, 1933, six years before the beginning of the European war in which Switzerland was to play a tangential but troubling role, the cage of the black panther at the Zürich

Zoologischer Garten was found empty. The animal, a recent arrival from Sumatra, had escaped in the night. In the weeks that followed, numerous sightings were reported in the Zürich area. The normally unflappable citizens were caught up in hysteria. There were hundreds of articles in the Swiss press. Traps were set, and a few half-wild dogs were caught. Tracks thought to be those of the panther also turned out to belong to dogs. Some people suggested that an exorcism be performed by the members of a religious cult. Someone else wrote to say that what was needed was a clairvoyant.

It wasn't until December, ten weeks after her escape, that the panther was found hiding under a barn in the boundary between the Zürich Oberland and the Canton of St. Gallen. The remains of roe deer found nearby were a clue as to how she had survived during a Swiss winter. The black panther was discovered by a casual laborer, who immediately shot and killed her for food.

Many movies made by Hollywood have engaged in thought experiments about Africa. Some, made for American whites, resurrect colonial fantasy ("I once had a farm in Africa"), with the African roles either brutish or naive. Others, made for American blacks, have a goal of uplift, cloaking the African experience with a fictional grandeur. These fantasies, white and black, are always simplifications. There are fifty-four African countries. What would it mean to dream with these already existing countries? What would it mean to dream with Mozambique, Sudan, Togo, or Libya, and to think about their politics in all their hectic complexities? What would it look like to use that as a narrative frame, even for works of fiction? Wakanda is a monarchy, and so is Zamunda. (No idea what Nambia is.) Why are monarchies the narrative default? Can we dream beyond royalty? In my wildest dreams, there is no king. I killed the king. The king is dead. All power to the people.

Only once have I ever owned a pet: a cat, about a decade ago. Her name was Mirabai, also known as Midnight. She'd leap up to meet me, this beautiful panther in miniature. Or she would go deep into prayer, as cats do, or knead some patch of sun on the wooden floor. But I could not train this sweet, playful, all-black kitten not to bite. I soon tired of having to take a course of antibiotics each time she bit me. Three times she bit me, and twice visitors. There was no hostility there; she simply didn't know how to modulate, and often drew blood. More seriously, I discovered that I have a severe allergy to cat hair. Not all cats, but most. I hadn't known. Poor Mirabai. I had to return her to the shelter. But in my heart of hearts, I'm a cat person. I can stand dogs, but I more naturally like what cats do and how cats be.

On my way to becoming African, I also began to become black, which proved a more complex journey. "African" was about sharing a mutual space with Africans: friends from across the continent, or people with whom I'd been placed in the same category. It had something to do with us finding ourselves strangers in the strange American land, but also with our shared experience of the background radiation of colonialism. The formalized white supremacy of colonial rule ended in Nigeria only fifteen years before I was born. It was still fresh! "African," whatever else it was, was about collectively undoing this assault.

"Black" was something else. It was in a sense more inclusive. It took in all that colonial hangover and added to it the American experiences of slavery, slave rebellion, Jim Crow, and contemporary racism, as well as the connective tissue that bound the Black Atlantic into a single territory of pain—which brought all of the Caribbean into its orbit—as well as European, Latin American, and global diasporic blackness.

But "black" was also more restrictive because, in everyday language, "black" (or "Black") was American black, and "American black" meant slave-descended black. In the terms of US discourse, this wasn't primarily about every black person in the world; it was something else, highly localized to the American situation. To be black in America, that localized tenor of "black" had to be learned; it had to be learned and loved. Black skin was the admission to the classroom (and skin sometimes didn't have to be especially dark, and sometimes it was just a shade or two off white), but black American cultural codes were the lesson. So I learned black, like Obama learned black, like black British living in LA learn black, like Jamaicans in Brooklyn, Haitians in Miami, Eritreans in DC, and Gambians in the Bronx learn black. We learned black and loved black—knowing all the while, though, that it wasn't the only black.

In the heart of the continent is a landlocked nation, small and peaceful. The inhabitants are thought to be a simple and unostentatious people. But this is one of the richest nations on earth, and one of the most technologically advanced. The country is set at a great height, ringed by mountains. Its political system is stable. There have been no internal wars for centuries. Fearful of the mayhem convulsing the world, the country stays out of international disputes and does not open its borders to migrants. But behind the quiet-looking walls is a remarkable industriousness in the fields of scientific research, weapons development, and pharmaceutical innovation. The country has solved the mystery of transportation: traffic congestion is unknown there, and high-speed trains silently crisscross the territory. Now, in a rapidly changing world, the inhabitants of this country must decide if they want to continue hiding themselves from the world, or if they wish finally to take more responsibility and use their wealth and technology to improve the lot of others.

I'm talking about Switzerland, obviously. But Switzerland is a democracy. Wakanda, not so much, and my antipathy to monarchies is intense, inflexible, and probably irrational. The hereditary right to rule offends me almost personally, whether I encounter it in fiction or in reality. I rate it, as ideas go, somewhere between eugenics and phrenology. Human history is full of monarchs. Let's leave them where most of them are, in the past. The societies I dream of organize themselves around knowledgeable democratic choice. The dream extends past even the nation-state. No kings, no queens. No royal presidents. Temperamentally, I'm a regicide.

The nations and cities of Africa, as they are now, are each so consumed with the complexity of being their distinct selves from day to day that they cannot take on the thankless task of also being Hollywood's "Africa." African countries have always been in conversation with the world; an isolationist blackness is incoherent and impossible: we already *been* cosmopolitan. In the modern world, black is as unimaginable without white as white is unimaginable without black. What we are is shaped by the other, for better or worse (for us, mostly worse), but interaction is real. The way out is through. We can't wish that away, not even as a storytelling fantasy.

As for kings, they exist even now, but they mostly occupy modest roles, at the level of the ethnic group or clan rather than as potentates over nation-states. These lesser kings have ceremonial roles within various larger political organizations. They know their place. Meanwhile, the few real national monarchies that remain are nothing to be envied. They're absurd throwbacks, no kind of future.

Truth is not stranger than fiction, but it is more specific, more contradictory, more hectic, more layered. "Africa"—vague or composite—cannot hope to match the complexity or interest of any actual place in Africa.

In the winter of 1902, Rainer Maria Rilke visited the zoo at the Jardin des Plantes in Paris and saw a black panther there. The poem he wrote in response, the earliest of his *Neue Gedichte*, is one of his most famous.

Sein Blick ist vom Vorübergehn der Stäbe
so müd geworden, daß er nichts mehr hält.
Ihm ist, als ob es tausend Stäbe gäbe
und hinter tausend Stäben keine Welt.
Der weiche Gang geschmeidig starker Schritte,
der sich im allerkleinsten Kreise dreht,
ist wie ein Tanz von Kraft um eine Mitte,
in der betäubt ein großer Wille steht.
Nur manchmal schiebt der Vorhang der Pupille
sich lautlos auf—Dann geht ein Bild hinein,
geht durch der Glieder angespannte Stille—
und hört im Herzen auf zu sein.

In my rapid translation:

His gaze, from the constant passing of the bars,
becomes so tired that it can no longer hold anything.
He feels as though there are a thousand bars
and behind the thousand bars, no world.
The soft strong supple steps
that turn in the smallest circle
are like a ritual dance in the middle of which
stands a great will, stunned.
Only sometimes does the curtain of the pupil
soundlessly lift—Then a picture enters,
goes through the tensed silence of the limbs—
and, entering the heart, ceases to be.

Rilke's poetry, at its best, is a marvel of sympathy. He ghosts himself into the lives of things, adopts the view from their perspective. The panther in his poem is black because of the color of its coat. But it is also a racialized subject.

All black panthers are black in color but cannot now evade cultural meaning: the caged cat, the escaped cat, the never-captured cat, the black people who are seen as animals, the 1960s comic book hero, the radical political party, the twenty-first-century film stars. All black panthers and Black Panthers are black—black like night and also black like me.

No translation of Rilke's "Der Panther" is entirely satisfying, so dependent is the poem on the propulsive rhythms of the German original. Only a *version* will do, one full of forgettings, misreadings, a stealth leap into the poem, an ambush:

A thousand bars flicker
in front of nothing.
A thousand bars
—his exhausted eyes
can't take it.
Soft paws, supple tread.
He circles,
dazed.
But sometimes!
The eyes slide open,
an image enters,
goes through the tense limbs,
and on reaching the heart,
vanishes.

In addition to my big cats and soaring raptors, in childhood I was keen on the Transformers, Voltron, Speed Racer, and a number of American superhero comic books. This was in Lagos in the 1980s. But by the time I was in my mid-teens, I had lost interest in all that: sci-fi, fantasy, video games, comics, cartoons. There are exceptions: I like *Solaris*, *2001: A Space Odyssey*, *Children of Men*, *Minority Report*, but that's a fairly narrow selection of dystopian futurism. I love Sun Ra's *Space Is the Place*, though that's something else entirely.

But the recent leotard-and-cape blockbusters generally bore me to tears. It faintly feels like a terrible thing to admit (what kind of monster doesn't love superhero movies?), but the world is made of what we're into and what we're not into, and there's consolation in knowing what's yours. In certain genres that I do not love, the louder genres especially, there's so much at stake that it can feel as though there's therefore nothing at stake. The fate of the planet, the destiny of the universe, and so on, are always one clever, decisive action away. The fight sequences stretch on, but the fights don't really feel like fights. Compare a battle in any recent big-budget superhero film to one in a Kurosawa samurai epic, like *Ran:* the recent films are all CGI, while Kurosawa feels like steel and flesh and dust and actual battlefield clamor. In a typical superhero film, the enemies are killed in great numbers, but death is curiously light, inconsequential, undeathly. (What would the climactic civil war in Wakanda have felt like had there been a serious reckoning with its death toll? It would have made apparent the movie's discomfiting secret: that it has two lead villains and no hero.)

Maybe it's a tonal thing. Or maybe it's the economic censorship, which is inescapable in any film that costs more than $100 million to make, and which is even less forgiving than ideological censorship: that money must be recouped and there must be profit. Or maybe it's that the films are made, as all films are, for those who love them, not for those who doubt them. I know I'm an outlier. The box office returns of the Marvel Cinematic Universe proves that heretics of the superhero-film money-laundering operation are outnumbered. But even for us, there can be the fine surprise, for example, of a film that strains at those conventions, attempts to establish new mythologies, and in the process invites even nonpartisans to think with its world, reactionary as that world might be. Coogler did that.

On a rainy Tuesday afternoon in March 2015, I visited the Parque Zoológico de São Paulo. A zoo, with its echoes of early science and colonial practice, can feel like the opening chapter of a given country. It's often as though the logic of a society's organization has been reduced to the fundamentals in a zoo, where there are the rulers and the ruled, types and typologies, symbols everywhere and meaning nowhere.

That day, I saw elephants, giraffes, a strange fox-like dog, chimpanzees, flamingos, a boa constrictor. Few solitary adults were around, but there were a couple of boisterous school groups. Perhaps this is one place where my tastes reliably overlap those of younger children. I go to zoos, and while I'm there, I think about what a zoo means—it's both defensible and indefensible—but I'm also absorbed by the gallimaufry and sheer strangeness of those ones on the other side of the barrier. Their gazes, dulled by human encounter, can no longer admit us into their existential circle but, like tarnished mirrors, still glimmer from time to time with recognition.

I do not recall now why I paused by the black panther's cage that day. I began to record a brief video on my phone. Soft paws, supple tread. She (or he) moved swiftly, worriedly. It was an intent rather than a distracted pacing. He (or she) was simultaneously gorgeous and frantic, loping, maddened, a grievously confined power.

In 1902, Rilke had written another poem, "Die Aschanti," about a group of West African men and women. They had been displayed in the zoo-like setting of the Jardin d'Acclimatation in Paris. The practice of exhibiting African people (as well as Samoans, Inuit, and Sami) in zoos, circuses, and world fairs was especially rampant between the late nineteenth century and 1930. The history of this atrocity is deep, but a signal moment was in the life of Saartjie

Baartman, brought from South Africa to England in 1810 and put on display in London.

In the 1870s, in the name of ethnographic research, there were human zoos in Antwerp, Paris, Barcelona, Hamburg, London, Milan, and New York City. The Congolese Ota Benga was confined to the Monkey House at the Bronx Zoo in 1906, and freed only after the protestations of African American activists. (He was to kill himself a decade later, with a gunshot to the heart. To the heart!) And in 1930, three years before the black panther escaped from the Zürich Zoologischer Garten, a group of Senegalese people had been put on display there.

"Die Aschanti" is a poem of disappointment. Rilke finds that the Ashanti are not African enough for him, not savage enough. One verse goes:

Keine wilde fremde Melodie.
Keine Lieder, die vom Blute stammten,
und kein Blut, das aus den Tiefen schrie.

In Edward Snow's translation:

No wild unheard-of melodies.
No songs which issued from the blood,
and no blood which screamed out from the depths.

It goes on. There are "no brown girls who stretched out / velvety in tropical exhaustion," there are "no eyes which blaze like weapons," no mouths "broad with laughter." The Ashanti are just there, self-possessed, with a "bizarre" vanity, acting almost as though they are equal to Europeans. "And it made me shudder seeing that," Rilke writes. He can only conclude the poem by declaring, "O how much truer are the animals / that pace up and down in steel grids."

That's racist.

Eusébio da Silva Ferreira was born in Maputo to a poor family during Portuguese colonial rule. He moved to Portugal and became the greatest of Benfica's players, and perhaps the greatest to ever have worn Portugal's shirt, for greatness is more than a matter of trophies and goal tallies. Eusébio was black and beautiful on the field, quick, quick, in that red shirt of his, blessed with a tremendous right-footed shot. He was the best player in the 1966 World Cup, this man of feline reflexes whom they called the King, the Black Pearl, and, above all, "la Pantera Negra," the Black Panther. Perhaps it is only too obvious that the first great football player from the African continent would be compared to an animal. But it is also true that neither the panther nor the player is diminished by the comparison, which after all seeks to put into words a beauty the heart cannot contain.

Had to look it up. Forgetting is impossible. It turns out a black panther is two different animals, and no animal at all. It is "no animal at all" in the sense that a panther is not a distinct scientific species. A black panther is two animals because a jaguar with a black coat is a black panther and a leopard with a black coat is a black panther. The blackness of the panther, in the case of the jaguar, is due to a dominant gene for coat coloration. In the case of the leopard, the blackness of the panther is due to a recessive gene. Both are melanistic variants, and when deh mutated gene for the bleck color is expressed, deh big cat receives the powa of deh Bleck Pentha.

* * *

Listen to Toni Morrison a second: "Saying something is pitch black is like saying something is green. What kind of green? Green like my bottles? Green like a grasshopper? Green like a cucumber, lettuce, or green like the sky just before it breaks loose to storm? Well, night black is the same way. May as well be a rainbow."

And there it is, the black rainbow. I learned black and I learned diversity in blackness. Turns out black is multifarious and generative. It is capacious and dissenting. Those who have to learn black also expand what black can be. My pain is black pain, my joy is black joy, my individuality is black; I arc blackly in the rainbow with all the rest of those pitch-black cats. Next person comes along to learn black will have to learn me too.

At least once a day, I think: *Another world is possible.* There's life yet in our dreams. The pan-African political project is still alive. The memory of whatever was good in the Bandung Conference or the Organization of African Unity still makes the heart race. Flashes of common cause among the Darker Nations can be illuminating and sustaining. But "Africa" as trope and trap, backdrop and background, interests me ever less.

I am more fascinated by Nairobi than by Africa, just as I am more intrigued by Milan than by Europe. The general is where solidarity begins, but the specific is where our lives come into proper view. I don't want to hear "Africa" unless it's a context in which someone would also say "Asia" or "Europe." Ever notice how real Paris is? That's how real I need Lagos to be. Folks can talk about Paris all day without once generalizing about Europe. I want to talk about Lagos; I don't want to talk about Africa. I want to hear someone speaking Yoruba, Ewe, Tiv, or Lingala. "African" is not a language. I want to know if a plane is going to the Félix-Houphouët-Boigny International Airport. You can't go to "Africa," fam. Africa is almost twelve million square miles. I want to be particular about being particular about what we are talking about when we talk about Africa.

I grew up with black presidents, black generals, black kings, black heroes, both invented and real, black thieves too, black fools. It was Nigeria, biggest black nation on earth. I shared a city with Fela Kuti for seventeen years. Everyone was black! I've seen so many black people my retinas are black.

But against the high-gloss white of anti-black America, blackness visible is a relief and a riot. That's something you learn when you learn black. Marvel? Disney? Please. I won't belabor the obvious. But black visibility, black enthusiasm (in a time of death), black spectatorship, and black skepticism: where we meet is where we meet.

Going on twenty-six years now. I learned African and am mostly over it. But what is that obdurate and versatile substance formed by tremendous pressure? What is "vibranium"? Too simple to think of it as a metal, and to tie it to resource curses. Could it be something less palpable, could it be a stand-in for blackness itself, blackness as an embodied riposte to anti-blackness, a quintessence of mystery, resilience, self-containedness, and irreducibility?

Escape! I would rather be in the wild. I would rather be in a civilization of my own making, bizarre, contrary, as vain as the whites, exterior to their logic. I'm always scoping the exits. Drapetomania, they called it, in *Diseases and Peculiarities of the Negro Race* (1851), the irrepressible desire in certain slaves to run away.

* * *

Ten years pass and I still dream about that cat. The eyes slide open, an image enters. Where are you now, Mirabai? Euthanized years ago by the animal shelter? Or successfully adopted and now gracefully aging in some home in Brooklyn? With people, young or old, merciful and just? Dream cat, leaping up to meet me.

How Not to Be

Priya Minhas

Growing up, my family spoke of women who broke the rules like the titles of *Friends* episodes. There was the One Who Ran Away with a White Man, the One Who Got Married Twice, the One Who Never Married, the One Who Was Probably a Lesbian, and the One Who Smoked Cigarettes.

Sometimes these women ran away from their communities, and sometimes they were forced to leave. Either way, they lived in exile, resurfacing only when they were spotted in the supermarket, or on the tongues of others as a cautionary tragic tale. I know little else about these women. They were often of my mother's generation, and their stories had been told, and retold, their choices discussed and debated, long before I was born. Some were victims, some were villains, others were both, but by the time their stories reached me, the entire lives of these women had been condensed into an adjective. We spoke of them then as our own common cultural references, my aunts referring to them as I do Britney's 2007 head shaving or Kanye's "I'ma Let You Finish." We labeled and separated them, as we often do with women. The short one, the dark one, the pretty one. The Kelly, the Beyoncé, the Michelle. The Baby Spice, the Scary Spice, the Posh Spice.

I lived in fear of becoming one of those exiled women. I imagined them perpetually wandering the aisles of a supermarket, waiting to bump into someone they knew, waiting to be invited back home. Still, from a young age, I understood that I was connected to them. Our connection may not have been traced neatly on a family tree, but I understood that even in their exile, their shame could be transferred in the retelling of their stories from one woman to another like fresh ink across a page. The retelling of these stories was an act of prayer, not meant to shame but to instill a fear that would protect me and prevent me from ever becoming one of them. This is how I was raised—how *not* to be.

How Not to Be meant growing up with the promise of a life better than my parents had known. A life in which I would quietly, and often unknowingly, cash in on privileges paid for by the ones who came before me. My sisters and I were supposed to be the 2.0, the reason it was all worth it. Every school photo and each certificate placed on the mantelpiece was a step toward fulfilling this promise, each one an offering, a single penny placed at the altar to repay their sacrifice.

As girls, we were to follow a set of unspoken rules passed down through the stories of these women. A watchful eye was placed on our bodies from the moment we were born, and a large part of our cultural identity rested entirely on how we used them. Such was my dilemma, and the dilemma of many daughters of immigrants whose purpose seems to be the preservation of "our culture" as much as the progression of it.

Our cultural identity was the language, values, and customs my grandparents first carried as memories from India, but it was also the new words, recipes, and rituals that evolved as our family settled. It was adding masala to the spaghetti and eating samosas for breakfast on Christmas Day. It was the grocery stores, video shops, ware-houses, and temples we built, and the communities that poured in and out of them. New roots were planted for us in these rituals. This was a way for my grandparents to create a more permanent state of belonging at a time when they could not pick up the phone or travel back home to be reminded of who they were.

The need to preserve and nurture all that was left of home was strengthened by the ever-present threat of having everything taken away. The fragility there, and here. Protecting these traditions was an act of self-preservation. We held on tightly to the things, places, people, and values that kept us safe, and could continue to keep us safe: a community and culture that reflected us at a time when our presence was often regarded as nothing more than a canvas upon which others could scribble out the terms and conditions of our stay.

My grandparents migrated to the UK with only the dream of opportunity. After years of watching the violence and destruction that came with British rule in India, they knew better than to carry over with them any hope for acceptance.

My sisters and I were sold a different dream, one of equality and assimilation. We worried less about our physical safety and more about the safety that came with "fitting in." In our pursuit of this, and in our ignorance, we often strayed purposefully from these carefully preserved cultural cornerstones. But as we navigated our path to belonging, there were three rules we continued to accept with the understanding that as brown girls it was "our culture": no sleepovers, no revealing clothes, and no boyfriends.

NO SLEEPOVERS

I grew up on the outskirts of London during the 1990s. As one of only a few Indian girls at school, I found my experience of girlhood consisted mostly of a slow surrendering to the idea that I did not have the right one. Instead, I had multiple versions of girlhood, none of which felt as though they belonged to me.

In some versions I grew up slowly, lagging five years behind the white girls, who filled water bottles with vodka and had their first kisses and broken hearts by the age of fifteen. In other versions I grew up fast, learning quickly which stories, words, and mannerisms to bring home and which to leave at school. Sometimes these versions threatened to collapse in on one another.

Having friends in my home carried the risk of exposing differences more easily hidden in the classroom. My mother switching to Punjabi on the phone or a framed photo of Ganesha meant explanations later. Constantly negotiating your difference as a person of color means you are always explaining and excusing the plurality that holds you together, as much as it threatens to split you apart. My parents feared me growing up too fast, but juggling an identity that felt plural left me feeling old when I was young anyway.

Still, I often did have friends over, and on one occasion a friend remarked how lucky I was to have more than one type of cereal at home. I remember her words now because they remind me that I did not recognize the warmth and abundance of my own home. The truth is, I envied white homes for their "normality" as much as I feared them.

My parents' reluctance to allow sleepovers grew out of a fear rooted in the values of the NO BLACKS, NO DOGS, NO IRISH Britain where they had been raised, the same values that had justified decades of systematic, physical, and verbal abuse toward people like us. Their reluctance acknowledged a deeper internalized fear toward white people and what they perceived as universal white culture. It was a fear rooted in memory. Of motorcycles being set alight, of being spat at, of being cheered out of a pub, of being watched, then followed, then beaten, of not being able to trust a schoolteacher, colleague, or neighbor to do anything but stand by and watch.

For the first ten years of my life, I lived in the same house in a town on the edge of London. My grandparents lived on the next street over, but we would drive to their house anyway, except when I threatened to run away, slamming the front door and walking over instead. My uncles and aunts lived in the same town too, and we shuttled from one house to another, often daily, stopping by to fix something, have a chat, drop the kids off, or deliver steel saucepans of leftover food.

When I was eleven, my family relocated to the United States. We flew back home to visit often, and during one of these trips I returned to our old house. My dad asked repeatedly if I was sure I was ready to see it, the same way he'd asked if I was sure I wanted to see my grandmother at her funeral. I stood in our old dining room, stunned by how small it was even now that it was empty. How it strayed so wildly from what I remembered. For many Christmases three generations of my family had piled into this room, sitting at tables—borrowed from the local community center—that snaked around the perimeter. The walls themselves must have expanded to hold us all.

I think often about the way I have recreated that feeling of safety. In the cities and towns I have lived in since, I place anchors by remembering which bartenders put the change directly in my hand rather than sliding it across the counter, finding an eyebrow lady who understands "Just a tidy," and knowing which shortcuts to avoid at night. People of color learn early to take responsibility for creating their own spaces and their own safety, whether that means choosing a university in a "diverse" area or simply looking for another person of color in the room.

I live in New York now, and the truth is that I enjoy the anonymity it allows me. Community brings safety, but it also brings "What will people say?" Sometimes it is a luxury that I'm now able to define myself outside my community.

Other times I'm so homesick that I forget I'm living here by choice. For the women who ran away, and for those who were told to leave, I wonder how and where they created a home, and what happened when they didn't have somewhere to return to.

In 1955, my grandfather arrived at Wolverhampton railway station, guided to the city only because he had seen the words written on a letter and nothing more. A taxi driver picked him up and, without asking for an address, transported him to the doorstep of an Indian family the driver knew. This house, and the man who opened the door and welcomed him in, became my grandfather's first home in England. He spent the next few years sharing rooms with many other men like him, who pooled together their salaries. When my grandmother arrived five years later, she made a home out of these rooms, cooking for at least ten men at a time, men who had arrived on the doorstep like my grandfather once had.

Over the years, cousins, aunts, uncles, and grandparents passed in and out of my childhood home. Sometimes staying for months, other times stopping by for the evening. Our living room was the remedy. These were the days when you could arrive without calling first, when you could leave your shoes at the door and be welcomed in with a cup of tea or glass of wine, and dinner was always ready. I think back to my grandmother preparing food for each of the men in those small rooms, and my mother, now in America, thousands of miles away from those cousins, aunts, and uncles, but still always cooking extra.

As I entered my twenties and made homes of my own, friends would steal a T-shirt and makeup wipes before curling up in my bed, too drunk to go home, falling asleep to the sound of one of us thinking out loud in the safety of darkness. One night a friend showed up on my doorstep after leaving her boyfriend. One woman's home becoming a sanctuary for another is a theme that has punctuated some of my deepest female friendships.

NO REVEALING CLOTHES

For a few years I attended an all-girls school in the UK. We all wore the same bottle-green uniform, and every morning the top of the bus, the back of the classroom, and the bathrooms would be filled with girls huddled together applying makeup or rolling up their skirts at the waist until the hems skimmed their thighs. The girls who, like me, had multiple versions of themselves would roll them back down and wipe off their faces before returning home. These were girls who dared not fly out of the school gates to flirt with boys but instead flirted with the idea of another life. Girls who knew to stretch the lie just far enough so that it didn't split entirely into two lives and force them to choose one.

Once my family relocated to the United States, I could wear shorts to school. My two pairs of denim cutoffs, one pink and one blue, are perhaps a seemingly insignificant detail, but wearing those shorts became just as much a part of our new American Dream as the yellow school buses, the Pledge of Allegiance each morning, and Chinese food that arrived in little white boxes on Friday nights. Before this, my sisters and I had worn shorts only on vacation. But now, in the suburbs of New Jersey, we were on a permanent one, because we were three thousand miles away from "What will people say?"

There is a photo of my grandmother taken shortly after she arrived in England. In it, her hair is cut short, falling just above her shoulders in relaxed curls. When I first looked at that photograph, at her standing next to a bike with her cropped hair, sleeveless top, and wide-leg trousers, I thought how she too had moved thousands of miles away from "What will people say?" But my grandmother cannot ride a bike. Her hair was cut during the year she spent in transit to England in order to make her look more westernized upon arrival.

Growing up, my relationship with my body, and what I did with it, centered on edging closer to whiteness. Whiteness—in pigment, not behavior—is celebrated in my community, and "You don't look Indian" was the "You're not like other girls" for brown people. I chased it and accepted all of those scraps of "Pretty for a brown girl" and "You could be mixed" that always left me feeling empty. I suppose at one time those words meant safety before they meant self-worth.

Fitting in, it turns out, is a very physical process. I have spent years in a battle with my body, trying to make it compliant to the needs of others. I have tried to shrink it as though that could shrink my difference. Am I more welcome if I take up less space? If I can perch on the end, squeeze into the middle, hover by the door or against the wall and disappear? I have spent hours threading, wax-ing, and bleaching to achieve a feeling of cleanliness and normalcy. Hours running from store to store, trying to pack my body into something that says "Girl who deserves the job" or "Girl who can drink like the white girls."

Growing up, I kept a diary for brief stints of time, discarding it whenever I felt my handwriting had deteriorated. I was too afraid to commit any real thoughts and feelings to paper, and instead I wrote lists—of all the things I thought I needed, to make being me a lit-tle easier. Things to wear and say to convince other people of my worth.

I wrote—very matter-of-factly—that I would like to stop growing hair on my arms and legs, around the edges of my lip and along my tummy. Which I wished were smaller too. I wished that I was allowed to shave, to wear crop tops and lip gloss and platform jelly sandals, and to pierce my ears. For women like me, who are rarely considered beautiful or powerful, there is always a list. And as a young girl, I had enough conviction to write it all down, believing everything that sep-arated me from acceptance could be condensed neatly into a page of bullet points.

It was my aunt who eventually pierced my ears. She was a newly trained beauty graduate at the time. She sat me at the top of the staircase of my grandma's house, marked my earlobes with a Biro, and told me to hold still. To everyone's horror, what resulted were two new holes resting just above where they were supposed to be. Those little studs, sitting so close and yet so far from where I had hoped, summed up so many of my attempts at chasing ideals not meant for me.

After the earrings, it was the large pink plastic bag from the British clothes store Jane Norman, which girls at school often repurposed as school bags. Jane Norman sold what I called "Friday night" clothes. Everything they sold was body-con, halter-neck, strapless, slinky, and mini. Jane Norman was for girls who hung out at under-eighteens nights, girls who could flaunt their sexuality without shame or surveillance, girls who could dabble in their womanhood without being burdened with preserving their innocence. I had no business being there.

After that pink plastic bag, I wished for a body slim enough to wear tight jeans and a plain white tee and, after that, skin hairless enough to lie out in the park with the blond girls in June. Edging closer to whiteness was my own Sisyphean task, pushing myself further away from looking like the "others" only to be repeatedly reminded that I would always be "other."

In America, I wore the shorts and the JanSport backpack and the American Eagle hoodie like the other kids. I went to homecoming dances and even had a white boy crush on me. But each day I spoke less and less, afraid that my accent would ruin the illusion and draw attention to the differences I had tried so hard to erase. Most days I didn't speak at all.

In aspiring to whiteness, there was loss too, because it required forgetting. Forgetting the words in Punjabi because I was too afraid to speak it outside my grandmother's house, letting my eyes glaze over at the mention of Diwali at school, lifting my shoulders in a shrug when someone asked whether dhal was spicy.

Sometimes I get a glimpse of who I could be if I stopped considering myself through the eyes of others. My potential spills out in front of me like a pint of milk that's slipped from my hand—impossible to

put back and for a second, as it pours uncontrollably, beautiful. It is
in my most mundane moments in New York, showing my skin without fiddling with my buttons or holding hands in public, that I am
sometimes reminded of how far I've spilled out.

NO BOYFRIENDS

I met my best friends in school. I suppose we were quite literally
put together, but in hindsight, it felt like an act of fate that each of
our last names began somewhere between *M* and *P*, placing us all
next to one another across two rows. Together we accounted for
nearly all of the nonwhite girls in the class, branding ourselves the
"ethnixx." We carved our girlhood out between those two rows,
passing notes up and down to one another, talking about nothing
and yet everything.

We shared an unspoken understanding that slowly shuffled my
versions of girlhood into one. We were careful to say each other's
names correctly, chiming in defensively whenever a teacher tripped
over their pronunciation. There was no need to make excuses for
why someone could not sleep over or to hide the dark baby hair that
stretched across our stomachs and forearms. We knew better than
to reference certain topics or anecdotes in front of each other's parents, and we knew to instinctively play alibi and cover for one another
when a parent called asking after us.

For the first time I saw my adolescence through my own lens,
and slowly my experiences were normalized. We each experimented
with rebellion differently, but more often than not, our attempts were
nothing more than small acts of subversion that we knew we could

get away with. Some of us feared aunties, some feared fathers, and others feared God. Most of the time, we kept the secrets of others rather than our own. We lied to our parents to protect them. To lie was to play adult.

For most of us, falling in love was out of the question until we were at least eighteen, or married. Still, we exhausted our emotions, phone credit, and internet allowance with stories of our crushes and unrequited love. We took one another's heartbreak and excitement seriously, as though these feelings had been reciprocated or existed outside our conversations and imaginations. We fell in love alone, together.

White people fall in love loudly. They have nine lives when it comes to falling in love. Nine love lives, that is. Over the years, I have watched white friends bring love interests in and out of their homes, onto their social media posts, and along on their family holidays. Even the most fleeting of romances are displayed with a confidence I can only recognize as recklessness. Rarely, in my own community, have I seen anyone introduce or even acknowledge a partner until it is confirmed they are the One. When I have been in love, I have protected and compartmentalized my relationship, sharing that person with only a select few and with bated breath. I have often protected others from my own heartbreak in an attempt to protect myself from "What will people say?" and from becoming the One Who Picked the Wrong Guy.

Brown love is public only in the sense that it demands accountability. Most of the images and stories I consumed growing up have led me to believe that brown women fall in love secretly and often with sadness or shame. They taught me that there is beauty, romance, and virtue in holding back, in cutting the action right before lips touch, and leaving any real display of physical desire, affection, and sexuality to exist within the imagination. So many of my own experiences with love, too, exist largely within my imagination. I have spent so much of my life entertaining those emotions only in the hypothetical that when I scan through my history of love interests, the reciprocated and the unrequited feel equally real.

I have never enjoyed going on dates because I have never managed to arrive for one without leaving half of myself at the door. Even the most promising ones require me to split myself in two—the other half of me watching the night play out, never quite believing it.

When I think about dating white men, I think of white women. Specifically, the white women who arrive at the same party or same bar and manage to compliment me and replace me on my own date in the same sentence. I have spent enough time watching white people fall in love to know the exact moment I become the sidekick. On every occasion, I have seen it coming. I've watched with admiration how easily and deliberately the white woman can lean her body into him, hold his gaze, and believe herself to be the object of desire without caution or shame.

In these moments, I wait for the anger to arrive. It's not that I'm invisible to these women. They see me, but they simply don't believe me to be there in *that* way. I don't believe myself either, so I scoot over at the bar or go back inside the party. I call it a night. They act with an entitlement that I'm reminded I don't have, laying claim in a way that I cannot. It's a feeling of smallness that will not entertain the illusion, even briefly, that it could have been me, in a world that has repeatedly told me it cannot.

I fell in love for the first time somewhat unexpectedly and yet inevitably. Having grown up with the understanding that I was not allowed to date, doing so felt like something to be feared rather than celebrated. I feared the consequences of showing love, which also meant I feared allowing myself to be loved in return. Giving in to my emotions, as honest as they were, felt like betrayal. I had been defeated and became the girl living a second life. I was consumed with guilt, and as one lie shattered into ten and then twenty, I felt myself becoming closer and closer to the women I had grown up being warned about. It's easy to speak openly of the women we celebrate and model ourselves on becoming, yet perhaps it is the women we silently swear never to become that influence us the most.

My heart aches for brown girls who fall in love in the shadows. Whose love stories are confined to deleted messages, libraries, lunchtimes, and their imagination. Who can only laugh at the idea of meeting a boyfriend's or girlfriend's parents, making it Facebook official, or being walked home right up to the door. These are the girls who knew how to curate and filter themselves long before social media.

My heart aches because these are the girls who have learned to accept being loved only part-time, who must endure the pain of heartbreak by themselves, and then carry the shame alone too. The girls who can't hear their parents say "You deserve better" instead of "What will people say?"

I once read that "a path connects one place to another, but it also measures the distance that separates two places. A line at once joins two points and keeps them apart." Through the hopes, fears, mistakes, and ideals of my heritage, I learned How Not to Be. Those three rules—no sleepovers, no revealing clothes, no boyfriends—formed the line that kept me connected to my culture throughout my girlhood as much as it kept me apart.

Turning the experiences of the women who broke the rules into little more than cautionary tales led me to believe there was one acceptable and universal brown girl experience. Defining myself by how closely I followed those rules led me to believe there was a *right* way to grow up.

So my girlhood meant growing up twice. My first coming of age was learning the rules. The second was breaking them.

After Migration: The Once and Future Kings

Walé Oyéjidé

Our story is one of migration.
Mediterranean migrations in half-toppled rafts,
winged migrations in first-class seats,
forced migrations in overcrowded ships,
scholarly migrations to enslaved-built universities,
postmarital migrations that spirit daughters away from their daddies,
and chain migrations that bring distant families together,
while tipping the population against invaders
who fear what it means to finally become the invaded.

Our story is one of finding home.

You may now hold the sacred protection of a navy-blue passport. But if you are a traveler who left half your life savings in the pocket of a grinning customs officer at Murtala Muhammed, you will always remember that disappointing your ancestors is a worse fate than deportation or death. After stepping out for groceries, you could abandon your wife and kids without explanation—only to resurface a continent away with a blond sweetheart and blue-eyed children who will never learn to speak your native tongue. After graduating at the top of your class, you could fill a Lagos warehouse with unemployed doctorates to run an email phishing startup that will bankrupt retirees in Florida. And after sharing a meal with sub-Saharan expats, you could flirt with tribal excommunication by professing that jollof rice made by Ghanaians is "actually just as good as Nigerian jollof if we're being honest." You could embrace all of these cardinal offenses in one afternoon. But none of them would be more dismaying to your West African family than if you admitted that instead of continuing your preordained life as a doctor, lawyer, or prosperity-preaching charlatan you would rather become a stay-at-home dad, designer, and writer.

Perhaps you've seen creatures like me before. Overdressed young fathers whose Chelsea boots and sport coats clash with the battle-tested sweatpants and stained blankets more experienced grandmothers bring when braving the Normandy-like terrors of a public playground. Our faces are filled with undeserved optimism. Our pockets are filled with photo-ready smartphones. But no backup toddler trousers, no juice boxes, and no cartoon-branded Band-Aids in case a child performance of *A Clockwork Orange* plays out beneath the monkey bars. In earlier times, you would have known men like us by our swooning paramours, and the trail of dead suitors who had sought to challenge us. But now you know us by the stuffed animals we brandish, and the trail of barrettes littering the road behind our careening strollers after we fail, yet again, to twist our daughters' braids correctly.

The notion of being a male homemaker flies in the tribal-marked face of everything strong men from the vast African continent are supposed to represent. We are, according to any of the historically inaccurate tropes you might consult, anything but tender and incapable of instilling discipline without the aid of a closed fist. For centuries, men from our hometowns strode from compound to compound—

surveying their lands, their multiple wives, and the many sons whose diapers they had never even considered changing. "That is women's work," they would have said. And they would have stood unchallenged. Back then, such flippant statements may have held sway when confronted by famine, plague, and well-armed European invasions sponsored by well-meaning Christians. But now, when held under the unholy tyranny of Student Loan Debt, no man—bold Nigerian or not—will dare protest domestic duties while his dear wife is the only one keeping godforsaken creditors from broaching the front door. Patriarchy has a strange way of bowing under pressure when love and economic reality rear their natural-styled heads. Still, if it isn't enough to deal with the chauvinistic moaning of elders turning in graves that have been emptied by colonizers seeking cheap resources, there will always be your mumsy to contend with.

It is often said that mothers from the Middle East lead the arms race in using guilt as a weapon. But during domestic disputes, only a Yoruba mother can package her feelings of betrayal in a silo of prayer before aiming them at her children with the indiscriminate precision of an Obama-sent drone strike. "You mean after all this family has suffered, you will not become a doctor?" she might ask softly, as you wipe the last morsel of her egusi soup from your plate and look up with the fateful awareness of a deer that sees the hunter's scope a split second after the shot echoes through the forest. Or during conversation, she might slip in a "But how can your wife pay the mortgage?" with the delicacy of a Russian mixing a polonium cocktail for an old colleague during happy hour. None of these proclamations is accompanied by the pomp and furniture-moving fanfare a wrathful father might exhibit. But each of them feels no less fatal when volleyed across the warm steam of a chai-filled teacup. It's not that the notion of rapidly shifting gender roles is foreign to our mumsies. Nor are their opinions about the independence of modern women any less progressive than ours. It's just that few women who have left their careers behind on a different continent relish watching their now-American sons spend a Wednesday morning casually prying open produce bags instead of casually performing open-heart surgery. Because we have no other choice, and because we would have it no other way, we nod respectfully at the pious whims of these mothers who have loved us at our very worst. Still, we defy them at every turn. Because the internal drive toward greatness points us in a different direction.

But where is greatness to be found if it isn't clinking around a third whiskey glass after another day spent chipping away at one's soul to preserve a job title that sounds impressive at parties? If it isn't in the Olympic somersaults one does to avoid Thanksgiving dinner questions about the flailing trajectory of one's career? And if, later, it isn't peeking through the trees like morning sunlight when a small girl on a swing screams to you, *"Higher, Daddy, higher"*? Perhaps it is found in something greater than oneself. If you're a stay-at-home dad from a culture in which manhood is synonymous with work, then you've also shut your eyes and walked across the fiery coals of your family's critiques with the serenity of a Buddhist swearing he will find Nirvana on the other side. But unlike the migrants I befriended in Italy, you've never shut your eyes to walk across fiery sands that put miles of desert between you and your family, before putting miles of water between you and the country you once called home.

For me, the journey began as all great things do: with the naive and self-important notion that one individual's actions can shift the course of an ocean. Or, failing that, one's efforts can help to stem the tide of negative perception washing over refugees before their feet even touch the first punishing waves along the Libyan coast. I was invited to travel to Florence, where I would present my brand's latest menswear collection before an audience of fashion dignitaries. There would be bright lights. There would be an army of makeup artists. On the runway, there would be human aberrations of such staggering height and beauty that anyone without the towering ego of a Nigerian would immediately feel inadequate. It was to be my first fashion show. And it was a reason—I had been told—for great celebration. But as Italian headlines told of capsized boats and smuggled people gasping beneath their overturned decks, I felt sober. It occurred to me that while many of us had grown accustomed to looking into our champagne flutes during times of tragedy, it was now a season for bold statements. "There will be professional models at this event, yes?" I asked one the organizers. "Would it be possible for us to cast migrants among them, so we can more positively illustrate the stories of people who are widely seen as burdensome victims?"

It was a simple request that turned out to have transformative results. For members of Florence's elite, who found themselves giving standing ovations to gorgeous refugees with no current place to call home, except the catwalk they momentarily had called their kingdom. For asylum seekers, who had become familiar with police harassment in Italy's streets, only to find themselves later being stopped in the road by tourists wanting to know which American rappers they must be because they were so well dressed. And for me, who met individuals whose iridescent smiles cracked through conditions that would smother most men. "This is what I was made for. I must have more of this," I loudly proclaimed. I was talking about the pastries in

Florence, it's true, but I was also referring to what I now regard as my life's work: the noble depiction of those whom our society has chosen to ignore.

And so, now I am a designer. In my former nation, it's the sort of vocation that inspires the same healthy skepticism one would afford a *democratically elected* leader or a poorly dressed pastor with fewer than two mistresses plucked from his congregation. On some days, the job places me in the middle of fresco-decorated rotundas in Tuscany, where the portraits of dead aristocrats observe me with a *How the hell did someone with your skin tone get in here?* stare that has been practiced for centuries. On other days, I can be found standing within circles of newly arrived migrants from sub-Saharan Africa. Upon hearing about my prized citizenship, they stare at their hands. Then stare at mine, before raucously declaring in their mother tongues: "How the hell did someone with your skin tone get in here . . . and how can we be next?!" The empire might well be enjoying its last desperate gasps, but until it collapses, each of us is going to take what we can from it. Thus, we stand patiently at its borders.

We're accustomed to queuing, we postcolonial blacks. Along with the resurrected Messiah and criminally hot tea that assaults the tongue with every serving, it's one of the many social fictions Brits sold us to maintain order and placate our otherwise restless souls. In long lines outside the empire's fences, we wait. A chosen few are armed with lottery-acquired visas. Others are armed with letters written by loved ones who embedded themselves in the West decades ago, like Cold War double agents afflicted with a guilty conscience. But the least fortunate are armed with every penny they could dredge from the savings of their villages. As they pour the dreams of their mothers into the bottomless pockets of people smugglers in Tripoli, they pray they will not be sold passage on a vessel with just enough holes in its hull to make it halfway, or worse, sold into the oblivion of an indentured servant army building more ski slopes in Dubai while wealthy blacks take selfies in the souks.

These are the men I meet in Italy, migrants who are windswept and unsteady on their feet. As if they have freshly fallen from heaven, only to flinch for the first time when faced with flagrant racism in the beautiful streets of Florence. They come from Guinea. They come from Nigeria. They come from Syria and beyond. They get fresh line-ups when they can. Because these men are brown and still prideful, and they refuse to look like wastemen refugees whose unkempt hair-lines now resemble the hurriedly scrawled borders of a colonizer's map. They smile while telling me they listen to esteemed poets like Kano and Kendrick. They send me messages to ask how my family is doing. Because they know what it means to miss someone who will love your disembodied voice on a dodgy connection, when she doesn't have the luxury of loving the real thing. Later, when I finally earn their trust, they tell me nothing of Lampedusa, the Libyan coast, or any of the places in between where men like them tread water for hours while watching women and children with the same dreams as theirs drown. They speak little of these terrible moments because they would rather tell me about the joys of home. The sounds that bounce off bustling street corners in Bissau. The curves of women dancing Azonto in Accra. The once-beautiful cityscape that used to be shown on postcards labeled "Love, from Aleppo." They tell me that sometimes it is better to remember these places for the ways they once were, instead of remembering why men like them eventually had to leave.

They also tell me about their current struggles in the complicated countries that bear ill-fitting names like "Home, for today." When they speak, they are every bit as erudite in their analyses of Chancellor Merkel as local Lagos hooligans are when offering critiques of Manchester City. To my shamed surprise, I find them to be more eloquent and informed than the televised pundits paid to stir up fear while railing against open immigration policies. And why wouldn't they be? Throughout history, immigrants have made a pastime of developing a strong, if impotent, knowledge of the rules written to keep them caught within death's jaws.

I see myself in each of these stateless men. Me, with soft hands that have plied at keyboards instead of working the earth or wrestling the waves of the Mediterranean. Me, with lettered accomplishments that garner acclaim instead of downcast eyes that encounter scorn whenever they meet the gazes of the local population. But me, with the same skin and unbowed spirit as theirs, nonetheless. For this reason, I have chosen to clothe my brothers. In vivid silks and brightly colored cottons, yes, but also in the love and nobility men like them have been denied for all time. Whether they are refugees or learned professors acquainted with the masterworks of a thousand dead white men, they are rarely seen as regal. This is something I find myself uniquely positioned to change. After all, what better case can a reformed lawyer turned designer bring to the bar than one in which he defends his blood and bredren against centuries of systemic subjugation? As the empire selectively swings its drawbridge open for some, others must climb in uninvited. Over barbed fences and across miles of sand. Over bureaucratic red tape and across seas of hypocrisy. As it always has been for people of our ilk, and as it will continue until we erect empires of our own, where we will no longer beg to be welcomed, where we will cordially build bigger palaces, and where we will silently wait when those who once excluded us come calling with empty palms. Our present circumstances may be humble, but our elegant appearance will announce the oncoming glory that awaits us.

When it presents itself, the glory will arrive in ways less grandiose and more wonderful than we might imagine. These days, few of us are atop horses and holding flaming swords. Few of us are immortalized as white marble busts, in rooms where tourists snap photographs while misinformed guides mistake imperialists for notables of history. But we are indeed present, and thriving in places where those charged with recording the greatest gifts to humanity rarely venture. We are present where all the best fathers are found. In parent-teacher conferences, where we make it threateningly clear that the subject of discussion will surpass the highest achievements of everyone in the room. In front of mirrors, where our reflections resemble Basquiat's greatest works after our children have subjected us to makeovers. And in museum aisles, where we point at empty spaces between masterpieces and say quietly to the kids whose small fingers are squeezed within ours: "This wall is waiting for you." Like a five-year-old girl suspended in midair with hands outstretched, and no sense that her feet will one day be cut by the rough earth set before her, the glory will fall effortlessly into our waiting arms.

Fatherhood struck me as it does most men: with the ego-shattering affirmation that from that moment forth, there would always be something greater, more beautiful, and more worthy of the lord's grace than I would ever be. Many fathers refer to that moment as "humbling." But what most of us mean is we are terrified at being confronted by the physical embodiment of our unpreparedness, our mortality, and a new obligation to make the world a better place for our children to live in.

My daughter was an adequate number of pounds. She had an adequate number of fingers. Samba played in the room—the songs of once-enslaved Yoruba people, whose Portuguese captors stripped them of their language but could never strip them of their joy. Her small hand reached toward the light as her half-clothed mother cradled her in both arms. Nurses bowed adjacent like visiting angels on either side of a triptych. Somewhere near Philadelphia, I beheld a renaissance Madonna who put every brushstroke hanging in the Louvre to shame. We named her after something St. Coltrane wrote, because it was the closest we could come to speaking in the same language as God.

There aren't a lot of directives offered to young men with daughters. And there are fewer still for those of us who must balance the fading history of a distant home with an encroaching Western culture. We are taught to show our sons how to ball their hands into fists. As if it is we, not an uncaring world, who should first introduce them to violence. But we are told little about how to raise assertive girls in a world men have shaped by silencing women. Our forefathers feared colonization, crosses, and Coca-Cola. But after immigration, we fathers fear raising children who will think it acceptable to slam doors or call us by our first names. Many of us learn too late that the seeming fragility of our girls is the great strength that will save us from our own undoing.

Things have grown clearer now that we are parents. The years spent studying like a wartime code breaker to figure out which accent to use in front of which audience. The evenings spent asking whom to pray to, and wondering which deity ignored the pleas of old countrymen who were unable to escape. The sacrifices of our parents, who withstood endless ridicule in a nation that refused to see them for what they were. And later, their comfort in our triumphs, knowing that the children they raised on foreign soil had become forces for the entire world to reckon with.

There are no right ways to survive as an immigrant in America. But when viewed within the context of a historical struggle for acceptance and self-determination, our reasons for being become apparent. Every song stands as a monument to those whose feet danced to the rhythm of shackles that failed to keep them in place. Every recipe recalls the traditions that held families together, despite the jagged coastlines threatening to keep them apart. And when accompanied by reminders that our daughters are the most beautiful gifts this country has ever received, each of the kisses we place on their cheeks resound as loving acts of revolution.

Our uprisings don't always come in the guise of smashed windows, overturned cars, or respectable slave owners forcibly torn from their stone housings in front of capitol buildings. Sometimes they come in the form of building-sized brown faces broadcast on cinema screens, portraying characters who are miles away from the token minstrels we have come to accept for want of more inspiring alternatives. If you're a cinephile who is familiar with obscure works created by unknown auteurs from Oakland, by now you may have heard of a little-known independent film called *Black Panther*. It enjoyed moderate success and was seen by a few scattered people across the globe, I'm told. Some time ago I became involved with the film in the same way that one does with a 419 scam ring: by responding "Yes! Absolutely!" to an unsolicited email that extolled the glory of black royalty while hinting dubiously at the possibility of future riches. My firm was asked to lend its design aesthetic to some of the project's personas. One of our scarves appeared in a pivotal scene, after the film's end credits. Naturally, I leapt at the opportunity to finally see my culture represented in cinema without being depicted as a punch line or a plot device for some well-meaning westerner struggling against the backdrop of a savage Africa only to fly home after bravely surviving malaria and getting the girl with the aid of a grinning black sidekick whose inner complexities would never be revealed. Most of us have seen those movies. Those of us with a conscience have cringed at the accolades they inevitably receive. From the outset, it was clear that *Black Panther* would be different.

The idea of "representation" is often hushed over at family dinners in middle America. All over the world, it is viciously derided by internet commentators whose zeal for "the good old days" conceals the fear and creeping erasure they feel when dark-complected people with better qualifications invade the sanctity of their once-homogenous lives. But less is heard of the impact that a fictional King T'Challa or Princess Shuri can have in places where more tangible role models have been made invisible by institutional discrimination. On a Sunday afternoon in West Philadelphia, while the opening bars of "Before I Let Go" echoed off the red-brick walls of a community block party like the final rebellious trumpets of an army that refused to surrender the losing battle against gentrification, a group of black children did somersaults inside a multicolored bouncy castle. They knew joy and flight in ways that could not be defined. Because they had not yet grown old and callous in a world that would define their ascendance as ceiling high before they even had a say in the matter. I stood nearby holding a camera, because the soul-shattering beauty of my daughter demands that I always have one at the ready. Spotting the lens of my instrument, two boys ran from the inflatable castle and made a beeline for my position. Unprompted, they stood before me with defiant eyes while crossing both arms in front of their small chests in unison. *"Wakanda forever!"* the boys shouted. It was a battle cry. It was a celebration. It was a re-membrance of days past and kingdoms yet to come. When a man sees the face of God, he is expected to bow his head in reverence. Instead, I smiled and depressed my finger on the camera's shutter button. The boys were immortalized on film. Just as my ancestors from Ikiré are immortalized in the oral histories our people have told for generations. And just as the golden moments those boys experienced in that theater will be immortalized when, years later, they tell their grandchildren about the first time they saw blackness shine gloriously on a pale white screen.

Acknowledged or not, we are children of a distant society that has reared us at arm's length. Regardless of whether we are held in its em-brace, we are no less deserving of images that show us at the height of our potential. In furtherance of this dream, there will be windows to break and there will be statues to tear down. But perhaps most revolu-tionary of all, there will be endless stories to write. And, increasingly, there will be audiences filled with *us* waiting to hear them being told.

But what does this nation make of its adopted? We, the sons of former diplomats who now smile politely while trying to maintain their dignity in the caricature-proportioned suits of lobby doormen? We, the daughters of former scientists who now taxi belligerent pas-sengers through Babylon's crowded streets? And we, the scions of half-English speakers who appear backward but are literate in the great philosophies of an older world? Those proud holders of navy-blue passports that were won through patience, bribery, and blood? Those devoted wavers of miniature red, white, and blue flags that welcomed them into a better life? We are accepted as long as we learn to blend in and bury ourselves within the boundaries of what is defined as a God-fearing citizen of the self-appointed Greatest Nation on Earth. We are the seeds of those young idealists who gave all, and would give more still, so that their children could have the luxury of choice. It took us too long, perhaps, to realize that it doesn't matter what this nation makes of us. It matters much more what we make of it and ourselves.

Through desert sands, we have migrated. Through neck-high waters, we have migrated. Through invasive customs searches, and through pinhole eyelets of legalese that ensnared the millions of cousins we left behind, we have migrated. For what we have given, for what we have built, and for all we have yet to accomplish, there is no nonindigenous man alive who dares tell us we do not belong. I am like many. A father. An artist. And, like most immigrants, a teller of obvious truths that are obscured by the fear of otherness.

Promises were made to those who arrived on this country's shores. There were full-throated declarations about equality and all men breathing free. Regardless of how uncomfortable those words may now make some sons of the men who wrote them, we intend to hold those promises to account. Among Yoruba people, it's not uncommon for some distant relative to arrive at your home uninvited, with packed bags and with no precise date on the calendar for when they plan to leave. Now, in the Land of the Free, our shops have been opened. Our foods can be found in street carts that outdo the most revered restaurants. Our students can be seen in the front rows, with heavy accents and small hands raised to annoyingly answer first, again. Our collective bags have been unpacked. We have made ourselves comfortable in the seats of our success. And like those damned Yorubas are known to do, we are *all* planning to stay—for more than just a little while.

On Loneliness

Fatimah Asghar

> *I would not have found this cracked jar if it weren't
> for my loneliness,*
> > *which sees gold in all that glitters.*
> > > —Dunya Mikhail

A few days ago I order an Uber pool on my way to my friend's surprise birthday party. I've just moved to Los Angeles and am new to
this city, my loneliness creeping up like an old shadow around every
corner. The driver double-checks my name. He asks me where I'm
from. I knew this was coming. The question "Where are you from?"
has punctured most days of my life, and has been both innocuous
and frightening. "Where are you from?" usually means "How did you
get here?" or the clearer: "You don't belong here." A few weeks after September 11th, I showed up for middle school soccer practice
half an hour early, and three older boys followed me around the park,
yelling, "Where are you from?" old beer bottles they found around
the park clutched menacingly in their hands. I rarely answer this
question honestly—the real answer is that I belong to many froms.
I was born in New York, grew up in Cambridge, Massachusetts, but
made Chicago my home after college. My mom was born in Srinagar,

Kashmir, but fled the violence of Partition with her family, moving to Lahore, Pakistan. I don't know where my father was born, but his family also eventually moved to Lahore. When I was young, both my parents died, and along with them, the stories that could have helped me answer the unending questions.

"Where are you from?" usually bothers me, but tonight I note his brown skin, and I know it's not the same thing as a white American asking me the same question. I note his Muslim name. His question is not an attack but an invitation, a cup of tea, from someone who also feels lonely in this country and is looking for a bit of home. There's no one else in the pool, so I don't have to put on for outsiders. He's from Lahore, but *actually* from there, as in was born and raised there, whereas Lahore is just in my blood, the clearest origin point of my lineage. My Lahore is romantic, a place my parents were alive and loved each other. It was their city, their home, their history that I can't access. A Lahore of the '70s and '80s. A city stuck in time. His Lahore is real, concrete. Modern, updated with cell phones and internet. His Lahore is stores and shopkeepers he knows. Where he had his first kiss, where he took his first steps, where he learned to drive and shave. But here we are, in an Uber in Los Angeles, linked by a different city halfway around the world, both real and imagined.

I've often, to no avail, tried to figure out how much of my loneliness comes from my race. Or how much comes from my queerness or my confused gender. How much comes from my bad relationships and desire to be loved. Growing up, I loved books and TV, often using those stories as a way to escape from my real life. But I wonder now how much of my loneliness comes from never seeing myself in those spaces and instead consuming so many stories in which the protagonist was always white. I recently saw a video of artist Kathleen Collins giving a talk at a university. She spoke about how, as folks from marginalized backgrounds, when we see only white people on TV, we begin to think of ourselves as not human, and our feelings as not worthy. Because we see only white people fall in love on screen, we mimic them, contorting our feelings into an approximation of white heterosexual love rather than Brown or Black or Queer love. Therefore, we are not only isolated from traditional representation but also isolating ourselves from our own feelings by not thinking that we are capable of defining love or anger or joy or hurt on our own terms. If whiteness is human, then anything else becomes inhuman. This is the crux of so much of our loneliness: the early set belief that not even our feelings are real, that nearly everything we do is mimicry or an approximation of whiteness, a cry to be seen as human.

As an artist, I'm always struggling to manage the well of my loneliness, how much of myself I can give away to satisfy others' thirst. Working in entertainment, it's not uncommon to walk into a room, pitch a South Asian or Muslim-specific idea, and have an exec say that they don't think their audiences will connect to it. In these spaces, even my loneliness isn't palatable. I wish there was a pie chart for loneliness, a way to submit a blood sample and receive hard data on how I can quantify it, what I can use and what I can put away, and why I'm always dragging my loneliness behind me, hoping someone will pick it up.

I'm an orphan. I find things funny that I shouldn't. When I make orphan jokes, no one laughs. My humor is purely mine, and my sister's, and slowly the people who love me and understand my brand of wickedness. But if I'm not allowed to laugh at my own life, then who is? My sister always doubles over laughing when she tells a story about how after my parents died, when I was in first grade and she was in second, I was crying uncontrollably in the lunchroom for no apparent reason. Her teachers had to pull her from class to sit with me because no one else could calm me down. I know why I was crying: I was being crushed by the weight of my loneliness. I didn't know where my parents were. I was just starting to under-stand that they were never coming back. But when we talk about this story now, neither of us can stop laughing. We find it so funny: the image of me as a first grader, in my hand-me-down American clothes, crying uncontrollably because I was realizing that I was go-ing to be alone for my whole life, while all the other kids happily ate their pudding nearby.

Part of loneliness comes from having to explain the things you think everyone should know but they don't. That nagging feeling that you are not normal. Whenever I'm having a conversation with someone new, there's always a moment when I feel I need to explain myself, or we hit a roadblock in the conversation. I remember get-ting into an argument with a friend I had known for years because he didn't know that my parents had died. He acted as though I'd be-trayed him, said that I'd been "withholding" something from him. I hadn't been doing it intentionally—it just never came up. I suspect he felt betrayed because he'd thought I was normal and I turned out not to be. But it's annoying to have to define or qualify myself in every conversation. Hi, my name is Fatimah and I'm an orphan. Hi, my name is Fatimah and I'm queer. Hi, my name is Fatimah and I'm Muslim. Hi, my name is Fatimah and I'm and I'm and I'm and I'm and I'm...

* * *

My Uber driver starts asking me if I've seen any Pakistani movies lately, if I listen to Pakistani music. Hearing the excitement in his voice, I feel like a disappointment when I say no. I often feel like a fraud when I talk to South Asian people who weren't raised in America. He asks if I speak Urdu. I give him the standard American bastard first-generation answer: "I don't speak Urdu, but I understand it fluently." Our conversation stalls; we are both familiar and unfamiliar to each other. Race often feels like a planet I don't understand, one whose rules I'm trying desperately to figure out. What makes us the same? What makes us different? We're strangers—I literally met him a few moments ago when I got into his car, and yet there are layers of shared understanding between us. Even in our moments of silence I feel sadness tinged with history and diaspora. A desire to connect, to bridge the distance of land, sea, and childhood in order to find a mirror we can recognize ourselves in.

At the same time, I know that he can hurt me more than the average person. When he asks me if I plan to marry a white man, it feels as though he's asking if I'm going to betray him. I can't tell him I might not even marry at all, let alone a man, because I don't want his judgment. Because his judgment would be too close, would be the judgment I feel in my family, the reason I'm on the other side of the country from them. I'll rationalize this to myself later: what makes him think he can ask me such personal questions; why is he making assumptions about me; I don't owe him an explanation; we're speaking completely different languages. And, yes, we might be actually speaking different languages.

I want to tell him that I understand Urdu by its texture. Here's a scene from my childhood: a friend comes over for dinner, and one of my family members asks them if they've eaten enough or if they want more food. I stare at them, waiting for the response, and they look confused, eventually whispering, "Fati, I don't know that language." I can't tell when my family is speaking English or Urdu; in my aunt's mouth, her voice is just her voice. The boat that carries the cargo. Perhaps this is because I am a poet, but language has always been a multidimensional plane to me. My college friends make fun of me for how wrong my grasp of English is, how I use words incorrectly all the time. "For a writer, you don't know shit about language." Yeah, yeah, fuck you. I'm constantly aware of how little I know of English. But my strained need to appease my colonized tongue keeps me stuck in this language. It's the only language I know well, yet it still denies me my freedom. I hold hands with words only to find out that they've betrayed me and mean something else. I'm a native English speaker, but Urdu was my first language. I spoke both Urdu and Saraiki before my parents died, and now I don't speak either. When I hear an Urdu word or an Urdu phrase, I understand it by the texture it gives me. The knowledge of its intention, the direction it pushes me toward. For example: "bas" means "stop," "enough," "this is the limit." Depending on how it's said, it's a cry or an apology. Is there an English equivalent for that? Is that language or tone? I'm not sure. When I ask my uncle how to say "I'm sorry," he says we don't have a word for that. The closest is "Mooje maaf kijye," which is more like "Lend me your forgiveness" or "Give me pardon." It's all mixed up in my head; I don't know where a word starts or ends, just the feeling that I'm left with when it's gone.

It's not that I think race is oppressive. I try not to trap myself in narratives that present race as automatically equated with hardship or negativity. Our identities as people of color should not be defined solely by our struggles. But, as we are perpetually made to feel like others in this country, that's how we are taught to understand ourselves. There's so much love in my race. I've been trying to think of my race as a site of joy. The feeling I get when I see a South Asian or Muslim person succeeding, like I've swallowed a handful of fireflies, lighting up my stomach. I glow into the night. When an older South Asian woman I've never met calls me bayti and she transforms into my auntie. When a bhangra song comes on during a party and all the South Asian people sweep in from the corners to form a circle. When I see a flock of South Asians in traditional clothing crossing a street in a crowded city, and we catch eyes. When my older family members ask if my tattoos are bird shit. My people, my people. How I love you on sight, how you make my heart beat a crowded symphony in my chest. Half the time I want every single one of you as my kin, and half the time I want nothing to do with you. Perhaps this is the source of my loneliness: belonging and not belonging, always, to you.

I both belong and don't belong to America. When I'm in America, I'm constantly reminded that I'm not actually from here, that I can never have the same access as white Americans. But when I'm abroad, I feel the most American I've ever felt: hyperaware that my cultural reference points are American, that I can't shake my American entitlement, that once I open my mouth and talk, I am perceived as an American.

I learned to be who I am by approximating who others are. When my classmates wore T-shirts, my auntie went to the fabric store and hand-sewed us T-shirts made out of a flower print fabric with a yellow background. My aunt is the best seamstress I have ever seen—

I remember when she made me a beautiful green velvet frock with a matching scrunchie from fabric she got at the store, and I proudly held her hand as I wore it to the fanciest place we could think of: the McDonald's a few blocks away from our house. When I showed up at school beaming in the T-shirt she made me, all my classmates laughed at me. All their clothes came from stores, where they could pick them off the shelves, stamped with brand names. Not made at home or thrifted from a bargain store. I wanted to be like them, enjoy their inborn American ease. But my approximation was always off, a little bit distorted. There's a photo of me from when I was around six or seven years old: I'm wearing a huge puffy pink princess dress with knockoff Timberland boots. The majority of my classmates wore Tims, and I wanted them. When I asked my family if I could get them, they agreed that they were practical shoes, good for winter and snow. We went to Payless and bought the closest things to Tims, and I practically lived in them until they were so broken down that I had to let them go.

At the mosque, I watched the other girls wrap their hair up effortlessly, not a strand poking out of place. I tried to do the same, only to have a random older woman come over to me and tug my dopatta over my head to hide all the wisps of hair I had let escape. At parties where there were South Asian people who had parents, I watched them interact. I noted the easy way Urdu poured out of their mouths, the way they complained about their parents being too overbearing or involved in their lives. The kurtas their families sent home for them from stores in Pakistan or India. Later, when my uncle died and I had to buy a white kurta for his funeral, I researched all the South Asian clothing stores I could get to by bus from my house. I arrived and fingered through all the racks, not knowing what would be appropriate, or how to negotiate in Urdu. I tried to practice in front of the racks of clothes and felt defeated. The shopkeeper took pity on me and became an auntie, helping me pick out what to wear.

When I told my uncle if I ever got married it would be for love, he responded with, "We aren't Amreecan. We were never meant to fall in love."

My Uber driver asks if I have heard the saying about Lahore, and I almost answer yes: "You haven't really lived until you've lived in Lahore." I've heard this a thousand times, along with the sayings about how Kashmir is the most beautiful place on earth. I wonder if every city has its own mythology, or if Pakistani people are just more romantic than most. When he speaks, it is a different saying: "A person who's lived in Lahore can't ever feel at home anywhere else." I ask him if this is true. He takes a long time to answer and then says no. He's lived in the US for fifteen years now, and the first time he went back to Lahore was after seven years away. All the streets had changed, and the shops had turned over. It was an unrecognizable city. And he felt like a stranger in the place that was supposed to be his home. He's only answering part of the question, saying that he doesn't feel as though Lahore is his home anymore. But he's not answering the harder question: whether he's found home anywhere else.

Before I knew the word for gentrification, I saw it happening in Cambridge. I don't know if what happened in his Lahore is gentrification or not. But I know we both grew up in places that are no longer home, places where we can no longer return. I'd come home every few months from college to fancy produce stores and chains where there had previously been run-down local bakeries and businesses. The new additions to our neighborhood—wealthy, white—spoke often of how *nice* these new stores were. Meanwhile, my friends' families found themselves unable to afford the apartments they had been renting for years. Growing up, I lived in a Cambridge that was very Black, Brown, and immigrant. When I meet people now who aren't from there but lived there as students or adults and they complain about how white or affluent the city is, I want to hit them. It bothers me that they can so easily dismiss an entire city without understanding that they are part of the problem. It bothers me that people don't take the time to see the Black, Brown, and poor people who have lived in a place for generations.

My Uber driver tells me he's in the US Army now, that he joined to help get citizenship. He's not allowed to visit Pakistan anymore because he's in the army, and they have rules against their soldiers going to countries like Pakistan. He traded one home for another. I wonder if this is a rule just for people like him, like us, or for all their soldiers. I don't know if he'll ever be able to return to Pakistan now that he's in the army, if that ban will ever be lifted for him. We might be American on paper, but we aren't granted the same privileges of Americans in actuality. Like how even though I have a US passport and haven't been to Pakistan since I was four or five, it's complicated for me to go to India because I'm of Pakistani origin. I would have to apply for a special visa and renounce any ties to Pakistan. I've had cousins who were denied visa entry into India and could not attend family members' funerals because they were Pakistani. The concept of being from "both" places or from multiple places is hard for governments to understand or acknowledge. Since I am not able to go to India, I am not allowed to return to Kashmir, where my mom's family is originally from, because it is on Indian land. I might never see the place where she was born, the place where my family lived for generations before the violence of Partition made them refugees. My loneliness heats inside me, reaching its boiling point. What is my home if there's no real place my people are from that I can return to? What is my home if I'm not allowed to go back to it because England drew some arbitrary line in a land they did not know, a line I now can't cross?

What does home look like when we've been displaced? The enormity of this question makes me feel like I'll never have a place in this world, makes me feel such a sharp loneliness. When I'm at my loneliest, I think about my mother. My displacement means nothing compared to hers. How many "homes" she had, how each uprooting was a kind of violence: her entire family forced to leave Kashmir, living in Lahore through multiple wars, getting married to a stranger and having to leave everything she knew behind for London and then New York. And her death, which maybe was a relief for her, was, and continues to be, a kind of violence for me. I try to build my home in people, but then they disappear. One of my poetry mentors, Willie Perdomo, once said something along the lines of "Home is nothing but a memory." It's a place we can only return to in our minds. And therefore, "home" is as unstable and impermanent as memory. We reinvent it at will. And each time we revisit it, we might accidentally change one detail, which ripples and ripples until the whole thing is distorted. Home is my childhood: the boys who followed me around the park with glass bottles in their hands, falling asleep on my Qur'an at religious school, my sister knocking all the air out of my body as she slammed her fists into my stomach. It's also dressing up as a bat and holding my aunt's hand on a Halloween night. Sitting with a boy I liked at the bus station for hours as we ignored the buses that would take us to our separate homes. Stretching before a two-mile run to practice, my whole team at my side.

My driver's phone goes off; another rider is added to our trip. We pull down a few streets to grab them, and as soon as they get into the car, we stop talking, our fragile Uber home interrupted by the presence of an American, a *real* American. The rest of the car is silent until he drops me off. And then I say goodbye, close the door, and never see him again.

Chooey-Booey and Brown

Tejal Rao

When the great American writer Jeffrey Steingarten was appointed the food critic of *Vogue* magazine, he made a list of his food phobias—foods, as he put it, that he wouldn't touch even if he was starving and everything else ran out. This list included kimchi, falafel, and desserts in Indian restaurants. Steingarten's plan, which sounded reasonable enough, was to expose himself to these foods, over and over again. To wear down his own sense of disgust.

Exposure is a proven method for dealing with food aversions. It goes like this: You have a little taste of what you don't like. Still don't like it? Wait a bit, and then have a little taste of it again. You repeat this, at intervals, and in some cases you can sort of trick yourself into changing your mind and liking a thing you did not.

The reason it works is because liking can be learned through repetition. Because a taste for something can be nothing more than a side effect of your familiarity with it (though it might be disappointing to think that way about what you love). In any case, the method worked for Steingarten with some foods. With others, it didn't.

"Eight Indian dinners taught me that not every Indian dessert has the texture and taste of face cream. Far from it," he wrote in his 1998 book *The Man Who Ate Everything*. "Some have the texture and taste of tennis balls." He sounded a bit like E. M. Forster, who in a report of a meal he'd eaten in India around 1912, referred to the sweets as "brown tennis balls of sugar—not bad."

Forster numbered the dishes he ate that night, publishing his notes in *The Hill of Devi*. By his own account, he ate awkwardly. He ate with his hands, cross-legged on the floor of a grand banquet hall, surrounded by busy servants, and feeling anxious the entire time because *what if he dropped stuff on the fancy clothes he'd borrowed?*

It was, technically, a work dinner. And Forster was pretty dismissive of the food itself. He seemed to find it heavy-handed and rough around the edges, describing some flavors as nothing more than the intense burn of chiles, and some dishes as so unremarkable as to be completely indistinguishable from each other. Three dishes "tasted of nothing till they were well in your mouth, when your whole tongue suddenly burst into flame."

If these descriptions seem a little familiar, and they probably do, it's because they've been so persistent.

You can hear Indian food characterized the same way now, more than one hundred years later, in conversations and in Yelp reviews and in the work of food writers. These clichés are supposed to fill me with rage, but I have to admit that I also enjoy Forster's descriptions in a very upside-down-smiley-face sort of way. There's something about seeing a writer, one who is generally quite good at describing things—a professional!—reduced to his most childish and useless words. Just look at number nine on Forster's list, the one I'll never, ever get out of my head: "Another sauce, chooey-booey and brown." This level of vagueness was the best he could do.

When I read Forster's book, I was in my early twenties, not yet an American, working as a restaurant cook in the United States. I disappeared into my baggy white uniform. Or that was what I wanted: to know exactly what my job was, to disappear into the *doing* of it. The job varied. In one kitchen, it was to cook lobsters, to pull the parasitic worms from monkfish livers, to wash the grit out of razor clams and slice them alive, at a diagonal. In another, it was to cut yuzu marshmallows into perfect cubes and cook chocolate caramels and churn five kinds of ice cream.

Weeks into one job, the chef noticed another cook taking time to teach me how to excel at some small but crucial task, routine to that kitchen. At lineup, more than a dozen of us were listening to him, waiting to hear what he'd say about the night ahead. A few of us had notebooks open, ready, pens in our hands.

"You! You must *really* like curry," the chef said, turning to the cook who'd helped me earlier, then back to me, then back to the cook. "Do you? Like curry?" he asked me very nicely, like he was asking about something fun, like he was asking at all. And because we often talked about food, it took me a few moments to realize what was going on. I can't remember if anyone laughed. The cook didn't comment one way or another; he just looked down at the floor.

I didn't feel close enough to the word to feel a rush of shame, but I knew I was supposed to. I knew that in the same way all brown people—whether their families trace back to Bangladesh or Pakistan or India—are perceived as Indian in the United States, all food cooked with a few dried spices or chiles, in anything resembling a sauce, is broadly categorized as curry.

The word in English was generic at first. British colonists used it to describe all of the new, foreign, and hard-to-categorize foods they encountered in India, a place they gradually, and violently, absorbed into their empire. What they couldn't distinguish, they saw as one

thing ("chooey-booey and brown"). And what they couldn't identify
or keep straight, they grouped under a single name.

Curry was *all* of India's food, made easy. And eventually, curry
really did become a dish, made for the British, in British India, by
Indian cooks—practically bullied into existence. A dish built to ac-
commodate a misunderstanding, to oblige a collective and willful
incomprehension of a vast, nuanced cuisine.

The eighteenth-century cookbook writer Hannah Glasse published one of the earliest recipes for curry in English in *The Art of
Cookery Made Plain and Easy*. To make a curry the "India way," she
instructed—as if there was *one* way for all of India, and she knew
what it was—you cut up a couple of small chickens and blanched
them in water, reserving the poaching liquid for the sauce. Then you
pan-fried the meat with some onions, in butter. When the onions
were browned all over, you added a mash of turmeric, ginger, and
chiles, and eventually the chicken poaching liquid, to make a sauce.
You thickened the sauce with cream and finished it all with a big
squeeze of lemon juice. Glasse's book, which was meant to "improve
the servants," was a bestseller for more than a century.

It took a little longer for curry to break through in the United
States, but in 1939, Charlotte Hughes reported in the *New York Times*
on "curry restaurants springing up here and there." By then, curry
wasn't just a dish or a range of industrially produced powders and
pastes. It was also a verb—you could *curry* a chicken. In the accompanying illustration for one article, an Indian man in a feathered turban
floats on a magic carpet just above the stove of a befuddled white lady
in a ruffled apron, his hands over the curry pot as if mid-incantation.
The caption reads, "Curry is a mystery to many American cooks."

Trudie Teele, an American missionary who had been stationed in

Rangoon and Calcutta for more than a decade, wrote a cookbook about curries and later opened an Indian restaurant on Fifty-Seventh Street. She was often quoted as an expert on the subject, and the *Indianapolis Star* once described her as a woman "determined to recapture for the homefolks the inimitable, tantalizing taste of real curry."

The Indian immigrant community that had settled in New York opened their own restaurants in Harlem and Midtown. A married couple, Habib and Victoria Ullah, founded Bengal Garden in 1948, just north of Times Square, with financial backing from Ibrahim Choudry. Victoria, who had moved to New York from Puerto Rico, worked front-of-house. Habib, who was from Noakhali and had worked on a ship that took him from Calcutta to Boston, ran the kitchen. Many of the Indian cooks working in New York at the time had experience cooking on ships, and their customers included sailors, students, expats, and Midtown's theater crowd. But few of those restaurants, or those cooks, made it into stories about Indian food.

"Indian cooks seem to work by instinct," wrote Hughes. "They couldn't begin to describe what they do. They've been doing it too long. You have to get at the recipe through an intermediary."

Despite the American obsession with authenticity, with "real curry," food writers were usually getting their recipes, and their ideas for how Indian food should be served and what it should taste like, through intermediaries, looking right past the expertise and experience of Indian cooks around them.

It meant early American definitions of curry were already removed, mistranslated, distorted. Simply brown your onion and garlic with a premixed curry powder, then add your liquid and citrus juice, one *Times* article instructed. And because so much of the American understanding of curry was based on that of eighteenth-century British food writers, Americans also considered jarred fruity chutneys, dried salted fish, and wafers of popadam to be crucial accompaniments.

"Curry is just a vague inaccurate word which the world has picked up from the British who, in turn, got it mistakenly from us," wrote the Indian cookbook author Madhur Jaffrey. Though she'd go on to write several books about curry, early in her career she resented the word and resisted its use.

Curry might have started as a kind of oversimplification, but it was transformed and reshaped over hundreds of years until the word spidered out to mean many things, and belong to many people, including Indians. What I wondered for the first time, when it was attached to me in the place where I worked, was if it belonged to me.

As the diaspora splintered and grew, so did the meaning of the word. The Indian side of my family, now mostly in Pune on the west coast, doesn't use it at all, not to name any of their foods. And the East African–Asian side of my family uses it only with one particular dish, kofta curry, or meatball curry. My grandfather from Kenya—I called him Deddy—made the dish as far back as I can remember, on special occasions and for family gatherings and big Sunday lunches at home.

To make it, the small, soft, juicy lamb meatballs are deeply browned all over and then simmered in a very lean tomato sauce spiked with garam masala and fried ginger and green chiles. Raw cilantro leaves speckle the meat. I make the dish in the same way, with some small variations, and call it by the same name. But ask someone else what curry means, or how to make it, and you'll probably hear a very different and equally true answer. Which is why "Do you like curry?" isn't only a vague and tedious question; it's one that's almost impossible to answer.

Curry doesn't refer to one dish, to one technique, to one point of origin, to one paste, to one powder. And it never did. It doesn't indicate a single texture. It isn't shorthand for a particular ingredient or precise set of flavors. It's a catchall, and few culinary words are better at flattening out all of the personal, regional, and historical specificity of an immensely sophisticated cuisine, expressed as it is in different languages, styles, and forms. This is not what I said, of course, that day in the restaurant. Because I said nothing. I was unprepared. I looked at my shoes. They were dirty.

"You must really like curry" is the kind of lazy, unimaginative racism I'd naively assumed people outgrew. It's soft, bouncy playground stuff ("chooey-booey and brown"), and I didn't imagine it would be so persistent. I'd moved to the United States almost a decade earlier, as a dependent on my father's work visa, with what I didn't then realize were a whole set of privileges, including a fluency in English and the right to work when I turned sixteen.

In Boston, where I went to college after 9/11, people were sophisticated and stealthy with their various brands of racism. So much so that I almost forgot about this variety. The people in charge, the people I reported to, the people who led the various institutions I was a part of—I was used to them practicing racism more privately and politely, which was often so much worse, because without help, it took a little more time to sniff them out and identify their damage.

The curry remark had been tiny but public. It had happened quickly, and then I wondered if it had happened at all. Because everyone was so quiet, pretended they hadn't heard it, or if they had, it was no big deal, it was nothing, it was just a harmless joke. *A harmless joke is what I told myself*, until it became clear that the cook who'd helped me once wasn't going to help me again.

My grandfather emailed me his recipe for kofta curry in the spring of 2010. It's an email I still reference every time I make the dish, and when I went back to it recently, what I noticed is that he didn't use the word "curry" in it at all.

Today is Madaraka Day. I am alone at home and the time is 11 o'clock in the morning. I thought, it is the best time to write you. Probably for six people you will need 1 kilo of mince meat.

In a bowl, add the meat, then start adding 1 teaspoon of garam masala, a pinch of red chile powder, 1 tablespoon of dhana jiru (powder of coriander and cumin seeds), 1 tablespoon of green masala (4 cloves of garlic, 1 small piece of fresh ginger, 2 green chiles put into a chopper and made into a paste. You will use what remains for making the sauce).

Also add in the bowl chopped onions of 1 small onion, chopped green coriander, and a pinch of salt. Mix well, and make small round shape balls with your hands and put them on a plate. Now what you have to do is to fry them lightly in a pan with a little oil.

The next preparation is the sauce. In a cooking vessel add the required quantity of oil, maybe a quarter to a half cup. Just check. When the oil is hot add chopped onions (2 small ones) until they turn into a golden brown, now add the remaining quantity of green masala and 3 liquidized tomatoes and keep turning the mixture with a wooden spoon.

Now a pinch of red chile powder, 1 tablespoon of dhana jiru, and 1 teaspoon of garam masala. Add 2 cups of water and salt as required.

Cook for 5 minutes or slightly more. Should you need some more water,
you can add it. When this process is done, add the fried koftas and
cook for 10 minutes. Finally for garnishing, sprinkle with chopped
fresh coriander. Well that is all.

I'd already moved into my first apartment in New York when someone told me the block was nicknamed Curry Row, just a little stretch
of it, beginning on Sixth Street, where a handful of Indian restaurants
glittered with hanging foil decorations and lit up at night with chile-
shaped lights. I thought it was cute. All these restaurants where men
sat down to play sitar and tablas, and Bangladeshi waiters occasionally
stood outside to encourage students and tourists to come in and try
the chicken tikka masala, sometimes even handing out morsels of it
on toothpicks.

My family didn't cook it at home, but we knew the dish well as a
restaurant curry created, by most accounts, in Scotland, where someone had the genius idea of adding canned tomato soup and cream to
chicken tikka to quickly turn it into a gravy.

Outside my home on Curry Row (I never, ever heard anyone call
it that, by the way, except to tell me it was called that) the air often
smelled of tomatoes, fenugreek, and cream. Coriander and cumin.
The savory caramel of browning onions. It was not exactly the smell
of my childhood home, but it was a smell I came to associate with
home, and if I walked down the street, especially in the late afternoon
when the puffy metal vents pumped air from the kitchens, I'd catch it
in waves.

That's when I remembered how my parents used to open the windows when they cooked Indian food and turn on the extractor fan to

full blast and light a candle or two on the kitchen counter. They used to close our bedroom doors. They used to worry about the Smell.

The Smell, if we weren't careful, could adhere to our sweaters, to our dresses, to my father's woolen suit jackets. It could find its way into our hair and the skin of our fingertips and the sticky depths of our armpits, and we would carry it out into the world, where it would give away—what exactly? Not the particulars of who we were. Immigrants who cooked Gujarati and Konkani food, by way of many other places. Immigrants who were also the sons and daughters of immigrants, and the grandchildren of immigrants who'd landed in the United States by way of Uganda and Kenya, jabbed this way and that by a series of both mundane and violent historical forces. Immigrants who, to be clear, enjoyed extremely delicious things in an often fragrant home.

If the Smell was present in the homes of aunties and uncles, my parents would discuss it on the way home, and not entirely without judgment. I noticed how when our neighbors commented on the Smell—"Something smells good!"—it didn't matter how earnestly they said it. Because who could be sure what they said behind closed doors? And the Smell was ours, belonged to us even as it left our kitchen, pointed back to us always, like a neon cartoon arrow with rows of flashing lights.

It was, once or twice a week, just the air we breathed. I loved it completely. It was so familiar as to sometimes even be unnoticeable. Because nothing could be more ordinary than mustard seeds and kadi patta leaves popping and crackling in hot oil, tipped into a pot of steaming kadhi, which we'd have with khichdi, all the while insisting that nothing, nothing at all happened at school today. My brother was not punched in the stomach. I was not asked about the color of my nipples. Nothing could be more beautifully routine than a few fragments of cinnamon and clove toasting for masoor dal. Or a pale green paste of ginger, garlic, and chiles sputtering very gently in ghee, cooking but not caramelizing at the bottom of the pan, to start some batata nu shaak.

It was many things, but really it was four hundred years of incomprehension wafting right into the hall, the driveway, the street, the cul-de-sac. And it didn't really matter what we called it in here, at home, because out there it would be curry, plain and simple. And nothing could clarify it, and nothing could keep it from drifting.

Luck of the Irish

Maeve Higgins

Cue the mournful fiddle music, please, and nod sadly as I tell you that when I was a child in Ireland, I stood often upon the shore and squinted across the Atlantic, dreaming of moving to New York City. And now bring in the beat of a bodhrán, our traditional wood-framed drum covered tightly in goatskin, to signify with growing excitement, triumph even, that I made my dream come true.

See me now, whirling around this city that never sleeps, bursting with that feeling you only get when ambition meets opportunity. Voices sing out: "Look at this good immigrant!"

But wait. Cut the music. This is all a bit much. My journey was not fraught. There was no huge obstacle to overcome, no great fortress to penetrate. In 1997, I was seventeen, and in that smooth "I want it, so I'll take it" way of a middle-class white person, I simply moved here.

I got a job as an au pair with an Irish family in Rye, a small and comfortable New York town. I did not need to apply for a visa, the mother of the family explained; as an Irish citizen, I was covered by the Visa Waiver Program, which allows citizens of specific countries to travel to the United States for up to ninety days without having to obtain a visa. I could just stroll up to the US immigration agent at Dublin Airport and show him my visa waiver.

Things got even easier from there. As an Irish person, I enjoyed

Preclearance from US Customs and Border Protection. This means that Irish people can go through a travel inspection that is basically customs as well as public health and agricultural clearance at their departure airport. This feature, found in many Canadian airports as well, is convenient, one less annoyance to deal with when you arrive jet-lagged and cranky.

Good for the traveler, and good for America. US Customs and Border Protection puts it like this: "DHS [Department of Homeland Security] firmly believes that establishing Preclearance operations in strategic locations will assist our efforts in identifying terrorists, criminals, and other national security threats prior to their boarding an aircraft bound for the United States." In the past couple of years, DHS is working to expand Preclearance to countries like Sweden and the UK.

I thought little about this system when I was a teenager and benefitting from it. Today, I have thought about it. Preclearance does indeed make travel to the US easier for citizens of wealthy, white, stable countries, and more difficult for people from poor black and brown countries under duress. Preclearance is calamitous if you need to claim asylum in the US, because you can only do that once you reach US soil. By preventing people from getting into the country, you deny them the opportunity to claim asylum. Not only that, Preclearance goes against the policy of non-refoulement (a term I had never heard at seventeen), which the United States claims to ascribe to. The 1951 Refugee Convention forbids a country receiving asylum seekers from sending them back to a country where they face persecution based on "race, religion, nationality, membership of a particular social group, or political opinion." By refusing admission to people before they even get to the US, the country can sidestep that rule. Of course,

I never had to worry about claiming asylum anywhere. In my life-time, the Republic of Ireland has overwhelmingly been a safe and peaceful place, a relatively prosperous one too. There are various in-dexes created by financial firms that rank global passports according to the access and freedom they provide to their citizens, and the Irish passport is one of the most powerful passports in the world.

Another thing I didn't worry about was overstaying my ninety-day visa waiver. I simply overstayed, slipping overnight into my new undocumented status. Most undocumented immigrants in the US have done something similar, arriving by plane either with a visa or a visa waiver, and then just...staying. Two-thirds of approximately 11 million undocumented immigrants in the US were once legal, until their visas or waivers expired. That's one reason I cringe at calls to spend billions on a border wall with Mexico when not only are more Mexican people leaving the US rather than going to it, the narrative of smuggling yourself in is far less common than someone who is already just here.

I cannot speak for other undocumented people, current or former, but I can explain why I stayed. It was because I felt like it. I was enjoying my time in the US and had taken a gap year before col-lege to do so. To remind you, I was a teenager and this was before 9/11, when immigration was not the viciously divisive topic it is today, and there was generally much less fear in the air around the idea of "foreigners."

I was friendly with an older group of undocumented Irish people I'd met through another Irish au pair. They worked in bars and on construction sites around the city and state and were generous with advice. "If you get into an accident, try not to report it." "If you get caught causing trouble, don't make a fuss; be calm, and give a fake name and social security number if you have to." "If you need to go to hospital, call this person, and they'll explain what to do."

Like most immigrant communities, we helped each other out. That means different things depending on where you're from. I was never frightened when I was undocumented. Being white made me less likely to be profiled by any law enforcement official, and speaking English and sharing many cultural tropes with Americans allowed me to fit in easily. I suppose it stemmed from the fact that in New York, and in the US widely, the Irish are a powerful group. Our political and cultural currency is stronger than most. The Irish diaspora provides arriving immigrants with a huge and solid foundation. The value of goodwill shown to the Irish by Americans, while difficult to quantify, cannot be discounted, particularly when contrasted with the suspicion and racism faced by people of other nationalities.

The thoughtlessness with which I behaved is what strikes me today. Over the past two years, I've made a podcast about immigration and interviewed many undocumented people, none of whom share my former nonchalance. Having met so many immigrants who are consumed by the need of papers, or "papeles," I acted with sheer breeziness, my comfort the surest sign of privilege there is.

In that gap year between my final school exams and my first year in college, I wanted to experience life in New York. It suited me. That is not a reality for many. The real fear felt by undocumented individuals and families with mixed status is growing by the day under the Trump administration. Living in the US without documentation is a civil violation, not a crime, but the detention of immigrants is gaining momentum month by month.

The day after Trump was elected, the biggest jump in stock went to the private prison industry, which also largely owns and runs immigrant detention centers. Shares of CoreCivic (formerly known as Corrections Corporation of America) and GEO Group, the two biggest players in the business, leapt 43 and 21 percent, respectively. Worse days for immigrants are coming. For the majority of the undocumented community, fear of imprisonment and deportation to a place away from their homes, work, and family have always factored into their lives and are reaching new heights today. As I write this, months after families were separated at the Mexican border, thousands of children have still not been reunited with their parents, and Temporary Protected Status has been stripped from half a million immigrants who argue that they still need it, badly.

Trump has played on the fear of foreigners from the time he began his election campaign, when he claimed Mexico was sending rapists into the US, right through to his first speech to Congress, in which he blamed immigrants for everything wrong under the sun, announcing a list, to be published weekly, of crimes committed by immigrants. His administration is desperate to equate immigrants with crime. All this, despite decades of irrefutable evidence that immigrants, with or without papers, are less likely to commit crimes than native-born Americans.

Trump's Travel Ban 3.0, rejecting people from Iran, Syria, Libya, Yemen, Somalia, North Korea, Venezuela, and Chad, is now the law of the land, having been upheld by the US Supreme Court in December 2017. This third attempt at a large-scale restriction of travelers from a variety of countries, mostly with a Muslim majority, has succeeded where the first two failed. Possibly because this proclamation, issued in September 2017, for the first time includes two non-Muslim-majority countries, North Korea and Venezuela, and clearly invokes perceived weaknesses in those countries' vetting capabilities. Travel Ban 3.0 is also different in that it has no expiration date. This ban strikes me as illogical too, given that relatively few immigrants from these countries make it to the US in the first place. Illogical, that is, unless the logic you're working with is "Let's make sure all the brown people know they're not wanted here."

None of this is new. Throughout its history, the United States has taken a racialized approach to immigration and naturalization laws. Between 1790 and 1802, Congress passed a series of naturalization laws, mandating that applicants be "free white persons" with "five years' residence in the country" and "good moral character." According to a 2002 report by the US Citizenship and Immigration Services historian, "US nationality law generally transformed northern and western European immigrants into US citizens." Non-European immigrants were less fortunate, many finding it impossible to even get here.

Ethnic bias also played a part in US immigration history with the infamous Chinese Exclusion Act of 1882, which remained in various iterations until World War II, when it became a little too awkward to discriminate against the nation's new allies, the Chinese. Then, as now, anti-immigrant sentiment was stirred up by an acrimonious presidential election, and white Americans were being squeezed economically. When the US Supreme Court upheld the legality of Chinese Exclusion in 1889, it did so on the grounds of national security. When first introduced, the exclusion act was billed as a temporary measure. You know, sort of like Donald Trump "calling for a total and complete shutdown of Muslims entering the United States until our country's representatives can figure out what the hell is going on."

Back then, there were no protests against the ban at ports of entry, and there were few legal challenges. But Mae Ngai, a professor of Asian American Studies at Columbia University, points out some of the details in the so-called Muslim ban that have a chilling echo of the Chinese Exclusion Act. "The logic of Chinese exclusion was a racial one," she says. "You could say the religious part of Trump's order pertaining to Muslims is a new kind of racism, but the original racist argument behind the exclusion act was that Chinese cannot assimilate, that there is something about Chinese that makes them innately alien and unable to assimilate. That's the same logic as Trump's view that Muslims follow a hateful religion and that Muslims don't love America."

In 1924, the Johnson-Reed Act was passed "to preserve the ideal of U.S. homogeneity." It limited the number of immigrants allowed entry into the United States through a national-origins quota and completely excluded Asian immigrants. Immigration and naturalization laws changed during the 1940s and 1950s, ostensibly to be fairer to Asian immigrants, but the changes amounted to only mere tweaks in the 1924 system while maintaining the quota policy.

As a result of the 1952 Immigration and Nationality Act, 85 percent of the 154,277 visas available annually went immediately to immigrants of northern and western European lineage. It makes me think of our current president, with his rage-filled longing for more Norwegians. It's so sad, really, that the old white man craves more blondes.

The 1965 Immigration and Nationality Act eliminated the use of national-origin quotas and committed the United States, for the first time, to accepting immigrants of all nationalities on a roughly equal basis. The following years saw an increase in Asian and Latino immigrants and a decline in Irish ones, who had lost their lucky edge because of the new quota system. However, as a brutal recession ground on in the old country, thousands of Irish people decided not to wait for a legal path in: they came to the United States as tourists and, as I would do years later, *simply stayed.*

Irish American politicians tried to figure out what to do with these undocumented Irish people, and in 1986 they came up with the Donnelly Visa. Ostensibly, this was a diversity program lottery and was quite openly a way to help those undocumented Irish regularize their status. US Representative Brian J. Donnelly, Democrat of Massachusetts, oversaw the first phase of the program, under which 4,161 out of the first 10,000 visas in the lottery went to the Irish. They used a loophole that allowed them to enter the lottery multiple times, even holding parties to fill out multiple applications on behalf of one of their own.

In 1989, the diversity program became a truly random lottery, with only one entry per person, and the Irish received only 1 percent of the visas. The top three recipient countries were Bangladesh, Pakistan, and Egypt. But a new program a year later again favored European countries. Known as Morrison Visas, after their sponsor, US Representative Bruce Morrison, Democrat of Connecticut, these were distributed over the next three years to immigrants from countries disadvantaged by the 1965 Immigration and Nationality Act. More than 40 percent went to Irish citizens.

In 1995, this became the diversity visa lottery we have today, the one that allows 50,000 people into the United States each year from countries with "historically low rates of immigration to the United States," according to the State Department. It's a program the current administration is now looking to axe, with the president regularly deriding it.

In case it isn't obvious, I should point out that most of the politicians who helped the cause of Irish immigrants in the past were themselves Irish American. Ted Kennedy, Tip O'Neill, and the aforementioned Donnelly and Morrison all claimed Irish roots. As do many in every branch of the US government today, most of them loudly and with no small amount of pride. Ironically, some of the most virulently anti-immigrant people in the White House today are Irish Americans, including John F. Kelly and Mick Mulvaney.

Vice President Mike Pence, who once tried to ban Syrian refugees from Indiana, often lauds his Irish grandfather's immigrant story. The grandfather, Richard Cawley, left Ireland in 1923, escaping a vicious civil war. Yet under rules in place at the time, Cawley would not have been allowed into the country had he been Chinese and likely would not have been able to get the job he did, as a streetcar driver, had he been black. And yet the *New York Times* quotes Pence addressing a group of Latino business leaders in March 2017, saying, "If you work hard, play by the rules, anybody can be anybody in America." That isn't true.

Race and ethnicity remain hugely significant in the story of immigration. After six months of washing bedsheets piddled on by toddlers for $150 a week, wandering around the city on my days off, not thinking twice about asking cops for directions, I didn't want to be an au pair anymore. I returned to Ireland. There were no consequences for my overstay. Had I been caught, which was always unlikely, I could have been deported and faced a ten-year ban on returning to the US. The rashness of youth could explain why I took

that risk, but I was wholly backed up by my confidence that this
would not happen, that I would not get caught. And I didn't. Your
chance of being arrested or profiled by the police or by ICE (Immigration and Customs Enforcement) is higher if you're black or
brown, and most Irish immigrants are white.

I do not wish to belittle the experience of many undocumented
Irish people here who try every legal way they can find to regularize
their status. Since Trump, they are worried now too. The most recent
figures show a 30 percent increase in immigrant arrests made by ICE,
with the number of Irish deported from across the US rising to 34 in
2017, up from 26 the previous year. In June of 2017 the Irish Government appointed an envoy to the US Congress to work on the issue
of the undocumented Irish living here, who will work under the direction of the Minister of State for the Diaspora and International
Development, Ciarán Cannon.

I met Minister Cannon at an Irish American event recently. I was one
of the nominees for "The Voice of Irish America" and lost out to a
lady who does cross-stitch, a fact that has given my best friend, Mona,
something to tease me about for life. Whenever I express an opinion
now, she tells me to sew it on a cushion and come back to her later.
Undaunted by my loss to a needle and thread, I used my voice to ask
the minister if he felt the powerful Irish Americans in this administration will help the cause of the Irish undocumented. "Of course it has
to help. They're the people we are engaging with, on both sides." But
he added, with a nod to Boston's Irish American mayor, Marty Walsh
(who is adamant on this point), that there must be a collective movement. "It's not realistic to expect that a stand-alone solution will be
provided for the Irish community... and it's perhaps unjust."

* * *

In March 2017, during the traditional St. Patrick's Day celebrations at the White House, a usually good-natured affair, Irish prime minister Enda Kenny struck a serious note, calling for a solution for the undocumented community at large: "There are millions out there who want to play their part for America—if you like, who want to make America great."

Kenny's message fell on deaf ears; in the first year of his presidency, Trump revoked the Deferred Action for Childhood Arrivals (DACA) program, leaving up to 800,000 people at risk of returning to undocumented status. His administration also ended Temporary Protected Status for immigrants from Haiti, El Salvador, Nicaragua, and Sudan. And he plans to cut legal immigration in half within a decade.

In 2013, I was invited to tell jokes at a comedy festival in Kansas City. The festival organized a P-3 visa, as I was an artist coming to contribute in a culturally unique way. I went over and did my work for a few days, but the visa lasted a full year. I lived in London at the time and hated it there, finding it as sprawling and lonely as all of its detractors say it is. I left London, and at a loss for what to do with myself, I went to stay on a remote island off the coast of West Cork. It was December, and I trundled around building fires and working up the courage to swim in the sea. I hadn't been back to New York for a decade, but I thought about the place every now and then. I can't explain why. I suppose it was a mixture of ambition and curiosity, but I felt I wasn't through with the city—I wanted to try it again. One night something magical happened with the wind and I had full phone reception for a minute, long enough to read an email asking if I wanted to do a show at the Irish Arts Center in New York—one show—at the end of January.

I sat up in bed and decided I'd go live in New York again. I clambered up onto the chest of drawers to get phone reception and replied, saying I would. It was just an email I answered. It was just one foot in front of the other. That's how things happen, I suppose. When there are few obstacles in the way.

A few months before my P-3 ran out, I applied for an O-1 visa, which means I am "an alien of extraordinary ability." It was granted. I'm now on my second O-1 visa, so I regularly tell people I'm doubly extraordinary. That's a joke, of course. I'm not extraordinary at all. It's dumb luck that I was born white and Irish. And that luck, combined with a history of racialized immigration policies, meant that I was allowed to move here, to a country whose leaders look at me and see themselves, and welcome me with open arms as they push others away.

Her Name Was India

Krutika Mallikarjuna

To her credit, the name listed on her Tinder profile was her middle name, Anita. And to mine, Anita was every queer girl's dream. She looked like she just walked out of an audition for Eliza Dushku's part in *Bring It On*. Dark, deep eyes that I drowned in; lush, wavy hair that made me itch to run my hands through it; and an easy smile—or rather smirk—that cut as quickly as it enticed. She flashed it enough over the first few rounds at my local that I thought, *Yeah, this is a vibe.*

Our thighs touched purposefully under the bar as we talked about our loved ones. Hers were hippies; they ran away together on a backpacking trip to Asia from which they emerged spiritually reformed, and pregnant. Lo and behold the magnificent creature sitting before me: brilliant (law school), driven (specializing in immigration law), and genuinely curious about people who don't look or sound like her (she asked why her palak paneer recipe was shit in such a heartbroken manner). I couldn't focus on anything except kissing her, so what caught my attention next was not what she said but the demure and self-deprecating way she said it.

"They, uh, they actually named me India," she said to me with a blush I would have found delightful had it not been accompanied by those words. "I was dreading telling you 'cause, God, it's truly terrible. I'm pretty sure I was conceived there."

I can't think of anything worse than knowing exactly when and where your parents fucked—expect maybe being reminded of it every time someone tries to get your attention. But sympathy isn't what flooded my mind. Neither was empathy, though if anyone deserved it, it was Anita. As I sat there slack-jawed, she stumbled all over herself to reassure me that her parents are the only people who call her India and that she was truly embarrassed by the obvious (micro? macro? just right?) aggression that this naming represented.

Of the many pitfalls of being a queer desi woman swiping through Tinder, I never expected to find myself getting trashed in a bar trying to forget that I was on a date with a white girl named India. I knew they existed out there in the post-Commonwealth world, especially one that worshipped pilgrimages to find oneself à la the Beatles or Elizabeth Gilbert. But it never occurred to me that I'd meet one in the wilds of Brooklyn. Though it certainly should have.

I swallowed a million questions with my next sip of mescal— questions not for Anita but for Anita's parents. *In what possible world is your connection to India deep enough for you to name your firstborn after the country? Did you live there for any extended period of time? Did you contribute in any measurable way to its economy, its society? Did you think about the dark and terrifying centuries of English rule that Indians only emancipated themselves from as recently as 1947? Did you consider how naming a white baby who embodies the platonic ideal of India's colonizers would make actual Indian people feel?* For two white folks who claim to love India, it's clear they never thought of it as more than a backdrop to their own story. The meandering path of Anita's parents might not have been paved with money or ease in the way we think of Wes Anderson's or Rudyard Kipling's, but it is undoubtedly a relationship that took more from the culture than it gave. No child should be punished for the sins of the parent, and yet there was no possible way for me to hear her good Christian name as anything but.

After that I stopped thinking about kissing her. Anita was still brilliant and beautiful and charming as all hell; her thigh still pressed up against mine in the booth. But I retreated into my own head, my own glass, and my own worries. She was the second, maybe third, woman I had ever been on a date with and the first after I had been outed to my deeply religious mother. What was supposed to be an evening to help me forget that my life was falling apart had turned into a blatant reminder of that fact.

I hadn't spoken to my mother for more than a tense minute at a time in roughly two months. Alerted by a fairly benign Facebook post promoting that I'd be a speaker at a queer Comic-Con panel, she called me in the middle of a workday. I leapt to answer because the only reason for off-hour calls from my family is to announce the death of a loved one halfway around the world. Granted they normally come in the middle of the night rather than the middle of the day, but still, fear gripped me. Skipping the hello, she cut straight to the point.

"Why am I seeing a post on Facebook for a...queer event...that you're tagged in?"

The word "queer" sounded especially so coming from my mother's mouth. It made me sick to hear it in the shaky tone I knew meant she was close to tears. First and foremost, I was furious that a woman I still consider the kindest person I know could show so much ignorance and fear about a group of people who had never done anything to wrong her. But in the silence between her question and my answer, it was shame that overwhelmed me.

My mother and I have always had a contentious, and fairly stereotypical, relationship. A deeply religious Indian mother, who never expected to leave the culture, customs, and city she had grown up in, she spent most of my childhood trying to protect me from being indoctrinated into Western ideals that, to her, screamed danger at every turn. No dating, no going out with my friends unless it was to a school-sanctioned event. I wasn't even allowed to pick out my own clothes for school until I was thirteen. I spent a lot of time lying to her. I used to sneak clothes into my backpack to change into at school. I'd tell her I was at my best friend's house when I was really just getting picked up from there by my illicit boyfriend. I was at a study group that met solely to dissect *The Matrix Revolutions* at the movies.

As a result, by the time I moved away to college, my mother and I had no real idea of who the other was. To me, she was simply the personification of overprotectiveness, someone who kept me from fully understanding and engaging in the world around me. To her, I was my father's daughter: brash, loud, intelligent, and far too questioning of authority to lead myself into anything but destruction. We loved each other deeply, but we didn't understand each other. When I was on my own in New York City, the burden of this barrier eased. I could filter my life for my parents, and while I presented anecdotes that cast me as in control of my life and making only good choices, all those anecdotes were still true. Their trust in me grew each time I conquered a new adult challenge. Steadily employed and also interning while acing a full course load? Check. Graduated with a job offer? Check. Found and paid for my first shared apartment in the city? Check. Successfully changed careers and landed at a prestigious media outlet? Check. Negotiated a significant pay raise? Check.

Somewhere along the line it felt like my parents had stopped waiting breathlessly for me to fail. I had a handle on things. My mother in particular seemed to have had a weight lifted off her shoulders. She could rest assured that she had raised me well, and despite all the fighting in my teenage years, I was headed in the right direction. America hadn't corrupted me. Rather than use our phone conversations to grade my life progress, she started to talk to me in ways that implied she was simply interested in what I had to say. As she began to see me as a person, I began to see her as the same. And I began to realize that while I've always loved her, I also actually liked her as her own person, beyond her identity as my mother.

This is what I was thinking about in the seconds of silence that ticked by on the phone after she asked me about the Facebook notification. I had a choice here: I could lie, as I had done for most of my childhood, and tell her the panel was just a work thing, or I could just come out and be honest about this huge part of myself I had been struggling with as a grown-ass adult. I came out. She broke down in tears. For the first time in my entire life, she hung up the phone without saying "I love you."

Doing the right thing left me bereft. I felt unmoored, adrift, alone like I never had before. Later that night on the phone with my dad, he assured me that she'd come around, that she just didn't have the context or understanding to think of my bisexuality right now. Months later, she would tell me she just knew it was something she did, or said, that must have made me this way. She was afraid that other people in our tiny, gossipy community would think she was a bad mother. My queerness was somehow her greatest failure.

It was the most devastating moment of my twenty-six years on this earth, that phone call. And yet there's something perverse about the way I enjoyed the lightness of being hollowed out, because at least I had been honest, and despite the fact that I didn't fully have the support of my loved ones, I was at least free to live my life. So I did. I drank, I dated, I fucked, and I enjoyed summer in the city—as long as I could repress the thought that perhaps I would have to learn to do all this without the support of my mother ever again.

The moments when the thought of life without my mother overwhelmed me happened mostly in private, when I wasn't surrounded by the unconditional love of my friends. I wasn't expecting these feelings to well up in a bar next to someone who, on paper, was my dream girl. We were simply getting to know each other, but I had already skipped ahead eight months to meeting the parents and couldn't picture anything but my dad apologizing for the fact that my mother wasn't there. There was no future here without my mother's tolerance. After another half hour of awkward first-date chatter, during which I was so distracted I asked her to repeat everything twice, Anita called it a night. It was a rare case in which we were both disappointed by how the evening went, and I knew that was solely my fault. As I expected, she generously extended an invitation to try the whole thing again when I had less on my mind. And like every asshole I've cussed out in the group text, I ghosted her. I fell into a deep depression that barely allowed me to get out of bed for work in the morning, forget about dating. In my darkest hours over the next several months, I questioned whether it had even been worth it to come out, seeing as marrying a man was still a definite possibility. My half life had been filled with things that make me happy, and I'd had the love of my mom. I thought maybe that should have been enough.

It would take repeated strained phone calls, months of therapy for both me and her, and the gentle urging of my dad before we were able to have an honest conversation again without screaming at each other. Minute by precious minute, my mother and I returned to our weekly half-hour kikis. Tension still lurked in each call, but after a while, thanks to support groups and therapy, she could bring herself to ask questions about my life again. Our implicit deal had become explicit: *Be honest with me, and I promise to trust you to handle your own life no matter how much it scares me.* I've never been prouder of her than when she tentatively asked me if I was seeing anyone. I was not, but I had been, so I offered up Anita as a noncontroversial anecdote that would not lead us into the territory of sex. She mirrored my silence from our initial bombshell conversation. I held my breath and hoped she felt the weight of the small victories that had brought us to this unprecedented transparency.

She started to laugh.

"Kruthu...are you serious? A gora girl named India?"

Exhale. Rinse. Repeat. I delved into details, embellishing whenever I could in a hammy way that I learned from my dad to make her laugh. When we hung up that day, she was still chuckling at the antics of white folks, the great unifier of brown people everywhere. But more important, she told me she loved me. And when I said it back, we both knew we meant it.

We didn't understand each other, but we wanted to try.

Shithole Nation

Jim St. Germain

1. HAITI. THEN.

Some of my earliest memories are from the top of my father's shoulders. There was no infrastructure in La Plaine, where I spent my early years, where hurricane season felt like the only season, and flooding was a way of life. It's just what happens in Haiti.

When the flooding started, Dad would throw a few of us on his shoulders and take the family to higher ground. One time, as we were running upland, my father realized my older brother Enrico was still on the other side of the road, an avalanche rapidly approaching, taking everything in its way. My father ran back just in time, and he grabbed Enrico before the floods did. There was nothing heroic about it. A father's duty. And after the ordeal, our house would be either destroyed or uninhabitable for weeks. The first decade of my life, this was my world.

I was born in La Plaine, a town a hundred miles north of Port-au-Prince, and light years away from the busy and touristy capital. Areas like mine have suffered the brunt of the country's stagnant economy, brutal regimes, and foreign intervention. We were surrounded by so much poverty that I didn't notice it. Except for on the days of excruciating hunger, which was most days.

Haiti is a place of rich heritage, of strong black men and women, and home of the only successful slave revolt in history. It's a place of exquisite beauty that's closed off to its inhabitants because most of us don't have the month's salary required to watch one of its sunrises while lying on its beaches. For two centuries—before an earthquake opened the world to its plight—Haiti had been ruined by American and French policies, while most of their school kids couldn't identify it on a map.

Our house was a shack: one room, dirt floor, no electricity, no plumbing, and a thin metal roof that let the rain in. It welcomed the water in, unable to flush it back out. We shared this shack with my aunt and her family, ten of us living in this space.

The average worker in Haiti makes a dollar a day, but we didn't make anywhere near that because the average person in Haiti is unemployed. Public school is rare in Haiti—there's simply not enough infrastructure or tax revenue to sustain it. The schools are private, and those without means, like us, aren't welcomed.

Prior to moving to Brooklyn, at eleven or so, I had attended one year of school in total. My father's friend, Mr. Eddie, set up a makeshift school in his yard called Aji Pepe, where we'd go sometimes, a few benches and the outer wall of a neighbor's home doubling as a blackboard. Sometimes Mr. Eddie would come over to the house and tutor us in reading or math. There was nothing to read in our house: not a book, not a magazine, not a newspaper.

My favorite time in Haiti was mango season. I would wake up at dawn, scouting to find the mango tree ripe enough for me to scale or assault with rocks. On any given day a group of us, barefoot, shirtless, and full of boyish energy and hunger, assembled under a particular mango tree and let the rocks rain. Often we would target the trees that weren't in people's yards as a way of avoiding an ass whipping. Some of us were particularly skilled at hurling rocks, targeting the thin string between the mango fruit and the branch. This method expended less energy, and the likelihood of destroying my meal before it reached me was drastically decreased. Often I hit a mango within the first few tries only to see it land in the filthy mud below the tree, and I would wipe it on my shirt before it felt the wrath of my hungry teeth.

I got by in other ways too, running errands for family friends, delivering food to grandmothers, helping Uncle Joslin as a mechanic's assistant, or fetching water for neighbors. I washed dishes and collected funds for neighborhood taxi drivers for a few gourdes or a plate of food known as arokan.

These were my hustles.

My father used to wake us up at dawn to take care of our hygiene in the back of the house. One day he was extra thorough, which for him meant rough. It was our big day. And he bathed us and brushed our teeth using a single bucket of water, then combed our beautifully nappy hair. Gentle isn't a part of his fabric, and the brute force of his handiwork elicited many cries of "Ouch!" from me and my siblings. Often, as he combed my brother Colin's hair, I'd sneak around the house hoping to avoid the wrath of his comb. Finally clean, we were dressed in our only decent outfits, sent by my grandparents in Brooklyn for the special occasion.

My father's best friend, Kesner, pulled up near the house in his old beat-up Toyota. This was as luxurious as cars got. We jumped into the back, and he sped through the dust along the bumpy road to Port-au-

Prince. The city itself is organized chaos: people everywhere selling fruit and bags of water, artisans selling painted wood-and metalwork to tourists, fried plantain and pork vendors, sugarcane in wheelbarrows, Barbancourt shots in small measuring cups, secondhand clothes from the States spread all over the street, because the street and the sidewalks are the same.

We were dropped in front of a building, white, beautifully painted, and stately with EMBASSY OF THE UNITED STATES written in gold letters. We took our place in a long line, were given a number, and waited. Big news was on its way. After ten years, we had finally been granted visas to join our grandparents in the States. My father's smile was accessible to us. He cracked open and let in a ray of sunshine. On the drive back, the usual hunger and frustration were replaced by hope and optimism. I didn't know those feelings could fill up empty stomachs.

On the day of our departure, Auntie Michelle was up earlier than usual, preparing breakfast. The smell pervaded the air and replaced the sound of an alarm clock. Flavored with burning charcoal, the spaghetti with boiled eggs, anchovies, and green onions demanded attention. Normally, if we were fortunate enough to have breakfast, it would be a piece of locally baked bread with Haitian coffee. Peanut butter was extra, and we called this "pain avec mamba." But today was special.

Auntie Michelle's cooking started the day, then came the early-morning well-wishers, and family members we hadn't seen in months, and unlimited smiles, and small gifts from neighbors with less than us, and my father's friends exchanging folktales. Even my mother was there to hug us goodbye.

I was lost in thoughts as my ten-year-old eyes began to trace the tire marks on the dirt road.

2. BROOKLYN. THEN.

We arrived on September 11, 2000. The unfamiliar light made the night look like daytime. The future didn't seem like a dangerous place, at least not right away.

When we arrived at our new home in Crown Heights, Brooklyn, I couldn't hide my disappointment. In some ways this place was reminiscent of back home. I recognized the smell of blunts burning everywhere, and the rap and reggae music blasting out of stationary cars. Everything seemed transactional, which was familiar enough. My father and his friends were chain-smokers and drunks; I'd had my first drink by seven and my first smoke by nine.

But my American dream was Kevin McCallister from *Home Alone*, forgotten in his two-million-dollar mansion on the west side of Chicago. The reality was closer to *The Wire*. There were parked cars on both sides of the streets and two brightly lit bodegas adjacent to each other. The streets weren't as clean as I had envisioned, and unruly teenagers seemed to exert whatever agency they had over the four corners of their world, and each other. The girls revealed more skin than I had ever seen before and appeared to have more control over their own affairs. The boys' style mirrored that of my diaspora cousin Rodlin when he'd visited us back home: fashionable do-rags, baggy pants over yellow boots that seemed more appropriate for a battlefield than for chilling on the block. Before long, my face would be introduced to the bottom of one of those boots.

Outside the school building the battle intensified. Small disagreements or ice grills could easily lead to someone asking you to square up, run your shit, get stabbed, or even get shot. I got it. I got the survival guide faster than most because I was an adaptable kid. It was my best asset. I transformed into whatever I needed to be to survive; I was amorphous. I began fighting classmates left and right, but unlike in Haiti, fights don't end in Brooklyn. It was a snowball effect. And soon I would be fighting sisters, brother, cousins, friends, acquaintances, foes, and, periodically, parents. Mothers and fathers weren't that far apart from their kids, mentally speaking, and had no qualms about busting another kid's lip if it meant protecting their own. The rules were blurred and perhaps invisible, so we took stake in each other.

As one of my favorite rap duos put it, "survival of the fit, only the strong survive." I was tested time and time again, on my way to school, on the playground, in front of my apartment building, in the lobby, at the door, walking to the bodega, in the classroom. No immunity.

Where I lived on Crown Street, between Nostrand and Rogers Avenues, it was a three-minute walk to my junior high school, its entrance facing the 71st Precinct. The short distance between the two didn't close the gap between terror and safety. Why would it, when we never got the sense that the cops were there to protect us?

High school was where it was all happening. Where I took an interest in girls, revealed through a toxic sense of teenage masculinity.

"Money, clothes, and hoes" was the mantra then. I began to carve out my space and pursued the girls the only way I knew how: "Damn, shawty, you gotta fat ass. Can I hit that? Do you mind if I walk with you?" Or a quick "You have a beautiful smile," which was the peak of my chivalry.

During one of our smoke sessions on the "Jewish steps," my homie Gutter, who was massaging his girlfriend's genitals, asked me to sit close to him to get in on the action. I was excited and huddled with all my other homies to tell them how loyal he was and didn't mind sharing.

Often we skipped lunch so we could play football, even though most of us were starving. The game was useful to the image we wanted to portray to the girls we wanted to get. I came from a place where a piece of bread was a luxury, but eating the free lunch now came with a social price, so I stayed hungry.

Once, during a game of two-hand touch football, I accidentally bumped into a girl while she was jumping double Dutch. I tried to avoid her swinging cord while running full speed in my Heisman swag, but I crashed into her and we both hit the gate. I didn't apologize. I didn't inquire about her well-being. And by the time school let out, her older brother was waiting outside with his entire clique. These guys were established in neighborhood beefs and already hardened by the street. They had earned their status, proven by the whispering around school describing what they were going to do to me. More important, her brother was known to be strapped.

I could see them from the window before the bell went. My heart dropped. I was sweating, but I couldn't show it. Not long after, seven guys pounded on my thirteen-year-old body. But through it all I held one kid and pounded on him, refusing to let go. It was the best way to get a beating and survive. The other students quickly turned into spectators. As they watched, they yelled variations on sympathy and amusement: "Damn," "Ouch," "They're fucking him up,"

"He's dead," "That's fucked up"—all euphemisms for "Welcome to America."

After, my grandmother blamed me for my own beatdown. She gave me warm salt water and a cloth, telling me to apply pressure to the wounds. "Adding salt to a wound" wasn't just a figure of speech; it was a typical Haitian remedy for most injuries, including bullet wounds.

Fights didn't end here. Everybody wanted a piece of the new kid, so I had to adjust and survive: two words that played in my head, a record on repeat. Like this, I began earning respect.

But money was the ultimate form of respect and protection, and I had no access to it. I tried the traditional route for a while. I wasn't afraid to work. I packed bags, delivered groceries, stocked shelves, and took out the garbage. Eventually my homie Big Head advocated for me to get a job at Food County Supermarket. It was located twelve blocks south of Crown and Nostrand, the East Flatbush section of Brooklyn, a working-poor Caribbean American neighborhood with mom-and-pop fruit stands, Chinese food takeouts, laundromats, barbershops, beauty salons, and check-cashing places attached to liquor stores. A relatively short distance, but anywhere outside the eight-block radius around where I lived increased the likelihood of violence.

Good or bad, I was liked by most of the OGs on my block. One, a well-respected hustler, approached me with an enticing opportunity. An ounce of regular greens—aka Arizona, or Ari—converted into dime and nickel bags could bring a 100 percent profit margin.

I had been unaware that, in America, there were conditions imposed on black and brown people that I would be subjected to simply because of my environment. We were surrounded by chronic poverty, and we used an affinity for materialism to mask our sense of powerlessness. Our schools were segregated and under-resourced, our homes, dilapidated buildings due to redlining—the federal government's way of ghettoizing brown communities—and our streets, heavily patrolled by the 71st Precinct. Easy access to both liquor and guns didn't help our causes. Drugs were the most viable economic path.

In retrospect, we were deprived of faith in our own upward mobility. We were downtrodden young men, full of hopes and dreams but with no access to social capital, therefore no access to any capital. We sought alternatives, but they were accompanied by heavy consequences: arrests, deportation and the breaking of families, never-ending court dates, bloodshed. The grinding machine of poverty was omnipresent, and it crippled many of us, some beyond repair.

The need to be resourceful was just as important in Brooklyn as it was in Haiti. On Crown Street, I would take out the garbage for Khalid, the gentleman from Yemen who owned one of the corner stores. I requested a milk crate from him and used my pocketknife to remove the bottom of the plastic crate, uncoiling a hanger to use as the wire. This was our basketball hoop. And the crates were our outdoor chairs.

One of my childhood idols, the late, great Biggie Smalls, said this about where we are from: "Shit, it's hard being young from the slums, / eating five-cent gums, not knowing where your meal's coming from."

These weren't just bars to us. Madison Square Garden was a mere twenty-minute train ride away, but it might as well have been a different world. The chopped-up concrete sidewalks were merciless, and there were no celebrities sitting courtside cheering for us. No one was cheering for us. It didn't take long to recognize that hoop dreams weren't going to be our way out of this bullshit life.

The blood of many of my friends stained these very same side-walks. People like Jigga, who was gunned down by Damien, some-one he'd known almost his entire life. It happened in broad daylight too. Right on the busy avenue. My younger cousin Breeze suffered the same fate just a few months after his eighteenth. I had been the first to introduce him to the streets. I carry that guilt like a heavy chain. Then it was Dread from up the street. Thrown off the roof to his death, brain splattered on the sidewalk for "disrespecting" a young cat who felt that Dread was stealing his clientele. And my friend Nate, gunned down while attending the funeral of another friend. He was pronounced dead before the paramedics even arrived. Or my friend Reggie, who was stabbed while sitting on the "Jewish steps" playing dominoes. And Patrice, who was shot in the leg over a game of dice. I can still see Shawn's face with his magnetic smile, revealing his flashy gold teeth, which were the envy of us all. Shawn had dark chocolate skin, a chiseled jawline, and stood at five feet six, stocky, with a goatee and designer braids. His ball-handling skills made Allen Iverson look like an amateur. He was gunned down too. And I can't shake it.

A young lady he was involved with got into a heated argument with another woman. I was sitting in the barbershop on Nostrand Avenue and Montgomery when I heard the commotion. I stepped out, and there was Shawn in the middle of it.

"You okay?" I asked.

"Yeah," he said. "These bitches tried to front on my shawty. Ain't nothin . . ."

I gave him a dap and went back into the barbershop. Because argu-ments like this were the air we breathed. But ten minutes later I felt something in the air. I walked out. Police cars and ambulances were now everywhere. I hurried up Nostrand Avenue to Carroll Street, where Shawn lived and hung out. I arrived as paramedics were wheeling his body into the back of the ambulance. Blood everywhere: the sidewalk, mailbox, bicycle, running down the drain. The entire block stood there stunned. The verbal altercation had led to a phone call, and a heartless coward rolled up and shot him on sight.

The fear was palpable. Danger was all around us. I learned on my first day in Brooklyn that elevators were death traps and I knew to take the stairs. One time I was on my way from the rooftop with a young lady who had just performed oral sex on me, colloquially known as getting head, brain, knowledge, domed, wisdom, or, simply, our little dirty dick suck. I measured my manhood by how many times I could get a young lady involved with me sexually. The roofs of most buildings around my neighborhood were used for messy teenage sex, to smoke weed, to hide a rusty shared handgun, or to look out for the police. And on this day the girl I was with suggested getting into the elevator. I went against my survival instincts and agreed.

Looking back, I always wanted to be a gentleman, but gentleman-ly ways are costly here. As the elevator descended and she fixed her hair, we abruptly stopped on the fourth floor. I stepped back to put distance between us, because another rule is to not be seen with a girl who just performed oral sex on you. What if she had done the same for several of my friends?

The doors opened and a young man I had never seen before walked in. As the doors closed, he flipped open a butterfly pocketknife. It was distinctive, with two handles that counter-rotated so when it closed the blade was concealed. He pressed it against my throat, his fore-arm pushing me into the corner of the elevator while his left hand simultaneously emptied my pockets. The girl freaked out and was screaming. All of this happened within seconds between the fourth floor and the main lobby. In the same elevator where I'd punched my next-door neighbor in his face for ice grilling me a few weeks prior. The cycle continues.

My friend Dr. Gore often says, "Hurt people hurt people." Like Shawn, and many of my friends who were killed, Jigga didn't have a choice in picking what type of world he had been given. He grew up with a Haitian father and a Trinidadian mother. They lived at 250 Crown Street, the building attached to mine, and he was one of the first friends I made on the street. On my way from school, I had walked past him and a group sitting on the steps of the building. Without saying anything, I squeezed through, proceeded to the gate, and rang the bell. Behind me, I heard, "Say excuse me next time, pussy." Being called "pussy" here without a fight was sufficient grounds to become somebody's bitch. I responded, and Jigga jumped up, coming toward me as my grandmother buzzed the door open.

Days later my cousin BIGS took me to the store, where we ran into Jigga. BIGS told him I was his little cousin, fresh from Haiti, and we became friends like this. Jigga would often protect me, or at least ask other dudes to shoot a fair one instead of jumping me.

I visited his apartment often when I didn't have anything, and he'd share what little he had with me: food, alcohol, weed, girls, his worn number-seven Air Jordans with dark charcoal and red stripes weaved in at the top and bottom. All the cool kids sported them, and Jigga had every single pair on the first day of release. Once the new ones came out, he'd pass down an older pair to me. He even gave me his favorite vintage Ralph Lauren varsity jacket, gray with black sleeves, leather patches on the elbows, and the signature "R. L." emblem embroidered on the chest.

The girls looked at me differently with my hand-me-downs, and I felt like my stature grew overnight. There was a magnetic pull to wearing name-brand clothing for kids who weren't able to attach value to meaningful things. Now there was something to work toward. When I began hustling, he'd often give me pointers, the dos and don'ts, the code of the streets. The things you can only learn by living them. Jigga told me who to trust, how to identify undercover cops, and the difference between Latin Kings, Bloods, Crips, Folks, and other gangs. I learned who the runners were versus the decision makers, and the OGs I shouldn't fuck with, the ones who had access to weapons and weren't afraid to use them. This type of mentorship was remedial education. There were rules everywhere, and breaking them here could earn you a broken jaw, or worse.

Jigga loved BMWs, especially the 745Li with the peanut butter interior. Haitian, Jamaican, and Puerto Rican guys often parked their cars in a line and let us play with the radio systems. We picked our favorite songs, making our own concerts, which were an invitation for the police.

Jigga was a son, nephew, cousin, friend, and leader. A paragon of urban youth, willing to risk it all for name brands, looking fly, and girls. He had a serious affinity for reggae and dance hall music and could memorize the latest lyrics from Jamaica in just three days. He kept to himself but was loved by many. He was sharp, talented, curious, and full of ambition. Sadness overcomes me as I think of the architect, investor, scholar, or family man Jigga could've been had he been born into a different situation.

Jigga and many others never had the opportunity to visit a college campus with mommy and daddy. No SAT preps, sleepaway camps, studying abroad, or prom dates. Instead, we were swept by the urban conveyor belt into Spofford Juvenile Detention, Rikers Island, and funeral homes.

I was well aware of another America. I knew it existed, and I didn't have to go far to see it. It was on the other side of Nostrand Avenue, where the orthodox Chabad-Lubavitch community was. There the women wore wigs and long skirts, pushed strollers, and chatted with their friends in Hebrew. They even had black babysitters. The men, wearing traditional orthodox black hats, white shirts, dark suits, and tzitzits, their absolute connection with God, and thick beards, gathered in tight groups, animatedly discussing affairs in Hebrew, Yiddish, or a mixture of both. They stared unabashedly while we sat on the steps of the synagogue, which we childishly called the "Jewish steps," blowing blunts while bopping to Jay-Z's *Hard Knock Life* soundtrack. Periodically, the men approached us and asked if we would mind turning on their lights or a stove. I'd agree to help. It was like this that I could look into another Brooklyn world.

Near here, east of Crown Heights, just a ten-minute walk or a few stops on the number 2 train, yet another world existed: Park Slope. In this neighborhood, many of the kids' paths were already carved out for them too. With million-dollar brownstones, yoga studios, therapy offices, outdoor cafés, gourmet supermarkets, well-funded schools, piano lessons, and parents who were always more involved than necessary. It was nearly impossible for the kids here to fuck it up. The streets were cleaner, and the police didn't feel like an occupying force. The "American Dream" was the floor here, not the ceiling.

But on my side of Brooklyn, just shy of my sixteenth birthday, I was already a regular at the 71st Precinct. I remember one officer said to me, "We should start charging your ass rent." But it was the city and state that picked up that tab. The daily hustles I partook in—the drugs, weapons, fights, boosting, truancy, suspensions, weed smoking, and a slew of near misses with fatalities—led to regular encounters with the police, until I faced two Class D felony charges for possession and intent to distribute drugs. The walls closed in. I was sentenced to the juvenile justice system.

I ended up in a group home. At first I fought my peers, got high, and lost my position as a leader. I suffered from withdrawal and, with it, a lack of connection to my family and community. But after an agonizing process of hard work, sacrifice, and steadfast pursuit of education, I pulled through. I was tutored by Joanna and got help from Iza with piecing a paragraph together. I was placed in the karate class with Sensei Tessa to channel my anger. I owe a lot to the support of staff members, peers, and mentors like my appointed attorneys and my former teachers—many of whom did not share a similar upbringing, socioeconomic status, education, culture, or skin color. So many pitched in to become the vessel I desperately needed in troubled water. They believed in my potential. They invested in me. I was introduced to books and soaked words in like dry soil.

I stayed the course because I knew what the alternatives were. I sought mentors and listened to anyone who was willing to teach. Reading helped me see America's social and political landscape for what it is. The responsibility to change was mine, and I embraced it.

Ultimately, I helped found Preparing Leaders of Tomorrow (PLOT), a nonprofit organization that provides mentoring to at-risk youth. My guiding principle is the axiom "Those closest to the problems are closest to the solution."

3. BROOKLYN. NOW.

It doesn't end. In April, Sayid Vessel, a twenty-six-year-old mentally challenged young man, was gunned down by the police on Utica Avenue for allegedly wielding a silver pipe the police claim resembled a firearm. His murder took place in broad daylight at the hands of police officers from the 71st Precinct, the very same one I had dealt with in my youth. I still walk by it today with my five-year-old son, Caleb.

Here are some of the things I knew about Sayid: like me, he grew up on Crown Street; we had countless mutual friends; his parents migrated here from the Caribbean; we were close in age; his mental-health issues were well known in the neighborhood; no one had been harmed by the time the police arrived. Nonetheless, the pipe he brandished was more than enough to warrant his public execution. That Sunday afternoon, I not only saw myself in this young man but saw us—I saw the kids I mentor, I saw my son.

I know this beloved Crown Heights community, its lively, hardworking, and diverse group of immigrants and Jewish residents. It's thought that the person who called the police on Sayid was a new resident, brought to the area by an aggressive wave of gentrification that is displacing and now killing long-term residents. Meanwhile, the same police manage to disarm white murderers over and over again, many of them taken alive after some of the bloodiest terrorist acts in recent memory. No surprise there. The animalistic behavior of police officers who produce black blood as red as the light on their patrol cars is as American as it gets.

We are under no illusions; our president has made his opinion of us and our heritage clear. President Trump has called Haiti a "shithole nation," willfully ignoring Haiti's rich history. It was Haitian strength and perseverance in the face of colonial brutality, after all, that made the Louisiana Purchase possible. If not for the Haitian people, the United States would likely be half the size it is today. But as long as people like Trump and their followers dismiss whole countries and populations as shithole nations and shithole people, we will stay trapped in our neighborhoods, police targets without opportunity.

The other day, I lost my cool with Caleb. I raised my voice to a level that's against my usual standard. He looked at me and said, "Daddy, you yelled at me, and I'm not your friend." For a brief moment I wished that he wasn't my responsibility to be afraid for.

There is this notion that we, as black and brown people, take great pleasure in talking about racism and oppression. One thing I am certain of is this: no oppressed person finds joy in addressing the very thing that stymied his or her fullest potential. I wish that, like my white friends, I didn't have to be held accountable for every mistake made by another brown individual. And that, like them, I was assumed "innocent until proven guilty." What I wish for, more than anything, is the ability to stare into my son's beautiful brown eyes and reassure him that, in his country, he will be judged by his hard work, grit, kindness, and commitment to what's right. And he will be awarded access to all that his country has to offer. That's every father's dream, including, and especially, black fathers.

But I must face this heartbreaking reality: in America my greatest joy is simultaneously my greatest fear. Caleb could easily be taken away from me, and no one would be held accountable. Sayid's murder is yet another blaring reminder that my beautiful boy isn't protected anywhere in his country. Not by the street violence that many of us fall victim to, not by the men and women who are sworn to protect him, not by the educational system, the job market, his intelligence, or his parents' socioeconomic status. And I can't perform my number one duty as a father: to keep him safe. Being his father is the equivalent of living with my heart outside my body in a war zone.

Last July, my memoir, *A Stone of Hope,* was released by HarperCollins. The book is an examination of my struggle and a call to action. After it was published, I began a book tour that took me to Los Angeles. Upon arrival, I drove through Beverly Hills, mesmerized by all the wealth: high-end luxurious storefronts, foreign cars, and people dining at expensive establishments who looked like they belonged. My Uber driver assured me that this grand sight was customary. WELCOME TO THE CITY OF ANGELS. A few minutes and two left turns later, he pulled up to the house where I would be staying, on a quiet, modest, and beautifully constructed street.

I woke early every morning and ran up the hill toward Fuller Avenue, where I made my way to the trails. One morning, on my way back, I slowed as I approached the house and passed a couple with their dogs. I greeted them before I opened the gate. Suddenly, I realized that the gentleman I had just passed was standing behind me, flashing me a wary look, peeking through the bush.

I felt a sense of rage taking over my body as I stood there, my hand shaking as I tried to fit the key into the lock. I got in the house and sat on the couch, my mind running wild, thinking about all the ways this encounter could've ended.

I thought about my son being confronted by this man's kids ten years from now. I thought about his inability to react as I just had, so different from what fifteen-year-old me could have done. I thought about this very same incident taking place at night. I thought about if this man was in possession of a firearm, as many of his countrymen and women are. What picture of me would the *LA Times* use in its morning news? I thought about my son. I thought, I must stay in the game. I have skin in it.

Blond Girls in Cheongsams

Jenny Zhang

XOXO was one of the slighter stores in Roosevelt Mall in the late 1990s. It was narrow but deep and had the sort of moody lighting that was romantic in the way seedy motels look romantic on the big screen—dim and pinky and brown. I liked beholding the XOXO sign, big, neon, and lit.

It was something the girls in my school would scrawl in peppy, loopy handwriting when passing notes to each other. Or maybe they never did, but it seemed only right that the girls who were cheerleaders and student council members and on the yearbook committee and the girls who baked cookies to raise money for charity and the theater girls who stayed after school to practice entertaining us for one night in the fall and one night in the spring would write "XOXO" to each other and to the boys they were dating.

In my high school on Long Island, I only knew girls who wore chopsticks in their hair to dances and none who knew how to eat with them. This was a far departure from the Queens neighborhood I grew up in, one of those actually ethnically diverse, actually working-class neighborhoods in which the kids of color far outnumbered the white kids, to the point that when in fourth grade we had a transfer student from Ohio with the kind of Irish skin that was so pale it flushed pink without warning, we mocked him ruthlessly, covering our eyes to indicate how his white skin blinded us, not realizing there was a whole other world where we, with our hair and our skin tones and our facial features, were destined to be the butt of most jokes.

It took the good old-fashioned American Dream of upward mobility—moving to the suburbs—for this to dawn on me. It hadn't meant anything to not be a white girl until I was surrounded by them. Suddenly I was the odd one, an immigrant who up until that point knew mostly other immigrants. It hadn't occurred to me that it was strange I had never eaten toast, that I'd had cereal only once before, when a houseguest brought a mini box of cornflakes with him and I'd been permitted to eat them dry, straight from the box like chips. The experience was terrible, tasteless, but still, I insisted, if only I were allowed to sample some of the other cereals—Fruity Pebbles and Lucky Charms and Cookie Crisp, or even Kix ("Kid tested. Mother approved.")—I might have a shot at becoming like the other girls, someone who ate cold cereal with a spoon for breakfast instead of hot rice porridge with chopsticks.

"Yep, I use them for everything," I said once over dinner at a Chinese fast-food restaurant downtown with my new friends, who held their chopsticks gracelessly, laughably, or else just used a fork. I was smug, still too young to know how much shame lay ahead of me, something that enough men in my life have since pointed out is about feeling bad about who you are, as opposed to "guilt," which is about feeling bad about what you've done. I used chopsticks to eat slabs of meat, runny eggs, spaghetti, birthday cake. That was what I knew, and the white girls in my school who showed up to school dances in nineties teen-girl formal wear—bright, shiny, satiny dresses—topped off with a pair of colorful chopsticks in their highlighted updos made me cringe.

There must have been other Asian kids in my grade, but the one I remember was from Hong Kong, and he was much more sadistic than the white kids in making fun of me for being Chinese. It was an odd time, especially because it was 1997, the year Britain was scheduled to hand Hong Kong, until then a dependent territory, back to China. In the West, it was referred to as "the handover," and in China, as "the return." Somewhere inside me, I felt he and I should have been co-conspirators, not enemies, and the distinction he drew, as well as the way the media discussed the "transfer of power"—technically, officially, sterilely, with little mention of the cruelty and arrogance of colonialism or how the people of Hong Kong felt about being ping-ponged between Britain and China— bothered me.

It didn't help that everywhere I looked that year, someone was wearing a mandarin collar or a dragon-and-pagoda-print mesh top. The Delia's catalog began offering a regular selection of Asian-inspired clothing. I tried saving up for a pair of Chinese Laundry shoes, only hazily registering that its chunky-heeled, faux-satiny sandals were always photographed on a white girl and never someone like me, a Chinese girl who had never been inside a Chinese dry cleaner's in her whole life because it was considered the most luxurious of luxury expenses, and so did not even recognize the stereotype this company was capitalizing on by calling itself "Chinese Laundry." I just wanted what the other girls had: trendy shoes, trendy clothes, trendy accessories.

If anything, I was thrilled that my ethnicity had made its way into the name of a coveted brand. When these poorly made, floral-print sandals, qipao-inspired dresses, and hair chopsticks started popping up in stores and catalogs, I thought this indicated, in some watered-down way, that finally the cultural products of the country in which I was born were very, very in.

That was also the year I started going to the mall as a social pastime. Before then, mall trips had been more utilitarian, accompanying my mother on two-hour-long drives to outlet malls in New Jersey, where there was no sales tax, or to Lord & Taylor's clearance stores, which still sold jackets with massive eighties-era shoulder pads. This was while we were living in Queens, and I was more interested in reading at home for hours than in going anywhere at all. But being a teen in a Long Island suburb meant weekends at the mall with my mom and my best friend, Diana, who still lived in Queens, and her mom. The four of us were "mu-nu," my mother would say in Chinese, meaning "mother-daughter," a connection I was eager to sever, just a little, in service of being more like the girls in my high school, who were dropped off at the mall or went with their older siblings who could drive.

But not me. Not us. The four of us went together, starting at Nordstrom because that was where the ample outdoor parking was, but when the sun shone too brightly, or the day was too cold, we'd go in search of the highly coveted covered parking outside the Bloomingdale's, a search that often resulted in protracted shouting matches. Once parked, we would snake our way through the department store until we emerged onto the mall concourse. Then we quickly separated and went off in pairs, my mom and Diana's mom to Ann Taylor while Diana and I went next door to Wet Seal, where I once spent far too long looking for a pair of lavender corduroy bell-bottoms that three of the most popular girls in my eighth-grade class owned, two of them wearing the bell-bottoms on the same day, the other on another, which probably indicated some kind of power struggle from which I was entirely excluded. As our mothers perused the boots at Nine West, Diana and I browsed the Limited Too, where every shirt was stretchy and sparkly, imploding with psychedelic prints, and the pants had such poor stitching, they'd unravel in the dressing room. Sometimes all four of us went into Guess together, my mother making a beeline for the few clearance racks and then immediately back out again. At the end of our mall run our moms would do a quick loop around Banana Republic and then wait for us while we tried on skirts in Contempo Casuals.

I was the only one who ever really advocated for going into the XOXO store, though. Marooned in a no-man's-land, next to those odd stalls in the middle of the concourse that sold things like nail buffer kits or foot massage machines that mysteriously doubled as humidifiers, it was too juvenile for our parents and too girly for Diana. But I lived for its clothes, which were out of my price range and never on sale. I had my sights set on a form-fitting brown rayon skirt with a dragon embroidered on one side and a less-than-demure slit on the other.

"Do you really want this?" my mother asked me kindly after the third time I picked it up in front of her and pressed it against my body.

"Yes," I said. "Yes, I do."

It became my most prized item of clothing. Wearing it to school with a pair of knockoff platform Doc Martens ordered from Delia's made me feel wonderfully visible. I was someone to see. A week after I wore it to school, I got a boyfriend who was in a hardcore punk band. A boyfriend! In a band! *I am really someone,* I thought. *I am someone's someone, so I am someone.*

★ ★ ★

"Did you know," Diana asked me while we stuffed our clear cellophane bags with sour belts at Sweet Factory, "that this is the second largest mall in America?"

"What's the first?"

"That Mall of America in Minnesota or whatever."

"Wow," I said, feeling a stab of pride that comes with associating yourself with something powerful. What was more opulent than the second largest mall in the richest, most powerful country in the world? Nothing, except for the first largest. Pre-Google, we didn't bother verifying, but we were wrong. It was the seventh largest in the country and second largest in the state of New York.

It was built in 1956 on the very airport and military airfield that the mall was named after—Roosevelt Field—where, a few decades prior, 150 people reportedly gathered to watch Charles Lindbergh take off in his modest plane, brightly named the *Spirit of St. Louis,* to complete the first nonstop flight from New York to Paris. There was a plaque commemorating his trans-Atlantic flight in the mall, which Diana and I always breezed past to get to the Disney store. Amelia Earhart used the former airstrip at Roosevelt Field as a launchpad as well, a fact many of my die-hard Long Island–born-and-bred teachers liked to share with us, repeatedly. "So when you're at the mall this weekend," my history teacher said, "think about that."

I didn't think about it at all. I was too busy writing a letter to Diana on Morning Glory stationery about the things I wanted to buy on our next mall trip: those black flatform foam slides with two thick white bands, a baby-blue spaghetti-strap tank top from Wet Seal, a cropped white T-shirt from the Limited Too to go underneath, dark denim bell-bottoms, brown corduroy engineer pants from the Gap, and everything, just every damn thing in XOXO.

Looking up photos of XOXO retail stores on Google now, I see again that I was wrong. In all the photos that show up, the store looks massive, spacious, blindingly white with garish lighting. I must have fabricated a memory of the store as cool, moody, and romantic. It looks like any store in any mall, if not on the uglier side of ugly.

Diana and I liked spending Saturdays playing board games—Dream Phone, Party Mania, the Game of Life, 13 Dead End Drive. But my favorite was Mall Madness. Every part of it pleased me: the irritatingly complicated setup, the soulless computer voice that announced the sales and went "Ching, ching" when you bought something. We played in maximum overdrive, upping the stakes to sixty items instead of just six to win the game. Sometimes after Diana left, I would keep playing by myself, swiping all the money from the bank and going on a mad spree to buy up everything until I had it all.

At Roosevelt Field, like most seasoned mall goers, we had a routine, and an exit strategy. Getting teriyaki chicken with extra sauce ("More! Sauce!" my mother repeated as we moved through every step of the food assembly line) at the food court signaled that we were an hour away from having to leave. Our last stop on the ground floor was typically Express, by which point, exhausted by whatever psychological forces made shoppers like us think we couldn't settle for the first or second or third or fourth or even fifth thing we wanted, we would make a mad dash to grab as many $7.99 sale items we could find in our sizes. One time my mother and I came across several racks of sweaters, tops, and pants that had been priced at $3.99, with an additional 50 percent taken off at the register.

"This has to be a mistake," I said. "Who cares?" my mother said, grabbing me after we had checked out and running out of the store as if someone was coming after us to make us pay back their mistakes. There were things in the store priced at $39.99 and even $79.99 that I'd wanted more, but instead we had bags full of $2 clothes. That was when I started making a mental catalog of things I would steal once I found a way to get back to the mall on my own, which was tricky, but not impossible.

At the height of the Asian-inspired fashion trend, Claire Danes showed up to the *Romeo and Juliet* premiere at Mann's Chinese Theatre in Los Angeles wearing a vaguely "oriental" printed Prada jacket over a vaguely "oriental" printed long skirt. I don't remember if I thought any of it was significant—that Danes, who exemplified the height of enviable, beautiful girlhood in her role as Shakespeare's Juliet, was posing for red-carpet photos in designer clothing that appropriated Chinese fashion while standing in front of the most iconic of Hollywood theatres, which was constructed in 1926 with imported artifacts from China, and partially built by hired Chinese artisans to resemble a giant red pagoda with a dragon across the facade, two Ming dynasty "heavenly dogs" on either side of the gate, even more dragons scattered along the copper roof, and lotus-shaped fountains sprinkled around the Forecourt of the Stars. This is the famous theatre millions of tourists visit every year, posing and taking pictures with the handprints and the autographs of Hollywood stars.

Meanwhile, in my corner of the world, I had to endure girls walking past me every day in the hallway after English class and yelling, "Jenny *Zhang*," as though my last name were a ready-made insult, until finally, after weeks of this, I pulled the main offender into the bathroom and said, "I will fucking hit you in the face until every bone is broken if you don't stop."

Commissioned by (and originally named after) the theatre magnate Sid Grauman, Grauman's Chinese Theatre opened to the public in 1927. America's first Chinese American movie star, Anna May Wong, drove the first rivet into the steel girders. The theatre was the height of grandeur and opulence. After all, what is more grand and opulent in the West than reproducing a long-held fantasy of the exotic East? It was renamed Mann's Chinese Theatre in 1973, when it was bought by a businessman named Ted Mann. Then, in 2013, a Chinese electronics manufacturing company bought the naming rights to the theatre and it became the TCL Chinese Theatre—making it the first time since the theatre was built that one could say the Chinese Theatre in Hollywood actually had something to do with the Chinese. Was it a handover? Was it a return? Or really, to be far less romantic, was it just one corporate power being bought by another?

On the official website for the TCL Chinese Theatre, the first words you see when you click on the "History" tab are, in all caps: "It was once stated that 'to visit Los Angeles and not see the Chinese Theatre is like visiting China and not seeing the Great Wall.'"

Around the same time I also started seeing the word "cheongsam" in my mother's *Vogue* and *InStyle* magazines.

"Do you know this word?" I asked, pointing to a caption of a celebrity in a cheongsam dress.

"That's a qipao," my mother said. "Kind of."

"Cheongsam" isn't a word that exists in any Chinese dialect. The earliest form of this garment came by way of the Manchus, who conquered China and established the Qing dynasty in 1644. They wore loose, high-collared, long-sleeved, A-line-shaped shirts that went down to the ankles, and required the Han Chinese to do the same.

The edict was eventually lifted, but by then it had become a fairly common way to dress. After the fall of the Qing dynasty in 1911, the style was revived in Shanghai in the 1920s, and the qipao (the Mandarin word for these high-collared dresses) evolved to be more fitted, ornately embroidered, and stylishly cut close to the body.

Once the Communists assumed power in 1949, qipaos were considered too ostentatious and feminine for a country in the throes of a proletarian revolution. Utilitarian unisex work clothes were in. Qipaos were out. The Shanghaiers who fled to Hong Kong carried the fashion over, where it flourished, and hemlines got shorter, the cut tighter. In the Cantonese dialect spoken in Hong Kong, these dresses were called chèuhngsàam. In English, the word was altered to become cheongsam, a word as foreign to me as Peking duck had been until my father explained that Peking duck was simply a manner of preparing duck that people in Beijing were known to enjoy.

There's this kind of irresolvable trap that occurs when you're too young to have any power but old enough to know that you want some. It's the trap of being too inarticulate to have the clarity people expect when you speak of the depressing black hole of systematic racism. What I wanted to say was how it felt to grow up in a country where the consensus seemed to be that Chinese culture looked best as an accessory on a white person. This trap made me think the classmate in the hallway making fun of my Chinese last name while sporting a Chinese character tattoo above her ass was the person I had to defeat, when, in reality, we belonged to the same world—a world where a qipao on me was a garish costume, but a polyester cheongsam mini-dress on a white girl was adorable.

My walking half an hour to wait another half an hour to catch an hour and a half bus to Roosevelt Mall to go on a stealing spree in Bloomingdale's, Macy's, and Nordstrom was a trap too. The spoils of my plundering—microfiber thongs, push-up bras, a random assortment of plain T-shirts and athletic shorts, anything that didn't have an electronic sensor and could be worn underneath my clothes—no matter how easy or illicitly thrilling, never looked good on me when I got home and laid everything out on my bed, because as any girl who has ever dealt with disappointment through retail therapy (or, in my case, retail theft therapy) has likely experienced, clothes never look good on a person who feels like shit.

The person I imagined myself being in these clothes was illusory. I knew I didn't need to spend money to become a valuable person, but what I didn't know was what kind of currency I could spend (or rather, earn) to feel worthwhile. What I wanted was a whole other system of values. Can I be the lout who quotes Martin Luther King Jr.'s "Beyond Vietnam" speech in an essay about nineties fashion? I'll be that lout. "We must rapidly begin the shift from a thing-oriented society to a person-oriented society."

After my freshman year of college, I spent a month in Paris, enrolled in a French immersion program. I packed my XOXO dragon skirt, wore it nearly every other day, felt and loved how it clung to my body, plumper from a year of finally being responsible for my own eating choices and a meal program that allowed me to eat as much cereal, whipped-cream-covered waffles, and syrup-drenched french toast as my heart desired. I had occasional impetuous urges to steal that were mostly curbed by how logistically difficult it was to swipe a baguette from a tiny, family-owned boulangerie, and furthermore by how wrong it felt to try.

When my parents and little brother came to visit me for a few days, I stayed in their dormitory room, which was located in one of the better resident halls of Cité Internationale Universitaire, where I also stayed. Their room was far nicer and cleaner than mine and even had a private bathroom.

"You stay here," my mom said, "after we leave in the morning. Take a shower; take a dump. It'll be more pleasant than doing it in the communal bathroom." So I did. I took a shower. I took a dump. I took another shower. I was late to my morning class and left a scattered assortment of clothes that I had brought over: a pair of loose, sheer, yellow pajama-style capri pants (I know, I know); a three-quarter-sleeved pastel paisley shirt with a flappy pair of neckties I usually left loose; and my XOXO dragon skirt. When I came back, the room was locked. I had missed checkout, and housekeeping had already swept the room. I asked the front desk if there was a lost and found but was told gruffly that it was up to the individual housekeeper who cleans the room to decide what to do with stuff that has been left behind.

"Sometimes," the man at the front desk told me, "it goes straight to the dump."

I found the housekeeper on duty and asked her if she had seen a dragon skirt, using my fingers to draw in the air the swirl of the dragon's tail.

"Un jupe brun?" I said, botching the French, becoming increasingly shrill and desperate. "Est-ce que vous avez vu?"

"Non," she said.

I went outside with the intention of dumpster diving for my skirt. It was gone.

Back home at my parents' house in Long Island, I went to the XOXO store in Roosevelt Mall and scoured the racks, even though years had passed since I had bought the skirt.

"Do you ever make the same item again?" I asked a salesgirl behind the counter.

"Dunno," she said. "Probably not."

It was 2002. Mandarin collars, dragon mesh T-shirts, Chinese Laundry sandals, chopsticks stuck into buns with a few spikes of hair pulled out, cheongsam dresses—they were all on their way out. A year prior, my family, like so many other families in New York on September 11th, had desperately tried to reach my father on his cell phone, knowing that he had to pass under the World Trade Center to get to his office in a neighboring building. In another year, I would be participating in an emergency protest and teach-in on the Stanford Quad after George W. Bush announced he was sending ground troops into Iraq. The kids who used to think my name was shit were now shitting on names like Osama and Mohammed, while sporting nonsensical Arabic tattoos instead of nonsensical Chinese characters. It was the end of one era but also the continuation of the same world in which we had always lived, except it was becoming increasingly clear to me who, exactly, was permitted to be free.

When I was caught shoplifting from Bloomingdale's the summer before starting university, one of the things they threatened me with was a lifetime ban from the store. "If you ever step foot in this store," the security guard said to me, "there will be a warrant out for your arrest." Still, years later, when I drive to Roosevelt Mall with my mother in the cold, wet season, we park outside Bloomingdale's, and as we walk past the hosiery and the hats and the jewelry and the makeup counters to get to the "outside" of the inside of the mall, I sometimes feel the smallest of thrills. The thrill of getting away with something. The thrill of no longer being trapped.

The Naked Man

Chigozie Obioma

A long time ago—I can't recall when exactly—my father, who grew up in a village and was still one of those who spoke in the manner of our ancestors, said to me: "Son, beware of the naked man who offers you clothes." In the Igbo culture, it is considered unethical to render a proverb and then interpret it. It is the sole responsibility of the hearer to investigate the intended meaning of the proverb. Thus, even though my father knew that I did not comprehend his words, he did not offer any interpretation. I had come to learn that the fast route to understanding such cryptic messages was to take them literally and hew out some meaning from them that way. This was what I did at first. But despite my best effort, I was unable to unpack the mystery for many years. I now believe that it is often in hindsight that one comes to the full understanding of what such hard sayings mean. And we often arrive at this revelation by accident or serendipity. Sometimes, that understanding can come through a slow unraveling or through a single event, and could take a long time. It was my time in the United States that would do it for me.

For me and other Nigerians, America was glorious—a paradise, shiny and prosperous. I still maintain that the biggest export from this country is Hollywood. Americans almost unilaterally paint a cultural narrative for the rest of the world to follow. And thus, one

image I had of the country was that it was cloaked in shiny garments. It was the land of the wealthy, of high-rise buildings and
yellow cabs, of scenic structures, of great educational institutions,
and of literary agents and publishers. Yet for a long time—unlike
my compatriots attending school with me in the little-known island
of North Cyprus—I did not think of moving to America during my
four years of study. Then, suddenly, a flurry of events occurred in
quick succession that swept me up like a weak stake in a violent
wind and hauled me toward America.

It was by 2010 that I had managed to struggle my way through an
undergraduate degree at a private university in North Cyprus. My
father had retired from his job and invested his gratuity in a business
that was vulnerable to the oscillations of the tenuous Nigerian economy. So difficult did things become that I worked carpentry, cleaned
empty houses for realtors, and still could not afford my school fees.
Then, just when I was tottering on the edge of a precipice, help
came in the form of an acceptance to a Virginia-based literary journal. The fee that this journal paid me for an excerpt from the novel
I was working on, together with a generous 75 percent merit-based
scholarship I got from the school for each semester, helped pay my
final year of school fees. I was thus able to graduate with the highest
CGPA in the university. The university then offered me a graduate teaching assistant position on salary and enrollment in a free
graduate program.

But by October 2011, a new problem had cropped up: I wanted
to complete my novel, *The Fishermen*. The publication of the excerpt
and its reception—mostly glimpsed through the many emails from
readers and agents asking to read more—had convinced me that if
I could complete the book, I might be able to publish it. But with

a schedule that required me to work in an office from eight to five every day, and sometimes on Saturdays, while also taking graduate classes and teaching two undergraduate classes, it was almost impossible to write beyond a page or two every week. The fortune that had come to me became the major barrier preventing me from achieving my biggest dream.

By now the desert wind had started to scald the skin, causing people to wear sweaters and jackets, and on one of those mornings, I went into my professor's office determined to do something. So strong was my frustration that I did not bother knocking on his half-open door. I stood on the threshold, greeted him, and said, "I want to ask you for a favor, sir."

"What?" he said, still tapping his keyboard. He looked up. "Close the door and come in."

Once in, I stood in the glare of the large portrait of Kemal Atatürk's face, surrounded by a sea of crimson.

"Can you tell them to take me away from the dean of graduate studies' office and just let me teach and attend classes? I don't mind—they can pay me half of the salary. I just want to finish my book."

My professor, Ünsal Özünlü, a Turkish man whose love for me almost equaled that of a father, shook his head. He turned his face down to his folded legs. For a moment, only the sound of students speaking in Turkish in the hallway came to us, one of them shouting the ominous word that means "no" in Turkish, "Hayir! Hayir!" Then, as if he'd suddenly remembered something, my professor said, "*The Fishermen?*"

"Yes, *The Fishermen*."

He'd read parts of the book and had encouraged me in serious ways. And when the excerpt was published, he'd read it with tears in his eyes.

"Chikozi, you can't do that. No," he said, his tone descending lower as he spoke. He shook his head again and tapped his one foot on the floor as he wheeled his chair to face me. "Do you realize that you get paid next to nothing? Eight hundred Turkish lira? How much is that, yani?"

"Six hundred dollars, hocam," I said.

He was quiet for a minute, then brightened and said, "You know, why don't you apply for a residency in America? One of the writers' residencies? If you get that, yani, they will say it brings good name to the university and let you go, and you can finish the book there. Or why don't you just apply for MFA, that bloody American thing? Do you know about it, Chikozi?"

I nodded. I knew about writers' residencies and had come across the MFA thing only recently while reading an interview in which the Nigerian writer Uwem Akpan had spoken about his experience in the creative writing department at Michigan. But until my professor mentioned it, I'd not considered the possibility of applying for such a program. When I left his office that afternoon, I felt like a fool. How was it that I had not thought of this option until a sixty-nine-year-old man suggested it?

By the end of the following week, I had applied to the Ledig House International Writers' Residency in upstate New York, and the week after that, to the University of Iowa Writing Center and the Helen Zell Writers' Program at the University of Michigan. In just two weeks, I had gone from frustration to making a big decision: a potential emigration to the United States, a place that, until two weeks before, I hadn't even thought of visiting.

* * *

When the acceptance letter came from Ledig House for a six-week residency, I was delighted but cautious. TRNC (Turkish Republic of North Cyprus), as the country of North Cyprus is called, is a pariah state, and visas are hard to come by for African students. When my visa interview at the US Embassy in Lefkoşa came, I went in nervous but certain that I had all the necessary documentation. The visa officer, a young African American man who wore an earring in one ear, grilled me for close to fifteen minutes. Then, through the glass cubicle, he said, "I must tell you that you have an uncommon application from the bulk we have been receiving from Nigerians and others here. So I won't reject your application. We will further review it and give you a call."

I left the embassy, relieved but still afraid. I had been singled out from the pack of applicants from African countries, a sign that gave me hope. That hope was dashed days later when a form email came telling me that after a review, my application had been rejected. I was still writhing from the blow when an admission letter to Michigan came. It had all the hallmarks of a successful visa application: full funding, a higher degree, and a reputable institution. I knew at once that my journey to the United States had begun.

As I had expected, things were different this time. The admission was for August that year, a time during which the school term would have ended. Since I had finished coursework, I agreed with my professor that it was best to work on my thesis and complete the master's degree while in the United States. To boost my chances of getting a visa, I returned to Nigeria, where I had stronger ties, and my admission was to a prestigious school and had come with many opportunities. I was therefore not surprised when, within a few minutes of appearing at the visa officer's counter, my visa was approved. I tried to shade my joyful relief as I boarded a taxi back to my uncle's house. The man in the taxi had an American flag on the dashboard. I told him I was going to America and asked if he could sell me the flag. He offered it to me for free, in exchange for a promise to help his children move there in the future. After I pocketed the flag, he asked me to take down his number. I did, without thinking of what I might do with it or how I, a mere student, might be able to help a man I did not know move his children to a country I was myself just about to move to.

I was holding that flag when I got out of the airport at JFK, and I kept holding it through the long bus ride from New York to Ann Arbor. All my savings had gone into making the journey to Nigeria, and it was my parents who had bought me the tickets from Nigeria to the United States. I had only about five hundred dollars left with me. By the end of the second day, which was when I arrived in Michigan, the flag had become crumpled. I stood gazing at its spindly stalk as I sat in the Greyhound bus station, contemplating what to do with it. It was precious in some way, a reminder of my recent triumph over what had seemed an insurmountable obstacle. But now, in this country of opportunities, a slice of which I had seen in the bursting flamboyance of New York, the crumpled flag began to feel like baggage from the past—an old garment. I stood up and threw it in a fly-infested trash can.

As with most immigrants, it took a few days, even weeks, for me to get over the euphoria of having come to America and to face its realities. But it would take months, even years, for me to fully understand the nuances of American culture and politics. At first, I interpreted everything I encountered, or that encountered me, through the lens of a Nigerian. Had I been more aware, I would have thought more about my first interaction with an American on US soil, outside of border control officers.

It happened at the JFK airport, less than an hour after I arrived. I had been dragging myself about the airport, unable to decide what to do or how to find the bus to Michigan, when a young, good-looking white woman with blond hair tied in a ponytail with a ribbon walked up to me. She came up to me and said she was hungry and looking for money to buy food. Her words struck me with great incredulity. I had heard that there were poor people in the US, but I had expected them to be immigrants who did odd jobs, or black people in poor neighborhoods, or, if they were white people, to be either on drugs or unable to work. For this *white* woman who looked so put together, even pretty, to come up to me and beg for alms? It was unbelievable.

I didn't give her anything because I was afraid the money I had was insufficient for me. She shook my hand and left, saying, "I understand." I didn't think about that encounter until one afternoon, two days later, when I was out walking with Jide, the other Nigerian student in the Creative Writing program. We had been walking the length and breadth of Ann Arbor in the hot late-August afternoon, looking for housing for me. Since classes had not yet commenced, the streets were still mostly deserted except for a few new students arriving with their parents in tow. We were trudging along the sidewalk on the way to a co-op housing facility when, as we approached a group of three girls coming toward us, something I hadn't expected happened. The girls paused, then, locking hands, crossed the grass divide and walked between cars parked on the side of the road. They stole glances at us as they walked until, seemingly satisfied they were now completely out of our reach, they returned to the sidewalk.

"Their papa!" Jide cursed under his breath. He stopped, turned back toward the girls, and, gazing from them to me and back, he said in Yoruba, "Look at these ones. They are afraid of two black African men."

Although I laughed at the time, the moment stayed with me. These girls were younger than the woman at the airport but also, in some ways, the same. There was something in our appearance, in the sound of our voices, and in who and what we were that seemed to have scared them. I pondered these things lightly because the need to get a place to lay my head was predominant in my mind. But once I got the apartment paid for, and once the department advanced a payment to me, I began to give greater weight to these kinds of encounters. I began to look and to see and to ask questions. In my second week in America, on a tour to places in Ann Arbor, I asked an elderly white woman, who had been very helpful to me, if there was a big black population in Ann Arbor—especially those from Africa, preferably from Nigeria. I wanted to know where I could get African food and supplies. Her answer was a swift "No."

Then she added, "There are in Detroit. But, uh!"

I looked at her. We had just gotten out of the car at the best cider place in town. She'd been touting this place as a must-visit even before I arrived in the States. She met my eyes and shook her head.

"Well, I mean, they don't have a very good reputation there. Crime, drugs..."

She must have seen a look of concern on my face, for my mind had cycled back to the woman at the New York airport and the girls who had avoided Jide and me. I wanted to arrive at a full knowledge of what was normal, what was usual. Was it the kindness of those here or their hostility? I wanted to know more than it seemed she—who had taken her time to show me around—was willing to reveal.

"Yes," I said.

"But it's more complicated than that," she said. We'd entered the building and were now sandwiched between tables filled with jars of cider. She bent toward me and said, "If you are new, an immigrant, like from Africa, they treat you differently."

Once those memorable words left her mouth, she picked up a jar of cider, pointed at the label, and began talking about it. She would not return to the subject that had kindled a small flame within me, even though I was certain she knew I was curious. I thought about those words, *They treat you differently*, again and again.

I was still thinking about them when I began going to classes and encountering so many beggars. Unlike the woman at the airport, they were dirty, unkempt, sometimes drunk, and mostly black. The sight of them haunted me, and often, I'd give generous alms. Many times I tried to engage them in conversations, to find out why they were begging. In response I got a blank stare or, sometimes, a deep confessional about a life in crime or some history of drug use. Whenever a new reality opened itself to me about America, I would recall the woman's words: *They treat you differently*.

Those words stayed with me through that fall of 2012 as I followed, from a close distance this time, the election competition between Barack Obama and Mitt Romney. In 2008, in Cyprus, my friends and I had stayed awake nearly all night as the prospects of the first black—and, as we were convinced at the time, "African"—president of the United States drew closer to reality. I watched one of the debates in which Obama, articulate and bold, skewered his opponent (who had said that the navy had fewer boats in 2012 than in 1917) with the quip: "We also have fewer horses and bayonets." I laughed for days, but even more, I began to wonder if he, Obama, was treated differently too.

As months passed and then a year, I began to realize that living in America meant more than one thing. I realized that I could be treated civilly by one person among the dominant group of white people and poorly by another of that group in the same day. I could be lifted by one person in that group and brought down by another. Jide, who was growing despondent about staying on in America, knew this too. But he seemed to think little of it as his resolve to return to Nigeria after his MFA grew stronger. He kept more to himself now, writing and meditating, while I turned frantically, daily, to the news. By the time the police shootings began to hit the news in 2014, I had come to understand much about the American political landscape and decided firmly not to engage in it. Since I could not vote anyway, I would not join in the vicious politics fueled more by hatred of the other side than by policy differences.

As everyday reality washed over me, the woman's words assumed an even more chilling effect. I found myself concerned as days passed that my novelty was wearing out the longer I stayed in America and that, sooner or later, I would be treated like other black men in this country. I was right, and it didn't take long. A man, Eric Garner, had been killed by policemen, and in response, protesters went about in force setting cities alight. I was crossing State Street in Ann Arbor on the way to my apartment when a fast-moving car veered from the intersection and came so close to me that it touched the bag I was carrying. As my mind swirled back to the reality of my great fortune that the car had not hit me, I saw that the man in the car, having pulled to an abrupt stop, had wound down his window. As I leapt onto the sidewalk, among a few bemused onlookers, he called after me, "If I hit your fucking ass down, they'll say it's 'nother white man!"

He slammed on the gas and sped away, through the WALK sign. I had not done anything untoward but crossed the road when the sign had said to do so. Yet I'd almost gotten hit by an angry man. As I walked, shaken by the encounter, it struck me that in that moment when I had not opened my mouth to utter a word and the man did not know who I was, it had not mattered that I was an immigrant. I was simply black. I was the other. And he would not have treated me differently, no matter what.

By 2015, I had completed my studies, and *The Fishermen* was being published in many countries. I was appearing in media around the world, and my work was receiving attention. I was traveling the US, and then the world. My new status meant I was indeed being treated differently—not always in a good way. Now every time I returned to the US, after waiting in line at the border control counter and answering a few questions, I inevitably would be taken into a room and detained for a while for cross-checks. After which, usually after an hour or so, they'd set me free and allow me to enter the country.

This happened to me many times in 2015, even after I switched visas from student to H-1B—temporary worker—because I had gotten employed as a professor at the University of Nebraska earlier that year. One of the cruelest detentions occurred in October 2015 on my way back from a hectic week in London. *The Fishermen* had been up for the Man Booker Prize but did not win. Although I had secretly feared that I was not ready to win such a top prize for my first book, I was still somewhat sad about the outcome. I arrived in the US two days after the prize ceremony, feeling worn out. I approached the border control counter with a heart full of prayers that I would be let through easily this time. I had a close connection I hoped not to miss. The officer, a man with a shock of gray hair that he kept scratching as he spoke, asked where I was coming from in a guttural voice.

"London," I said.

"What for?"

I cleared my throat. "I went for a prize ceremony for my novel."

He raised his head and made eye contact with me for the first time. "You wrote a book?"

"Yes, sir."

He turned over my passport, gazed at the green cover with the fading print that read ECONOMIC COMMUNITY OF WEST AFRICAN STATES. I am not one to guess at people's unacted intentions or to hear their unspoken words, but I could tell that the man was surprised.

"Hmm," he said and then pointed at the biometric machine in front of the counter. "Your left fingers please."

As I placed my fingers on that biometric machine, I was thrust into a psychological space where everything feels balanced on the thin line of the threshold between success and failure, where the mind works like a loom, spinning thoughts and felting them up into a fabric. Why did he ask me these questions? Was he impressed with me? Was it that he'd compared me to others from my country or continent and thought I may be better off? I had no way of knowing. My immediate fate was to be decided in the moments after the green lights of the biometric machine flashed. And indeed, once they did, the man said with a countenance that was so harsh one would have thought I had insulted him earlier, "Go and stand in that corner. An officer will come and pick you up. Follow him."

In that room on that day, I was furious. There were a lot of people there, including a man from some Arab country who was being sent back. The man was in distress. Two Arabic speakers in Qatar Airways uniforms were scrambling to translate his increasingly anguished words, and his wife was struggling to contain his tense gestures. I watched in the subdued light from a single bulb at the center of the room, the sound of the airport filtering in as troubled susurrations. As I sat there, watching and thinking about how I would spend the night in Chicago, having missed the last plane to Lincoln, Nebraska, my father's saying came to me like a thing from some other world.

And in the way my mind sometimes works, turning words into images, I pictured a naked man standing by the side of the road with a basketful of clothes, thrusting them at anyone who passed. In my mind, the man was somewhere in Nigeria, on a familiar street in Makurdi. He stood there on that street corner, unshaken by the voice of the Arab man pleading as two men in uniform forced him out of the room. The man who sat by me turned and whispered to me through labored breathing, "He had a visa. How can they deport him?" I shrugged, for on that street corner back home, a man sartorially graced in a suit and tie had stopped and taken a cloth from the naked man.

It crossed my mind that I could be that Arab man being dragged away. I thought of the possibility of things going that way, and a strange relief came upon me. I thought of home, Nigeria, and what I missed about it. I thought of Jide, who had returned just the previous year after studying in America for a few years. He was happier, freer amongst his own people. I saw now why he'd always felt strongly that he must return to Nigeria when the norm was that if you left home, you stayed wherever you went. It occurred to me, then, that America was not the man in shiny garments as I had often believed it was. It must have been this realization that had moved my friend so forcefully, and driven him out of the country. Perhaps he'd come to see that America was a naked man who hid himself behind the cloak he holds up for others to take. And I, like many others, have now started to see his nakedness, exposed in the bright light of the living day.

Your Father's Country

Alexander Chee

W*ould I die here?* It was August 8, 2017, and I was sitting on the tarmac in Seoul, waiting to fly back to America, and this was my first thought as I saw the president's tweet threatening the nuclear destruction of North Korea. I was in the last minutes of the trip, trying to edit a photo on Instagram as the other passengers boarded. The photo had been taken from my room in the hotel directly across from Seoul's City Hall, where I knew to stay because of the discounts on their beautiful rooms due to the many protests. There was a black spot on the lawn from where the conservative protesters demanding the release of the ex-president, Park Geun-hye, had been standing until just before I arrived, and I wanted the photo to include the view of the mountains, the Koreana Hotel—one of Seoul's oldest, where lovers go to get engaged, for good luck—and the black spot marking the lawn. But all of it wouldn't fit.

I had come to Seoul to interview the filmmaker Park Chan-wook for *T Magazine*, and to me, a longtime fan of his, it was the assignment of a lifetime. I had rewatched his films in the weeks leading up to our meeting in order to prepare, and sometime during the flight over, I began to feel as if I were in an as-yet-unmade Park film about a writer sent to interview Park.

Usually, in a Park film, a misunderstood hero or heroine is pitted against the world by what seems like fate and is destroyed and remade by how they cannot escape it, turning them into the butt of a cosmic joke. Coincidences often signal what seem like impossible plots against the main character. The last film I'd been rewatching on the plane was *Lady Vengeance,* the story of a young woman falsely convicted of murder who sets out to avenge herself on the murderer after her release from prison, painting her eyelids red to mark her mission. She kidnaps the murderer and gathers the parents of the children he's killed to punish him personally. As I stepped up to offer my passport on arrival in Seoul, I felt a chill as I noticed the red eyeshadow on the young woman officer stamping my passport—the same red eyeshadow as Lady Vengeance. She even looked like her—delicate features, and a stern seriousness despite her colorful eyes, as if she wasn't wearing any makeup at all.

After that, the feeling kept growing. I even made it something of a game, a possible frame to the profile. The photo I was editing, for example: the spot on the lawn, the shadow of a crowd, with no crowd, long after the crowd had left. Park likes to use images that way. I just hadn't been able to figure out what my Park film story line was.

And then I saw the tweet.

Just before I boarded the return flight, I realized I didn't want to leave. After years of being alienated from this country by my father's family, I had made friends here, had even come to miss Seoul when I wasn't here. As I searched Twitter for context of Trump's threat to North Korea, the cosmic joke in my Park film was finally plain. I had found my place here, perhaps in time to prepare to die here too.

The black spot marking the lawn, the shadow of a crowd, with no crowd—that was all that was left to see of the former president, the daughter of an earlier president-turned-dictator, Park Chung-hee, a man who ruled Korea for four terms until he was assassinated in 1979 and replaced by President Chun. She was the first woman president elected to the office and seemed at first to be the opposite of her authoritarian father. Her downfall began, however, with the Sewol Ferry disaster, in which an overloaded passenger vessel overturned while carrying students on a school trip, and more than three hundred people died, including rescue workers. The deaths, her poor reaction to the crisis, and the deadly unregulated nature of Korea's particular brand of late capitalism shocked the public. She had already been involved in other corruption scandals before this, and protests over the disaster and then the investigation into it grew into crowds filling the streets, famous to us now around the world.

Her final scandal involved the revelation of undue influence over her by a close friend and advisor, Choi Soon-sil, herself the daughter of a powerful man, the head of a Korean religious group known as Yongsae-gyo, often referred to as a cult, and perhaps known to us outside Korea as the "Korean Rasputin." The friends were in their own sort of Park film: two women with very famous fathers who had emerged from the repressive past of Korea to preside over the country together. One, the public face; one, apparently, the private; and now all they had done seemed to come down to this angry dark smudge on the lawn below my hotel room's window.

When I checked my notifications, I noticed a comment on one of my pictures of the new water park in downtown Seoul, created by the new president when he was mayor of the city. He'd ordered a poisoned underground river cleaned and had turned it into this. "Aren't you afraid of getting incinerated? I want you home now." Instagram is usually an anodyne scroll through the lives of your friends and your favorite artists and celebrities, like a magazine in which you are the only context—politics doesn't usually intrude, if you can even call the threat of nuclear war "politics." Stunned, I gave up on the photo and, as I waited for the plane to push off from the gate, returned to Twitter to figure out what this friend meant, where I discovered everyone back in America panicking about the possibility of nuclear war.

I had not been afraid before this. The trip, just five days long, had been, until then, nothing less than a dream. The interview with director Park had included an unexpected invitation to his home. Park is a self-taught auteur and is, to me, one of the world's great film directors. He lives north of Seoul near the border of North Korea in an artists' colony, a town created for artists, next to a school for stuntmen, where he dreams up his genre-bending masterpieces. As I sat on the plane, waiting for takeoff, my mind's eye was still full of the handsome stuntmen sunning themselves on the front sidewalk of the school, as if it were a muscle beach.

At night, after my interviews were done, I had gone out for meals and drinks with my friends there, writers mostly—mostly Korean American and living in Korea for work. There was a playfulness to life there that I hadn't felt in a long time, running around in the dark of Jongno, posing for photos, staying up late, and eating at the food carts there with a somaek—a shot of soju dropped into a beer. I had spent a lot of time with my good friend Joe, with whom I have a kind of friendship I think of as very Korean, something I've only seen between men there, despite us both being Korean American—notable for an affectionate loyalty for which one dares just about anything. Joe had come with me to help me interview Park, for example, even renting the car to go to his house once we were invited, and giving me notes on the translation.

It had all felt like the opposite of the Korea I knew from the 1980s, as if both the country and I had passed through an enchantment, transformed.

The thought I'd had on the way to the airport was *Would I live here?* and I remembered it as I heard the engines of the plane pulse to life. Was this what it meant, that I didn't want to leave?

My trouble with my family in Korea began before I was born, when my late father sacrificed his family's approval to leave Korea after his military service in the early 1960s, married the blond American girl his mother had asked him not to marry when he left, and had three children with her. I was the oldest, and the oldest of my line of Chee, technically the next patriarch. But I was happiest when I did not speak to his family, because these intense conflicts from their past seemed to constantly engulf them, each visit an attempt to ensnare me or my siblings, to enlist us for one side or another. Before his death, my father visited this country most often to settle their fights, and without him, their fights now renewed themselves, and stayed unresolved.

When I look back on the past decade, I can see that the more I became close with my friends, the more I became, through them, closer to the country's culture and history. I no longer needed to reach out to my family there and put up with their abuse. My family, who had so often criticized me for not knowing Korea better, turned out to be the obstacle.

Even as I read through the mix of disaster fantasies and bad jokes on Twitter, I knew the chances of a nuclear blast at that instant were minuscule. And yet with Trump, you just don't know. This is a man who bombed Syria over dessert on a Saturday at his club. I never posted the City Hall photo. Looking at it now, I see why. The black spot on the grass looks like the aftermath of an explosion. The montage I was imagining for my character had me in my airplane seat, remembering the new river park, the clean air, the artists' colony, just before it was all lost to nuclear fire.

There's another feeling I get from Park's films that I've been thinking about: of a Korea I still remember from the 1980s, when I came to visit my grandfather during the authoritarian rule of President Chun Doo-hwan. I can still remember my grandfather's driver rolling up the windows of the Mercedes-Benz, hustling us away from the tear gas being used on demonstrators, and me feeling the urgency of the students appearing, suddenly, out of the clouds moving down the streets in the distance. And smelling the gas as it entered through the air conditioner. My grandfather held a handkerchief over his face and passed one to me also.

The Korea I knew around the time of President Chun was one filtered obstinately by my family, an aristocratic family flashy with new money, thanks to my grandfather's hard work. I remember when I heard about Gwangju and the democracy movement, the reason for the tear gas in the streets, my first thought was *My grandfather has a hotel and casino there.* I had spent a few nights there on a long trip around the countryside at the direction of an aunt and uncle, and I had spent those nights sitting in a disco, swirling a brandy and Coke around in my glass and listening to singers cover American pop songs in Korean.

Even after we passed through that cloud of tear gas together, my grandfather never once told me about what the students were protesting.

Only when we went on a trip to a mountain park later that same summer did I get closer to the truth: a young man introduced himself to my brother and me as an organizer of those protests—he was the first one to tell me about the Gwangju democracy movement. He recognized us as Americans and wanted to inform us about the movement and the protests. "We are trying to reunify Korea," he said. He told me there was a student movement in North Korea also, and when I asked if he had communicated with them, he said, without faltering, that he had not but that they knew these students existed. They were sure of it.

This is the kind of person Park makes films about, and it is part of why I love his work. Park's films tell stories about people possessed by a love that borders on the fanatic, people who will risk their lives for someone they've never met but are sure exists. The films portray the desperation behind that sort of a senselessly romantic fatal gesture— and the humanity of that person as well.

The single visible sign that something was wrong with the country, to me, besides the protests, was the armed guards in the airport when we arrived, whose weapons shocked me. I was told that they were present as a part of preparedness for North Korean attacks. I would think of them years later when I saw armed guards in American airports, and then in our train stations too.

The last time I was in Korea, for family business, which typically meant family struggles, I went to see a Korean fortune-teller in Seoul. This is not undertaken lightly—they deliver truths you cannot easily escape from, if ever. He was blind, as was his wife, and he lived in the fortune-teller neighborhood, an in-demand advisor to very powerful Koreans. He'd been a soccer player as a young man, and a blow from a ball had cost him his sight but had also left him with this gift. A friend had arranged our meeting—her family had been going to see him for years. She came with me and translated. He told me many things, most of them good, and then, as he finished, he said, somewhat abruptly: "Korea is a beautiful country, but there is much about it that is not beautiful. But it is your father's country, and so it is your country too."

His fingers had been moving along the braille surface of his laptop, his way of reading his notes, and it had fascinated me. But what he said to me was not something he had been reading—his fingers had stopped moving as he spoke. His suddenly still hands underscored for me the shock of his words—that this was my country also—and I felt how much I had wanted someone to tell me this. Not the way my father's family had, as if they owned me. But the way this man had, as if I belonged.

Most of my sense of belonging here has been built that way—away from my family. It is not very Korean, but it is the only way I know to belong. I had long confused my ambivalence over my connection to Korean culture with my ambivalence toward my family. No longer.

Would I die here? As the plane lifted off the ground and I could see the city, I remembered again the dark spot on the grass in front of City Hall. Yes, I knew I would if I had to. That day it meant dying apart from my husband, my family and friends back in America. But I knew I would die here if I had to, and it would be a happy death, because it was born from that same shock of belonging, some deepening of the earlier one. As the plane returned me to America, I knew I would die here because I wanted to live here. That these were the same feeling.

In the last seconds before we took off, I was still in that Park film, but the story had shifted. The writer who believed he was going to die was going to survive. The film now possibly about a writer discovering that Korea is the free country with a democratically elected president, elected by a majority, and the United States is the one with the man elected undemocratically, and bent on ruling as a dictator.

I don't know where my Park Chan-wook film ends. If it's over, or if I'm still in it. Maybe the ending is in Seoul, at some distant point in the future. I almost look forward to when I will know.

The Long Answer

Yann Demange

Where are you from?"

It's a question I've always had a hard time with. And since moving to the US four years ago, I'm asked this question on a regular basis.

Maybe it's the combination of a brownish face and London accent coupled with French names that throws people off. Who knows? But this question, and hearing it asked over and over these past few years, has forced me to confront my unresolved questions about my identity, how I grew up, and how those experiences led me to being a director. After all, in longer conversations, the question "Where are you from?" is often followed by "What made you get into film?"

People tend to like things compartmentalized and simple; a simple answer to a (seemingly) simple question, right? But it's never been that simple for me. I've never actually had any sense of a "national identity" or, for that matter, a sense of belonging to any one tribe.

I'm mixed race: a French white mother and an Algerian father. So "I'm a Londoner" is my standard go-to short response when that "Where are you from?" question comes up. That's the simplest answer I feel comfortable giving without getting into it.

"Ah, so you're British..." is the response I often get in the US. I always bristle a little at that one. "No, I'm a Londoner, not British." I don't usually follow up with an explanation of what I mean: *It's complicated, so let's stick to the short answer, bruv.*

For what it's worth, here is the long answer:

I have never been able to identify as British. Not when I was called "Paki" by Brits for most of my childhood. Culturally, I don't feel British either. Rightly or wrongly, "British" always felt too wrapped in colonial connotations that I wasn't ready to accept as part of my identity—I ain't taking that on.

I feel the same about being French: Yes, I am a French passport holder, yes, I am legally French, but I haven't lived in France since the age of two. Being half Algerian, I can never really comfortably take on "being French" as a sole national identity either. France's colonial past—130 years of occupying Algeria, racism, the body count of two wars, and the legacy of the postcolonial Algerian experience—isn't something I feel comfortable glossing over either.

That said, when Zinedine Zidane led a French team, made up almost entirely of the descendants of immigrants from the "colonies," to win the World Cup in 1998, I celebrated for sure. He symbolized something that transcended football at a time when Le Pen was in power and France was becoming increasingly polarized. It was a special moment. I wish Zidane could make a comeback...

Twenty years later France went on to win the World Cup again. They were great, this new generation of players that included Pogba, Kanté, Mbappé, and Umtiti, men who are all vibrant and own their diverse Frenchness. They were inspiring. And their diversity, and what this means for French identity, didn't go unnoticed. In a loaded joke on *The Daily Show*, host Trevor Noah congratulated "Africa" on their World Cup win. What he was getting at was that France owes its victories to the descendants of people from their colonies. But there is defensiveness if you dare utter this out loud. When these kids win, they are French, and that is that. But during the day-to-day, if you don't happen to be a football star, or scaling a wall like a superhero to rescue a child, like Mamoudou Gassama, you don't get welcomed into the fold.

The French ambassador Gérard Araud's reaction to this joke was hilarious: "Unlike in the United States of America, France does not refer to its citizens based on their race, religion, or origin. To us, there is no hyphenated identity. Roots are an individual reality. By calling them an African team, it seems like you're denying their Frenchness. This, even in jest, legitimizes the ideology which claims whiteness as the only definition of being French."

The hypocrisy is incredible.

Even with all this in mind, I can't call myself an Algerian either. I grew up largely estranged from my father, and although I studied Arabic a little at one stage in my teens, I sadly don't speak it, which pains me.

Add to the mix that my mother was raised Catholic, but isn't religious, and my father is Muslim. Yet neither "gave" me a religion to follow or wanted to dictate a cultural identity for me, so it's safe to say I was left a little confused.

I once heard someone say when anything is possible it becomes too overwhelming, and it can lead to feeling like nothing is possible at all. My parents left me to figure out my identity. Neither claimed me for their tribe.

So at a very early age, one thing became clear to me: I'd always be an outsider.

Eventually I came to realize I'd always be a Londoner too.

Being a Londoner is something I could always accept and own. It transcends any national connotations for me. It's a vibe, attitude, swag, banter, and it doesn't have a flag, passport, or past atrocities attached to it in the same way.

But I'm also a particular type of Londoner. One of the multi-cultural mongrels who came of age in the 1990s and found expression in the rise of the Jungle, Drum and Bass, and then the UK Garage music scenes. A common language emerged across races that bound working-class Londoners living within the "melting pots," as opposed to those posh Londoners who lived in close proximity to us but didn't experience diversity beyond sharing a postcode.

Londoner: this was an umbrella that kept me dry as a teenager and into my early twenties. But I no longer live in London. That moment, that subculture, well, it isn't really around anymore (around as I knew it, that is). So I'm still searching for an identity, one that isn't tied to something fleeting but lies within.

So that "Where are you from?" question: more often than not, what people are really asking is "What's your 'tribe'?" And, essentially, I've always been tribeless.

It can be an innocent question, and maybe one you have to expect as a foreigner with a funny accent. But it strikes to the core of something I have found profoundly complicated and difficult to resolve. An annoying existential issue I can't shake. I thought I could ignore it. I arrogantly thought I had transcended it in some way through being a filmmaker and finding a form of expression that favors the outsider's eye. But this—this being an outsider and seeking a sense of belonging—is something I can now see has been a theme running throughout all my work so far.

The question "Where are you from?" goes to the heart of an identity issue I found myself forced to face all over again when I was where I felt more out of place than ever: in a white privileged Hollywood bubble.

Moving to the States was never a goal of mine. It happened after I made a UK indie film called '71. Surprisingly, the Hollywood film industry reacted really well to the film. Opportunities I couldn't ignore suddenly presented themselves, so I packed up, left my council flat in London, and off to Hollywood I went.

It was exciting, and all of a sudden I went from being the guy who couldn't get into parties to being seemingly popular for the first time. It's a bubble, of course, one that has a finite window. I knew this, and I was determined to make the most of it while it lasted.

I always think of that period as though I was invited into an amazing buffet. I knew they were gonna call time on me eventually, but I was stuffing my pockets with the smoked salmon, like Dan Aykroyd in *Trading Places*, before someone said my moment was up.

Slowly, as the dust settled and the political rhetoric of the ongoing election debates was kicking in, I started to feel a strange loneliness and discomfort. It wasn't until my niece and nephew, two cool mixed-race Londoners in their twenties, both came to stay with me for a few days that the penny really dropped. I was in a bar one night with them, our third night out in a row, and my nephew casually asked, "How come everyone is white wherever we go? Where is it more…mixed…?" I mean, some of the East LA hipster spots had a marginal bit of diversity, but it was shocking to us how little socioeconomic and racial mixing there was.

I'd gone from living in a particular part of London that was a genuine melting pot of diversity, coming from a family of multiple ethnicities, to living in the most segregated society I had ever experienced. And—get this—I was bunched in *with the whites* for the first time in my life. *Me?* One of the privileged whites?

Don't get me wrong. London is no Mecca of Equality. We may

have diversity among the working-class communities, but that's not to be confused with opportunities within my own industry. In fact, the diversity I'm speaking about is woefully underrepresented in the stories being told back home. When it comes to film and television, London's lack of representation is shocking.

They are behind the US, for sure.

In fact, along with many of my—shall we say "ethnically diverse"?—peers from the UK, I had to migrate to the US in order to have a real chance at a career with some scale. Diversity in the industry is surface level back home, as are the stories told in film and on TV, and the material the gatekeepers gravitate toward. The glass ceiling gets hit fast.

Nobody in the game is *racist*, of course. Everyone is liberal and open-minded. Yet every production company you'll ever walk into is almost entirely white, with everyone coming from a very small pool of the same posh schools. It's not something you're supposed to say out loud, for fear of sounding ungrateful and inviting some sort of backlash, but it's the truth.

When it comes to film, they continue to hide behind the old "foreign sales" argument that stories with any "diversity" are not castable and therefore won't sell abroad. They always bend over backward to find a way to jam in a white protagonist, whatever the story. I believe this, in some part, is a contributing factor to the increasing tensions back home, and the strong right-wing movement. There is a lack of empathy or understanding of the "other." How can people empathize with the parts of society they only see represented in headlines and rhetoric? Thankfully, the foreign sales model is dying off, and hopefully, so will the lie it perpetuates.

In LA, there were opportunities for me. But I felt completely out of sorts in the city itself. The experience triggered all my adolescent identity issues. And I'd never experienced being at the white privileged end of a racial pecking order before. Who was going to be my tribe? Where could I fit in?

In looking for an answer, I had to go back to my multicultural family:

I was born in Paris in 1977, and two years later I was an immigrant. My family moved to South London, then West. My mother is light, can't go in the sun, whiter than white. My father was born and raised in Algiers, grew up during the war for independence from France, and moved to Paris at eighteen. I have two older brothers, each with a different father—one is Afro-Caribbean; the other is Argentinian and half indigenous.

All three of us, my mother's sons, are mixed race, three different mixes, and each comes with its own particular set of identity issues to navigate. I remember each one of us wrestling with the question of where we were from, what we were supposed to identify as, and not being able to help one another. We were family, but our roots led to different tribes.

One thing was for sure: the white side of our family wasn't gonna claim us for *their* tribe, and they couldn't even if they wanted to. Mum had started her own new nonwhite strand of the Demange family, and we were, to begin with, basically a London-based unit of three.

My mother and father broke up soon after they came to London, and I ended up being fostered between the ages of four and twelve while my mum found her feet as a single mother and immigrant. I had two four-year stints with different families in Essex. The first was with a French-speaking household, and the second was with a white Cockney family.

I have never quite shaken the accent that gave me.

I'd see my brother and sometimes my mother on the weekends. It wasn't a "care home," and I have no horror stories to share. The families who took me in were decent people. But they weren't my family, and they certainly weren't my tribe.

I wasn't well received in Essex. I remember trying to reason with some white Cockney kids calling me "Paki" at school once: "I'm North African. I ain't Pakistani." A blank look. "You're still a fucking Paki." And that summed it up. "Paki" was how they saw anything "other," between their understanding of complete whiteness and what they could clearly discern as blackness. So a fight would have to be had—nothing dramatic, just kiddie stuff, but it was frequent enough.

I put a version of this exchange in my very first short fiction film. Film has given me a way to explore some of these themes of "otherness." I hadn't really taken the time to analyze the choices I have made in the stories I've chosen to tell, but of late it's become clear that it's all rooted in the things I'm discussing here.

When I was with that Essex foster family, I remember having to see social workers. I had pretty full-on behavioral issues by the age of nine. I was a bit of a nightmare kid, and I cringe when I think back. Anyway, the social worker was trying to get to the root of my bad behavior. I wouldn't listen to anyone, not the teachers and certainly not the Cockney foster family I was living with. The only person I'd listen to was my older brother, and if there was ever an issue, they'd get him on the phone.

I remember the social worker saying my "problem" was that I was "anchorless." That word has stayed with me. But I wear an anchor ring now, so I guess I have sorted that out...

My eldest brother, who is seventeen years older than me, was my hero growing up. Once my father was gone, my brother filled that role. He was anxious to help me avoid the painful experiences of racism he'd had growing up in France and was still experiencing as a young black man in London. He was there during the Brixton riots and had his fair share of battles with racists.

He was cool and had a sense of himself. I'd watch him play bass for hours on end, usually playing along to Jaco Pastorius's riffs on Weather Report's "Birdland," on manic repeat. I wanted to be like him... but I couldn't.

I remember how confident he was when he came back from a stint living in New York in the late eighties. It was an important, empowering trip for him. He had discovered his blackness. He was wearing Spike Lee merchandise, reading African American literature, had started playing basketball, and was wearing caps, which, believe it or not, was fucking radical in London at the time. His year in New York had given him an attitude and confidence that I loved; he'd found a personal way of owning and being proud of his blackness. It was unapologetic, and I wanted in.

He'd include me in his experience as much as he could but at the same time was mindful that I was not the same race as him. I remember us having a heated exchange over my love for N.W.A, the *Straight Outta Compton* album being the first vinyl record I ever bought myself. I was obsessed with hip-hop culture and black movies, but there was an implicit understanding that I was immersing myself in another tribe's culture, not my own, and it had to be done with respect and careful consideration.

This was round about the time that Tim Burton's *Batman* came out, which was the same year Spike Lee's *Do the Right Thing* was released, the latter being the cultural phenomenon of the year and a bit of a game changer. My brother came home wearing a T-shirt with the Batman logo, except it said BLACKMAN. I remember thinking that was the coolest thing in the world. I wanted one! It was awkward for my brother, but he had to explain why I couldn't wear that. He was black. I wasn't. "I know, but we're family, right...?" "Nah, cultural and ethnic identity don't work that way, bro."

But I hadn't known where else to look. There were no North African kids at my inner-London comprehensive school. The playground seemed divided into whites and blacks. So I ended up with the West Indian kids, along with a few of the South Asian kids. They were the ones who would have us. We were "in" but also the "outsiders."

The confusion even extended to my name.

My given first name is actually Mounir, but my brother convinced my mother to change it to Yann. He had experienced so much racism as a young black man in France, and he told my mother I would have the same fate as an Algerian. So Mounir was moved and became my middle name once my father left, and I was too young to have a say.

At this point they thought we'd be moving back to France soon, and my brother wanted to protect me. The way he saw it, I was "white passing," so why flag up my ethnicity with my name? His skin color couldn't be hidden, but perhaps my Algerian side could.

I wonder if on some level he was right. Would Mounir Hanine have been a filmmaker too? Either way, it was a change motivated by love, for sure, but it definitely accentuated the identity confusion to come. Perhaps Mounir Demange would have had a clearer sense of tribe. Perhaps he would have been "claimed" or embraced by the North African community more...Who knows?

During the school holidays my middle brother, who is seven years older than me, would come to visit us in London. He never lived with us in the end. He was having his own complicated identity struggle, wrestling with being part indigenous South American yet looking the whitest of the siblings and growing up in the roughest part of Paris.

Barbès in the 18th arrondissement in the early nineties was no joke. Funnily enough, his biggest antagonists growing up were the local Algerian kids. I won't attempt to tell his story—I don't know it well enough—but I should add that he was also a bit of a hero for me. He started martial arts at seven years old, was a great graffiti artist, and was the one who read in our family. Devouring books, he'd tell me stories and expose me to different philosophies and points of view. He was a good storyteller, and this too had a big influence on me. I remember when he got a Native American's head tattooed on his chest. I thought it was the coolest thing ever, that expression of identity, and at fifteen I went and got one done too. My mother went mad. My middle brother was always very kind about my tattoo mishap and never mentioned it. But my eldest brother laughed his head off. "You're not part indigenous, bro!"

Seriously, what the fuck was I doing? Cultural appropriation, I believe they call it. On top of it all, it was a fucking shit tattoo, done by a shit artist. The amount of comments I've had off North Africans who have seen that tattoo...

"Is that an Indian's head...?"

"Yeah."

"...Why?"

"Oufff, it's complicated, bro."

The tattoo aged badly, and I eventually just lied to people and said it was a portrait of my mother. I'd be straight-up deadpan about it, and that would nip the conversation about my shit tattoo in the bud nice and quickly. Let's not mention the tattoo again, please.

But I really wanted my own culturally empowering moment like my eldest brother had experienced in New York; it felt like the missing piece I needed. I called my father. I wanted to go to Algeria and meet my family. He was delighted. There was a further complication at this point, though, something he wanted to tell me:

I had one more brother I didn't know about. We shared a father, and we were only five months apart. A bit of a surprise. His mother was Algerian, which meant he was 100 percent Algerian, yet his mother wanted him to assimilate, so she'd given him a French name too! She wasn't teaching him Arabic either! My father has never called him by his French name to this day. Just like he has never and will never call me Yann.

I went to Paris to meet my "new" brother. He was living the Parisian urban Algerian disenfranchised experience. (Later, in our twenties, whenever we hung out together in Paris, we were always seen as Algerian, and as a result I palpably got a glimpse of what that meant in Paris. We could never get into any bars or clubs together, the vibe always tense and hostile, and we could forget about being able to get a taxi.)

It's strange, but when we're together we both feel it, that somehow we're undeniably part of the disenfranchised postcolonial North African diaspora tribe, yet we're also estranged from it in some ways. Since then, I have come to learn this is quite a common condition, because many first-generation North Africans were so desperate to assimilate, settle, and put the conflict behind them, they often didn't pass their culture on to their offspring. This legacy is unraveling in a big way in France right now.

I needed to go back to the source. So in the summer of 1991, I went to Algeria. I remember the feeling when I first got there, of looking around and seeing that the majority of people looked like me. It was undeniable that I was from this tribe, genetically speaking at least. I couldn't speak Arabic, and though I was making an effort to live as a Muslim at the time, I didn't know how to truly be one.

I was still an outsider.

The thing that was emotionally powerful for me was meeting my grandparents, aunts, and cousins. I'd never had grandparents before this. They took me in their arms and cried. No reservations or holding back. Just an outpouring of love. I was moved to tears. They were strangers to me, but I was not a stranger to them. I was family, and they made me feel it.

When I was there, I got very sick and no one could figure out what was wrong. It was some sort of virulent food poisoning. I was delirious with fever, puking and the rest. They took me to various doctors and two hospitals where I was given a load of injections, but nothing worked.

My family there believes in alternative Islamic healers. When my aunt had severe anemia, they took her down to the Algerian Sahara, where a healer said prayers and put drops made from herbs and plants in her nose and eyes. Apparently all the yellow from her skin started pouring out of her as he chanted... I couldn't buy this, but I let it go...

Yet conventional medicine didn't seem to help anyway. I was getting worse. At one point I remember waking up, fevered and delirious, to my grandmother and aunt praying over me in their hijabs, sprinkling some shit on me—can't for the life of me remember what.

I couldn't share their beliefs, but being that close to someone with utter conviction in their faith and watching the "performance" of the ritual was hypnotizing and soothing. I surrendered to it, just letting go. It's like how a performance in a film can transcend your personal beliefs and make you emotionally identify with a character's point of view. Anyway, the experience felt powerful, and I got better.

Probably the injections.

I stayed in Algeria for a few weeks. It was an important trip for me. I was having my own mini version of my brother's New York trip. Something in me was being soothed. It took me a while to let go and think of these new people as family. Once I did, I really fell for my grandparents. My grandfather wasn't much of a talker, but it was fascinating to hear him describe growing up during the French occupation. How strange to think I had "history," that I had a tribe I had been estranged from, that I was part of a larger narrative I wasn't aware of. As far as he was concerned, I was one of them and that was that.

It was on this trip that I first saw *The Battle of Algiers,* when my cousins screened it for me. My family was incredibly proud of the film, as many Algerians are, but they were particularly proud and obsessed with the film because my aunt starred in it. She played the beautiful woman who plants the bomb in the milk bar. This was the only time she ever acted in anything.

The director Pontecorvo used a lot of nonactors, making the film, something I would later do myself. I loved the fact he used real people and channeled who they were and what they could bring. Not only does this give the people you are depicting some ownership over their story, but the sense of authenticity and the experiences they bring to the process can help a film to feel truly immersive, rather than a story "told," I think.

So I had "returned" to the family, and I would now come every school holiday and get to know them all properly and perhaps start to have a sense of tribe. Or so I thought. It was 1991, and in the background a political conflict was brewing. The FIS (Islamic Salvation Front) had won the local elections, so the government cancelled the national elections. It wasn't really safe for me to go to certain places. With my Nike Air Max and London ways, I was the kind of "not true Muslim" who would be deemed a heretic and possibly attacked.

The shit really hit the fan a few months after I returned to London, when an all-out civil war broke out. More than 250,000 people died over the proceeding decade. Every time a school holiday came around, it was too dangerous for me to risk going back to see my family. They wouldn't risk me being there while it was like this. I never saw them again. I have not been back to Algeria since that original trip. My grandparents passed away, and it was even deemed too unsafe for me to attend their funerals.

Throughout all this, knowing my aunt had been in *The Battle of Algiers* strengthened my love for film. As absurd as it sounds, on some level I think I felt like I had discovered an inheritance to some sort of personal lineage in movies. It gave me a kind of connection and claim to film. I may just be projecting this onto it now, of course, the human need to try to make sense of, and find meaning in, narratives being so strong.

Either way, at around this time I started watching a lot of films. In them I sought comfort and some understanding of how I could find a place in the world. It wasn't a conscious search. I'd watch anything and everything I could get my hands on. I watched all my mother's French movies: a lot of Belmondo flicks (she had a thing for him), Truffaut, Godard, and a lot of trashy French pulp. At the time, Channel 4 showed films from all over the world at night. Carpenter movies, Walter Hill, Kurosawa, Melville, Fellini, Peckinpah, Scorsese,

Spike Lee, Sidney Lumet...so many amazing films. And the BBC backed some incredible voices, like Alan Clarke and Ken Loach, both of whom have been big influences...with a sprinkling of Hammer horror to freak me out too.

I never thought of film as a possible career path; the notion would have been absurd to me at the time. It was simply my medicine, my comfort and escape. Film showed me there were so many people out there, living so many different lives, and they were all really complicated. I found comfort in that.

I started making short films as a way of exploring the themes that preoccupied me. I have no idea how it happened, but I eventually ended up as a director. It's still very surreal to me that I have been "let in." Somehow I've found a way to use my "inside outsider's gaze"— as long as I don't get found out, that is.

As I started to work more, I didn't want to be limited to my own personal stories. I began to repeat myself as a writer and learned to value collaborating with other writers, coming up with stories I wouldn't necessarily have thought of.

Top Boy was my first chance to do that on a bigger canvas, more so than my previous short films or TV work. It was, at the time, the most personal piece I'd made in television. It offered an opportunity to explore some themes I was preoccupied with. It also allowed me to put in some experiences I'd had growing up in London. The drug-crime genre was just a through line from which I could explore things I knew and cared about: being a young boy, being raised by a struggling single mother, wondering which tribe to join.

For Ranell, the thirteen-year-old protagonist, the question was whether he would join the gang or go it alone and be his own man. I didn't share his narrative, but I found ways to connect to him. For instance, I could never sleep as a kid, something that remains a problem to this day. I'd often stare out the window at night, not having the intellectual capacity to make sense of any of it, particularly during my years being fostered. Nothing has changed, of course...I remember putting that in the series.

I went on to do a similar thing with '71, which is set in Belfast at the height of the sectarian violence during the Troubles. It tells the story of an eighteen-year-old English soldier separated from his platoon and stranded after a riot. His journey unfolds over twenty-four hours as he tries to survive and get back to safety. When I first read Gregory Burke's incredible screenplay, I saw that this was an opportunity to make a personal film.

This story was, after all, about tribes.

What I saw in the protagonist, played by Jack O'Connell, was a boy looking for his people and a sense of belonging. This was an aspect I brought to the story. I could project some of my own struggles onto the characters in the world I was an outsider to. It seems to me that boys seeking a tribe and seeking the paternal are often the ones recruited to join armies, gangs, and militias. They are promised family, but of course a terrible betrayal takes place as these boys are so quickly sacrificed and pitted against other boys seeking the same, boys they often have more in common with than those they are taking orders from.

Kids being robbed of their childhoods is something that makes me angry and something I've found myself subconsciously revisiting.

I've just finished my first American movie, based on a true story, called White Boy Rick. A father-son story set in Detroit in the mid-eighties during the crack epidemic, it's about a fourteen-year-old named Rick, the only white kid left in the east side of Detroit after "white flight," who becomes completely immersed in the African American community. He's an outsider, an "inside outsider," like so many of my protagonists have been.

Matthew McConaughey plays the father. Alongside this major star, I cast a fifteen-year-old street kid from Baltimore as the lead. A kid who himself lives immersed in a tribe that isn't his own, which is something you can't fake at that age. He'd never so much as done a drama class before.

I arrived in the US to make the film at a strange time. Trump was gearing up to run for president, and a Brexit movement was brewing back home. We know how that all turned out. The landscape has changed. People seem increasingly reluctant to engage with the "other" right now, and there is a global shift toward nationalism. Everyone is tribing up again and calling each other out. Lines are being drawn in the sand.

"Show me the boy, and I'll show you the man." At forty-one years old, I can hear that saying ringing in my ears. I haven't managed to outrun the question of identity. I find myself back where I started, only follicle-challenged this time around (the bald tribe being the one I unwillingly find myself claimed by).

I guess my tribe is the tribeless. I have come to terms with the fact that I will remain a perpetual outsider. That doesn't mean the loneliness and sadness that comes with it at times will ever go away. I certainly haven't found any profound answers. I suspect my list of questions is only going to keep growing.

Maybe in my case identity isn't something that can truly be squared up and "resolved," but I know I have to keep engaging with it, as it keeps evolving and shifting. But it's also clear that the problem of identity and tribelessness is why, and how, I got into making films.

It's all linked to the question of "What stories am I going to tell?" with the opportunities that have now opened up . . . "Whose stories do I want to focus on?"

Being in a city where I don't fit in, I'm now a different kind of outsider: not a French Algerian in a black London school, but a French Algerian Londoner in white Hollywood. But now I know who I am. I am an outsider. Yes, I'm still seeking. Yes, it's still confusing, but what I do as a filmmaker is embrace that question mark.

I know firsthand the importance of telling the stories of people who are underrepresented, particularly during a time when the discourse is becoming increasingly black and white. As the capacity for empathy toward people deemed "other" to one's own tribe gets more diluted, there is a responsibility to tell stories that engage them, whatever their tribe.

Fuck being judgmental or self-righteous; there's too much of that going around right now. That, sprinkled with a little too much earnestness . . . it's nauseating. Who are we to judge? People's lives are complicated, after all. It's by digging deep into that complexity that we find the universality in their experience. There's no universality without specificity.

So I'll continue to explore outsiders in storytelling in the hope that it may someday unlock something for me, or lead to some sort of inner peace.

And I'll continue giving my short answer to the question "Where are you from?" . . . Because as you can see, the alternative answer can go on for-fucking-ever, innit.

An American, Told

Jean Hannah Edelstein

1.

I was six the first and only time I watched *An American Tail*. (Who would choose to feel such pain more than once?) I remember viewing it a little too close to the television, sitting on the brown-and-orange shag carpet of the family room in our raised ranch in upstate New York. *An American Tail* is an animated film about Fievel Mousekewitz, a Jewish mouse who flees Ukraine with his family for America when the shtetl they live in is destroyed by Cossacks and the mice lose their home to the Cossacks' murderous cats.

On the ship to the new country the mice dance and sing their way through the horrors of steerage with a cheerful tune about how "there are no cats in America / and the streets are paved with cheese." It all seems so promising, but then Fievel is swept overboard in a storm. He survives—of course he survives, he is the mouse protagonist of an animated children's movie; the filmmakers were not monsters—but the rest of the film follows his trials as he finds his way through early-twentieth-century New York City on a plaintive search for his family.

My father had only just recently added a VCR to our very basic home entertainment system, and for the most part we didn't watch very much television, but I suppose my mother had other things to do that afternoon when she settled me in front of the set and put the video in.

I was the middle of three children: she had a seven-year-old and a newborn on her hands as well. I don't remember how much awareness I had of the stories of Jewish immigrants coming to America, if I related so much to Fievel's plight because I knew my father's family had taken a similarly choppy route. Or maybe, like most children of a certain age, the thought of losing my parents was just my idea of hell on earth.

I cried as soon as Fievel was swept away from his parents in the storm and I cried as he looked for them and I cried as he and his mouse sister sang their signature plaintive song, "Somewhere Out There," which became a Top 40 hit. It was a romantic ballad, which was quite weird since it was sung by a mouse brother and sister, but it was the mid-eighties.

At some point my mother came into the room to investigate my crying—which was, I'll note, on a different floor from the kitchen where she was making dinner, so I must have been crying at top volume—and suggested that if I didn't stop crying she would have to turn the movie off. I begged her not to: I had to find out what happened to poor Fievel, how he overcame the terrible fate of leaving the only home he'd ever known and becoming separated from his family in the process.

I did not consider, through my tears, that my mother and Fievel had something in common: that she'd left her home, her country, and her family to come to America. That maybe my mother could better tell me how it felt. For though my mother's transition across the ocean had been rather more comfortable than Fievel's, she too had left a great deal behind: her blood family, her friends, her career.

My mother came to the United States from Scotland in 1980. She wasn't pushed out of the country where she'd spent her whole life; she was pulled, by love. My mother met my father in the mid-seventies, when he was an American postdoctoral fellow at the University of Glasgow. They lived in the same apartment building near the campus: a grand terrace turned into a stack of bedsits.

My father's family had come to America like the Mousekewitzes, as I mentioned, sometime around the turn of the twentieth century, having left because of the persecution of Jews in Russia and the surrounding states, and landed on Ellis Island, the immigration inspection station where transatlantic immigrants of that era arrived and were processed and welcomed in (or turned back). Standard. The American Dream had worked out for the Edelsteins, at least to an extent: each generation became more affluent and better educated. My father, a second-generation American, remembered his grandmother speaking Yiddish and Russian but didn't speak them himself. His grandparents were not educated, but his father had gone to a state university to become an optometrist, and my father got a PhD from Harvard in nuclear physics.

Like any family, my father's family endured its fair share of real sadness, even trauma: one great-grandfather left his wife and children in such abject poverty for a period of years that the kids had to be sent to live with relatives. (The couple reunited, lived together to the end of their lives, but, according to my father, never again shared a bed; divorce was not an option for immigrants like them.) My grandmother, my father's mother, died from cancer in her early forties, and a few years later her sister became very ill too. There were arguments, estrangements, judgments. But my father's family achieved a kind of middle-class stability that was probably beyond what my great-grandparents imagined when they were refugees boarding boats in the Baltic. But it might have been something like what they'd hoped for, in the abstract: safety, homes, health care, no hunger. When my father left America, it was because he was following a job and had a sense of adventure, not because he didn't have a firm sense of home.

My mother did not have an American Dream, or at least not one that burned long and hard in her heart. She was thirty-three when she left her country, and she left because my father had lost his job and was struggling to find another good one in the United Kingdom—he was a medical physicist—though he'd tried very hard. By the time *An American Tail* was released to teach children like me the basics of immigration, she was raising three children in a country she wasn't from, in a small town where people never stopped asking her where she was from. Many of them were people whose families had come from the Old Country like my father: through Ellis Island, in kerchiefs, generations working their way up from the slums of New York and Newark to the relative gentility of an upstate postindustrial small town. These were people who understood the American Dream and who—perhaps—did not understand why my mother did not dream it. My father did not really dream it either: far from it. He had a family he adored and work he was interested in. He also had the confidence that comes from being born in a country where your parents were born too: the comfort that comes from first-generation parents smoothing out the wrinkles their immigrant parents could never quite iron.

My mother could have become a US citizen, but she chose not to; she loved the country she was from. "In Britain" she tended to say when something happened in America that she didn't like. "In this country" she tended to say, before talking about something in America that didn't please her. "Your mother is so nice," American women would say to me from time to time, enough times that it was notable as a thing women would say about my mother. It was notable because they said it in a way that sometimes felt to me like they were not just expressing a fact; it was something of a surprise.

2.

I was also six when I joined the Girl Scouts at school. I joined because it was inexpensive and convenient, meeting in the elementary school library or at the troop leader's local home. I joined, I'm sure, because my mother had fond memories of her own time as a Girl Guide. I'm not sure my parents considered the military underpinnings of the organization, or the patriotic ones, but I learned to swear to serve "God and my country," despite the fact that God was not a man my two-faith family followed with any vigor, though if I named him in vain, my mother would say, "Let's leave God out of it." She had moved away from the Church of Scotland she had been raised in when she married my Jewish father; we were raised celebrating holidays from both traditions but with no specific religion. Still, some habits stuck with my mother, as they do with us all.

Being a Girl Scout was, of course, about fitting in: literally wearing a uniform and achieving a hierarchy of skills that had been deemed useful and appropriate by a body of overseers. When my mother was in Girl Guides, she told me, she completed a badge demonstrating her ability to make a cup of tea. In America, we got patches for being able to roller-skate. Maybe that's part of the reason why my friends A and B, also the daughters of immigrants, joined as well. Even then it was made clear in the Girl Scout bylaws that Girl Scouts did not discriminate against those who did not quite fit in. Maybe it was evident to our parents that being Girl Scouts would help us to understand how to do certain things in ways our parents—learning themselves as they went along—could not teach us.

A's family was from China by way of Canada; B's, from Iran. One night at a gathering of mothers and daughters—I believe it was a potluck dinner—I noticed that my mother and B's stood during the Pledge of Allegiance but didn't speak the words. I asked my mother why not, afterward.

"We're not American," she said.

I nodded. I'd never thought about it that way before, but that was what my mother, B's mother, and A's mother had in common. It even kind of made sense, that some people might not want to be American, though everything beyond the limits of my immediate family seemed to tell me otherwise. I had seen that the lives of my relatives in the UK were not necessarily better or worse than our lives, that unlike Fievel Mousekewitz they did not have a burning longing in their hearts to leave their country behind to come to ours. I wasn't quite sure how to square that with the fervency of the Pledge of Allegiance, of the "sweet land of liberty" and so forth.

A and I remain close friends, thirty years later, but she still gives me a hard time about the Girl Scout meeting when I was tasked with introducing her to the group. Quite often when we're together, especially if someone asks how we know each other, A tells them how upset she was when it was my turn to share an interesting fact about her.

"A is Chinese!" I exclaimed, beaming. I thought this was a thing we had in common. We were both children of people from other countries. We both knew what it was to have a parent with an accent, to go red with embarrassment when other kids noticed that the foods we brought in for lunch were not the same foods other kids had. At seven, I did not understand the privilege granted to me by my whiteness: I didn't realize that the color of my skin gave me an advantage because it was the same as the skin of the kids whose families believe they have owned America forever. I didn't realize how much I could get away with.

"I was so embarrassed that Jean said I was Chinese," A always says when she tells the story. At seven, she already had been aware that some things marked her as different and might not be regarded by everyone as good, might be held against her in a country that was less free than our teachers and Scout leaders had us think.

3.

I was twelve the first time I attended a swearing in of new citizens. As I recall, the citizenship ceremony became a school assembly because my friend J and her family were becoming US citizens, and some well-meaning teacher decided it could be elevated into a teachable experience for five hundred adolescents. J and her parents and her sister were from India. I don't remember what brought them to our town; quite a few Indian families had ended up there because they were following careers in engineering or medicine. J was in the grade above mine, but we played in the school orchestra together and struck up a friendship. I'd heard J was not cool, but then neither was I.

Immigration was big on our social studies curriculum that year, which is to say that we learned about Ellis Island but not about any of the other ways people came to America, or the people who came after Ellis Island shut down. We didn't really learn much at all about any immigrants who didn't fit the mold of Fievel Mousekewitz or my great-grandparents.

When we were told to bring in photographs of our immigrant ancestors to post on a bulletin board, I brought in a photograph of my mother and brother. So did the other kids who were first generation, or immigrants themselves. But we didn't learn much else about these close relatives: where they arrived, why they came to America, whether they'd want to go back (of course no one would ever want to go back...).

On the day of the ceremony, the school cafeteria, which doubled as an auditorium, was bedecked with red, white, and blue. Each class was assigned an immigrant, which even then struck me as a little strange; ours were a pair of children from East Asia, too young to understand what was going on. The small kids with their adoptive parents and their sibling stood awkwardly at the front of our classroom. The children wore tidy tailored clothes in the style of American churchgoing children. They held American flags in chubby fists. I'm sure we ate cookies or cupcakes frosted with red, white, and blue frosting.

At some point in the afternoon the whole school filed into the auditorium to watch the new Americans pledge their allegiances and really mean it (I had been doing it for some time, I'm sure, to be polite). Some weeks earlier we'd gathered on the same chairs to hear a salesman pitch us on selling magazines to our parents to raise money for school dances, which in its own way felt very American. The top sellers received prizes, of which the most desired was a toy cell phone the size and shape of a brick. My mother did not allow me to participate.

"In Britain," my mother said, "schoolchildren aren't made to sell magazines to raise funds for the PTA. Not like in this country."

This felt like something to file in my list of things that I wasn't allowed to do because my mother was not American: wear fashionable American-flag-motif clothing, spend the summer at sleep-away camp, eat sugared cereal with toast and orange juice and call it a "complete breakfast."

On stage at the citizenship ceremony, J and her sister and parents stood among the adoptees, whose parents said the oath on their behalf if they were too small to speak for themselves. The school cafeteria was decorated with bunting, and there was something in the air more than patriotism: a sense of transformation, or of something being corrected.

The next day on the school bus J sat next to me, as had become our habit. "I have news," she said. "I'm moving to Australia."

I laughed. What a hilarious joke to tell the day after the whole school had gathered to watch her become a real American.

"No," she said, "really. My parents wanted to make sure we became citizens before we left so that if we wanted to, we could come back."

"But," I said, "the assembly—"

J shrugged.

By the time I went to my second citizenship ceremony, nearly a decade later, I understood there were reasons to become a US citizen besides a deep yearning to say the Pledge of Allegiance and mean it. My mother agreed to become a citizen at last because the family lawyer recommended it, because she'd been living in America for twenty-odd years, because the laws had shifted and she'd not be compelled to give up her British citizenship for a US one.

My mother took the ceremony seriously, raised her hand to agree to the things the government demanded. But when she was told that she must bear arms if called upon, those of us in the seats who were there to support her failed to stifle our giggles.

4.

I became an immigrant when I was twenty-two, but when you're a white woman from the United States and you go to live indefinitely in London, people call you an expat. That's just one of your many privileges, the things you get away with. People also ask you when you're going home. That they ask, and don't tell you to go, is a crucial distinction in the way many white British people regard you as opposed to other immigrants. Another advantage. British people are very polite to you, but many of them still can't help but make it clear that you should be thinking about leaving. You make friends with other people from other places, then, because they won't ask you when you're going. Their silence grants you permission to stay.

There are many reasons why I went to Britain: I was in love with a man who held an Irish passport but couldn't easily live in the United States. I was entitled to a British passport. I didn't especially feel proud to live in a country ruled by George W. Bush; I had long ago stopped saying the Pledge of Allegiance (a high school teacher had tried to get me disciplined for this and expressed disappointment when she found out it was my constitutional right to refuse).

But I think the biggest reason of all was the belief that I would belong there, that maybe the not-quiteness of my American girlhood would be resolved if I immersed myself in the British culture my mother still cleaved to and that lay just out of my grasp.

Or, at least, if I went to a country where I didn't fit in for obvious reasons, it would be better than living in a land where I seemed to not fit in for reasons sometimes too subtle for me to detect.

What are the things that I did to make myself fit in? I dressed like my British girlfriends, which meant buying a lot of pairs of black tights from Marks & Spencer. I drank a lot: pints, gin. I worked for an MP, and I worked in various cultural industries. I dated British men and listened to their anecdotes about where they went to school. I kept a stiff upper lip when they broke up with me (I didn't, not really; I cried a lot, and no doubt that was very un-British). Sometimes they ended it because they just weren't that into me. Sometimes, I think, because I was interesting but I just wasn't British. Sometimes they replaced me with women who looked like English roses, which of course was well within their rights, even though I had learned to say "tomahto."

"I'm as British as you," I'd say to the people who questioned it, who were never people whose Britishness was questioned. They were not my Jewish friends, not my friends who were people of color, not my friends who had EU passports, and not my friends who had found their way to London with the aid of a British parent. The people who questioned how British I was were secure in their belief in where they belonged, what belonged to them.

And yet I could never change the minds of the people who denied I was as qualified a Brit as they were. Nor the minds of the people who remarked on how I'd failed to lose my accent, as if losing an accent was a thing a person should do. Nor the minds of the people, when interviewing me for jobs they would never give me, who suggested I would do better in America, smiling, because they weren't being racist. The people who asked me when I was leaving were people who could never fathom why I was there in the first place; they couldn't fathom me. But then I couldn't fathom what it was like to have always lived in the same country, to have two parents who had always lived in that country.

I knew I could never change their minds on the nights in East End pubs when the Smiths would come on the sound system and my Essex-born boyfriend and his home county friends would rise to their feet and dance and sing as if there was nothing more hypnotic in the world than Morrissey's voice. Just the first few bars of the songs would make my heart sink, because I knew that no matter how hard I tried, I would never be recognized as one of them. I could never fully share their preoccupations or discomforts. I also wasn't sure that I wanted to. Perhaps this was another thing I inherited from my mother: a resistance to fully taking on the conventions of a country I didn't grow up in.

Maybe there's a country in the world where you're accepted, you belong, no matter where your life started.

Maybe there isn't.

5.

I became an immigrant again at thirty-two, if you consider the strict definition of the word: a person who migrates to a different country. I moved back to America after ten years in Europe because I wanted to be closer to my parents. I didn't want to move back, not really, not then, but it felt like the right thing to do.

I moved before Trump: when it still felt like America was a place that welcomed people, or at least had some intention of doing so. I moved just before the president emboldened the worst of Americans to be open in their hatred of immigrants. I moved just before this hatred began to be enshrined, more and more, into law.

It had been a long time since I had lived in America, and I realized that fitting in was no longer so much of a problem. No one asked me when I was going home.

Actually, I'd say sometimes, "Until recently I was living in Europe!" because that was such an important part of my identity, or had been for so long: an American Who Chose to Leave.

But no one I said that to seemed to think it was very interesting or significant. In New York, no one has ever told me—with my white skin, my curly brown hair, my slightly Jewish nose—to go home. And maybe that's all my ancestors could have hoped to achieve for their descendants when, like Fievel, they got on a big boat to leave a country they would absolutely never see again.

Maybe that's what my mother longed for sometimes, during those years of parenting, when she was made to feel just a little bit alien. Maybe that's all anyone can wish for when they decide to make their life in another country. Maybe that's the true American Dream, not gold- or cheese-paved streets. Maybe we all just dream of what it would be like to live in America, allowed to just be.

On Being Kim Kardashian

Chimene Suleyman

I was three months new to America during the hour Kim Kardashian was a brown woman. She walked in a bloodred jumpsuit that was not the color of blood at all and lay roses for a million Armenians lost to genocide. She ate Armenian food and dressed in traditional garb with the nerve of a person who would not be accused of confusing custom with costume. Because she was one of theirs, and it became this way when a young girl adorned her neck in jewelry as though she were not only a fellow but their queen, and an old woman kissed her face in the street as though there is magic in a grandmother's embrace that can make you belong.

And when my television was turned off, Kim Kardashian was again a white woman, of spray tan, not West Asian tan, of Bo Derek braids, not fabric headdress emblazoned in coins. Because this was still a woman showered with riches for very little, who chewed through black men at an uncomfortable fetishistic pace, who greeted us with the mistakes of white people who had been white all along. But there in my living room, Kim Kardashian and I were briefly the same, softening into something brown, remembering the dazzling embroidered waistcoats over patterned dresses, the decorated palms of henna, the elongated nose that surgery would not wholly disguise, and Kim

Kardashian was how I knew brown women with light skin to be, confused by it all.

Because with those fortunes I might have excised my sultan's nose too, and hadn't I already spent a lifetime combing the curls out of my hair, unprofessional and messy, as my mother called them? My mother, who would boast of Egyptian heritage while wanting nothing of its thick, textured head, and she was not alone. There were the rest of us too, who were light enough to be brown and then white in the space it took to air a television show.

On a road beside the waterfront, meters from Brooklyn Bridge, I am a white woman. A man I did not know told me so in the doorway of a popular Dumbo bar. "You," he said in the moment, "are a white bitch." I thought on this. For thirty-two years I had been—to men like this—a brown bitch. For the last three, I had been a white one.

There had been, of course, a time in London under the damp ceiling of a Cannon Street pub, where the colleague of a loose acquaintance supposed that I did, in fact, deserve whatever camel-fucking country I am from. But in America no such thing was happening. I may tell my Brooklyn neighbors that I am Turkish Cypriot, but they do not hear. "It is an island," I say, "its most easterly tip reaching toward the edge of Syria and Lebanon, its south coast toward Egypt, the north running parallel with Turkey." "So—Turkey?" they say. "Fine," I tell them. "Turkey." It is easier somehow—I am Turkish, with fistfuls of henna and palatial fabric on skin that is Kim Kardashian brown.

But erasure is twofold, after all, for in America it is my accent that walks ahead of ethnicity, where I may insist I am Turkish yet "I am English" can be heard. To my Brooklyn neighbors, I am *Downton Abbey, The Crown,* and *Doctor Who;* I am fanciful, regal, and classy; fish and chips, the Beatles, and "I love the way you say that!"; Hogwarts, Brexit, and Churchill. In America, I have become the accent of my colonizer.

That is to say, New York has hijacked the way I speak. I am reduced to using the voice I reserve for rooftop publishing parties and white people I don't know. I round off my vowels and remember my *t*'s. I may spend a lifetime asking the waiter for a glass of wa'er before he understands: water, I stress, wattter. They are stilettos in New York, not stile'os. Thank you, not fank you. It is not that I have grown tired of translating to sneakers from trainers, rather that I have grown tired of translating to trainers from creps. On being shoulder-barged by a man on the subway, I would like to call such a person *chief* without being mistaken for elevating him. But on these streets of New York, I am neither Turkish Cypriot nor Turkish nor the Londoner who found recognition in the underbelly of streets of confused and chaotic difference. I am, simply, English. Their English. "Say that again!" English. BBC English. The Queen's English.

"But I ain't English," I tell them. My voice, as I understand it, is not English. We studied the language not in Shakespeare but in the canon of UK Garage, Ridley Road market stalls, and Peckham barbershops. Teased syllables in the streets around Holloway on match day, and the top deck of a Camden night bus. Our accents were taught to us by those who spoke Turkish first, and English after; Yoruba first, and English after; Hindi first, and English after; Twi, Greek, Polish, Hebrew first, then perhaps nothing after. Our *English* brimmed with Jamaican colloquialisms, a London patois rich in the tones of West Indian migrants, and their kids who carried it, evolved it, turned it, delivering whole sentences until it was established. Our *English* was not English at all. Our *English* was never fish and chips and Big Ben; it was chicken and chips and antiestablishment; roadside chirpsing and rebellion; it was stop-and-searches on a bad day, gun fingers on a good one; *our English* was immigration, subversion, and unending defiance.

On this evening outside a bar in Dumbo I am an accent that is not mine. I am a white bitch. I am the voice of a British nation that never quite knew what to do with brown bitches like me. "I'm not white," I tell the man, remembering this: "I'm Middle Eastern."

Let me tell you that I didn't mean it. That there was no conviction, and what I meant is that I am from the Levant, Turkish Cypriot, Turkish, Muslim during those cultural hours that have grown to suit me. I am a Londoner, a Finchley girl, a Spurs fan during those cultural hours that have also grown to suit me.

What he meant is that I am not black. He had a point. Still, inebriation outside a bar in Dumbo had rid us of any nuance. So had an America whose presidency is built on crude lack of subtlety. So it had happened this way: we were black or white, right or wrong, patriot or traitor. Life had become binary now, so you must pick one.

Everything is lighter now. And we had disregarded the warning signs; considered those who objected to appropriation and touching afros as oversensitive. But white boys with guitars who collected awards at black music ceremonies had warranted further analysis. So did the white girls who twerked onstage and received credit for inventing the move. Or the white faces reciting "Namaste," not in the Indian subcontinent but in Williamsburg yoga studios. It had been there already, insidious and casual in the day-to-day, brewing until finally white supremacy and fascism was mainstreamed, then installed in government. America has produced a president lighter than his predecessor, lighter, in fact *whiter,* than some presidents before his predecessor. But the joke is as follows: the man is orange, tangerine, mango in shade, a walking mass of apricot, carrot, or Cheeto. Maybe, had my ethnology aligned with the visibly grotesque, I too would initiate a new race, singular and orange, distinct in glowing color and substance, unrelated to anywhere else.

But Trump is white. He is as white as the cult of whiteness that brought him, not independent from it, nor its founder. Because America has not been free of racial superiority until now, and Donald Trump is neither capable nor required to convert the unprejudiced into fascists. Trump's expertise was never in convincing a nation of what they needed but in giving a nation what they already wanted. A nation who should not be white at all yet sees only through the lens of whiteness.

Here is a man who may well subscribe to the temperament of reality TV, of candid straight talk and keeping it real, but the freedom to speak outrageously and with reckless abandon was all along the bedrock of white supremacy. With it, the confidence to act however they wish and still remain confident that the law makes an exception for them—the police officer who murders a black child, the civilian who marches armed and dressed as militia, or the president who grabs a pussy, then tears up the constitutional protection of religious freedom.

When bigotry arrives camouflaged as fear, the outcome may see whole nations and their religions blanketed with the burden of extremist terrorism. Likewise, dogmatism disguised as danger will have Antwon Rose Jr. shot in the back at seventeen. When fanatic bias goes undercover as trepidation, fear becomes its own currency. Synthetic terror rattles in the veins of those who use the law as their own grievance counselor—the shortsighted intolerance of a Starbucks employee who calls the cops on black customers waiting for a friend before buying coffee, the fragility of a woman witnessing a black barbecue who calls the cops, asserting they have no right to be there. America, it seems, has been victim to, and terrorized by, its own ignorance.

So you must claim him. He is one of *yours*. A product of symptoms from long before 2016. Born to an America of lynchings, segregation, and internment camps, of capitalism and privatization, where newspaper headlines and movies gave us black gangs, Arab bombers, and immigrant rapists long before the president did. Where legality and freedom of speech, at whatever cost, have become the shatterproof defense for illogical cruelty. America's enthusiasm for intolerance, it seemed, was not centered in Trumpism; instead it was a template for a nation that had learned to divide and keep dividing until there was no group large enough left to fight.

With this in mind, I return to that night outside a bar in Dumbo, where the man I did not know called me a white bitch, then insisted if I do not like how things are I must go back to wherever it is I am from. I had heard these words spoken before, listened to them outside a petrol station along the A12, seen them written beneath my articles, and blocked them from Twitter. But the requirement had always been to leave England, not return to it, and perhaps the man's girlfriend knew this, on some level understood the disorientation on my face as she explained that these were just words people used now, words that fell unmanaged from their mouths, the vocabulary to make America great, whether again or once and for all; and intolerance would find us, whether black, white, or Kim Kardashian brown.

Perhaps, outside this bar in Dumbo, what he had meant is that

I am an English bitch. That I have been an English bitch for three years, which is also the length of time I have been a white bitch. Because in America a failed businessman with no smarts can become president, and a woman with a remolded bottom and no discernible talent can become a millionaire, and an English accent can make you the smartest person in the room before you've even finished a sentence. Because to be white here meant, on the face of it, I was safe from being shot dead by the police, that I would be offered the apartment I liked, would be the model applicant for a bank loan, would be shielded, guarded by an outlandish power. And a part of me liked it, liked to bite back at JFK staff who gave attitude and pressed me when I returned from long trips to Turkey. The part of me that, pushing four fingertips against the scan, remembered the child who watched her father always pulled aside for further inspection, how he had warned me first that this would happen, how he was guided away from us, until his bags and his pockets and his skin were searched. And now I enjoyed my own arrogance, beneath the manically lit airport ceiling, to give lip or refuse a loaded question on why I had traveled frequently to the Middle East, to be obnoxious in this way; and I polished my accent, which had become my invisibility cloak in these moments, held my British passport tight as though I were addressing all those years, as if to say, "Now what you gonna do about it?"

What I had wanted to know all along is if I spoke without this voice, the kind they believe they are hearing—if I sold them cheap cigarettes and late-night deli sandwiches, carpets in Sheepshead Bay and Midtown falafel, as they might expect my people to; pronounced my words with harsher *r*'s and softer vowels—would they still think of me as white? If I wrapped my hair in yemeni, shayla, or niqab—simply, in *hijab*, as my grandmother had—would I be white then too? And it was on this night outside a bar in Dumbo that I recalled the disorder of being everything and nothing at once, and so I said, "I'm not white. I'm Middle Eastern." Which is to say, *Step back. You don't know me.* But he had turned to face me by then, and I don't remember if he laughed or if he only looked as though he wanted to, and asked, "Are you Iraqi, bitch? Are you Syrian?"

Had I thought to at the time, I might have asked him if the only Middle Eastern countries he knows are the ones repeated in the news because of their violence. If so—and it is only geography steeped in the offenses of America and the West we are listing—I can name for him many more. I may draw a map on the road between us, circling a chalk outline of the aforementioned island of Cyprus. I will tell him that here, only sixty miles from the Syria he believes he knows, my parents were born to a British colony. That this colonization, this American interference, erupted into civil war between Turkish and Greek Cypriots. I will tell him that my father's father was murdered with an axe to his head. I will say that my father was a child soldier, a prisoner of war, a refugee.

I may tell this man, beside the waterfront on a street in Dumbo, that ten years after a man I should have known was gone, Turkey came from both sea and sky, and the island divided in two. I will show this man newspaper headlines and Wikipedia entries describing the intervention as the "1974 Turkish *invasion*," as though Turks had not lived and been killed here before, as though Turkey claimed no right to save the lives of my parents. I will tell him that there is no need to erase my heritage on this street in Dumbo beside the waterfront when Western history had already done so. *Don't worry,* I will say. *You have done nothing new.* And yet the *invader,* the barbarian, the savage, the terrorist—are we white then too? Perhaps it is easier to think of us as white; perhaps the body count of brown people will lessen this way.

A friend tells me I am white here. Another says I am "spicy" white, swarthy, tawny. In college I was asked to mentor a boy because he was sallow like me, the teacher said. Not brown, but sickly brown, unhealthy in our brownness. He cared as little for the role as I did. He smoked weed and wore a loose tie beneath his blazer. I let him— this boy as pallid in his brownness as I am, who could have been *fully* white had it not been spoiled, perhaps ruined, by an air of illness. I never did find out where he was from. Spicy white, my friend says. Italian, maybe, or Portuguese, this friend means. I think back to a time on the train, hurtling toward East London, and the man I never saw again. "Paki," he had called me, chin resting on the dark blue lapel of his smart polo shirt. A glimmer of difference has always been enough to cause offense. I wonder, was I spicy white then as well?

Still, what we understand to be white comes with its own price list. You may know this if you have ever taken orders from a sign that reads NO BLACKS, NO DOGS, NO IRISH. Perhaps, too, if you are Eastern European in any suburb of the United Kingdom where UKIP votes hang between neighbors, or Italian in any part of Bensonhurst, or Jewish in the eyeline of a Nazi or the KKK. White supremacy benefits no one, not even those who think of themselves as white. Remember this:

I first hear the term "White Turk" on a panel in Izmir where I am discussing *The Comedy of Errors.* What I would like to do is lean across to the author co-leading our presentation and ask him who he is talking about. Over dinner, I hear it again. Then, the next day at lunch. I suppose, now knowing what it means, I had spent those few days working and dining in White Turkey, had spent it with people who were secular, intellectual, and *Western*. People who sharply distinguished themselves from the demographic of religious, less-educated, and rural Turks, of which there are many.

I thought on this. Whiteness had always been keen to claim intellectualism as its own. Likewise, to position Islam and Middle Eastern conventions as mindless and problematic, conflicting with progressive values, conflicting with *whiteness*. But there are still the Turks who do not want to be *white*. Perhaps if you have seen your neighbors killed by Western powers for praying in a mosque and not a church, playing doumbek and not percussion, shooting guns into the sky at village weddings and not Texas gun ranges (or schools), you may want to hold your identity more dearly, retain your Anatolian distinction, a memorial for the brothers and sisters who have had their traditions pried from their hands by US drones. Or you might want to rid yourself of your differences, throw in the towel, surrender Allah to US forces and be done with it. Maybe, if you are not just a Turk but a *white* one, you have understood you have a higher chance of survival this way.

Yet I think of the Muslim ban, as we have come to understand it, and whether we expect US officials to first ask individual Yemenis, or Iranians, how deep their relationship with God is. Whether they prefer the music of Farid al-Atrash or Post Malone. Whether they are a modern wearer of jeans or would rather move in shalwar. If their mother has never worn hijab, will it make any difference to letting them in? No. Simply put, there is no need to cover your hair to still be considered a raghead. In a world that has used "They all look the same" as a basis for foreign policy, many of us are only *white* by name.

When they say you are a white bitch, they mean you had it easy. That your life was gifted, stolen, pillaged, from creations elsewhere, because good lives are not distributed equally. And haven't we as a family always spoken of whiteness as a curse, a blight that arrived on our lands, then changed them beyond repair. But white lives are not even white lives, and a Pole in Ilford or a Jew in Charlottesville might tell you the same, that the parameters of whiteness are always changing, and so it is that I have become a white woman on canvas, but on paper I am still everything that had killed my grandfather.

On this night outside a bar in Dumbo I refused the accusation that I am a white bitch. "I'm not white," I declared, protesting all I had known whiteness to mean, and then I was hailing a cab, sliding into it, ridding myself of a foolish argument on a street corner with a man I did not know, when he said: "Fuck you, Kim Kardashian bitch."

Where there was no range for brownness, there was still Kim Kardashian. There was still ambiguity, an exoticism whiteness could still claim as its own, sunbeds without the racial profiling. And there was Princess Jasmine and the Prince of Persia and Aladdin—characters, just as Kim Kardashian is a character: was I a Syrian bitch character or an Iraqi bitch character? But I was not drowning in a boat; or handcuffed on the front pages of the *Daily Mirror;* or holding some noble American hostage on *Homeland;* or Abu, who was a monkey, or the genie, who was blue; or a ravenous sheikh character; or a bejeweled, belly-dancing character; or anyone in *The Mummy,* brimming with white actors and CGI; or an Iraqi character on *Lost* played by a person of Indian origin; or a Palestinian character on *Community* played by a person of Indian origin...

And where were our faces? Our beautiful faces, that were not beautiful South Asian or beautifully drawn but ours, in abundance—in government, on billboards selling Gucci or Adidas or Pepsi, collecting a Grammy or Emmy, seizing it close to our chests before thanking crew and cast and Allah alike?

Where were we? In all our vastness and difference, in our beautiful darkness and beautiful lightness, our cascading straight hair or wiry curls. Had you been allowed to see what we truly look like, in all our difference, I may have known myself. I may have loved my ugly sultan's nose, which was not ugly at all. I may not have wondered why it arched down my face, longer than the noses of the European girls, the *American* girls, the white girls I could have been but was not. For had I not spent a lifetime molding and arching my body to fit the look I almost achieved but still missed?

I had spent a lifetime being Kim Kardashian brown, which is to say I had been without race. I was not the rich darkness of Sri Lankan brown or Bengali. Nor the deep bronze of the Caribbean. Instead I had not known myself to be brown at all, just that I was *not white.* And such a distinction was made by virtue of pain—we had been killed, imprisoned, and colonized, and was this not what whiteness did to those deemed not white or not white enough? So I had learned to identify myself by everything I lacked—I was neither safe nor beautiful, and how can one be white without either?

On a road beside the waterfront, meters from Brooklyn Bridge, I said these words to a man I did not know: "I'm not white." Words

I had said to myself before, when I had believed my nose was not beautiful, that my hair was not beautiful, that my hips and my chin and my name and the accent thick between my parents' lips were not beautiful. "I'm not white," I said, long before a night in Dumbo, not with resilience but with disappointment. I had become defined by all that was wrong with me, not all that might be celebrated. Because I had not yet seen it—that we were beautiful palatial fabric, we were the brilliant blue-eyed amulet protecting from all that was evil, we were fistfuls of henna, and a nose bent and long and magnificent, a nose fit for sultans. We were the kissed hand of an elder pushed against our forehead, and the high, sweet whispers of the ney flute, expanding and almighty and holy. We were the thick stretched skin of a darbuka drum, where fingers and palms struck at an exceptional pace, flexing and echoing, a single powerful note, beaten and beaten and beaten again, still glorious, still alive.

Tour Diary

Basim Usmani

The Kominas are a punk band. We started around 2006. Currently it's me on bass, Karna on drums, Sunny and Shahjehan on guitar. We're unsigned, unmanaged, but out of a sheer force of will, and thanks to our fans, we've toured the world and crisscrossed the USA more than a few times.

Being a punk band and touring is hard because you have to cover the expanse of the country, and that can mean spending days in a van. And who knows what to expect when you're four weird brown dudes in a van, crossing White America. What follows are notes from two tour diaries I kept from 2016 through 2017, which chart the ups and downs of heavy touring, and my mental health. To kids just starting bands, or going on tour themselves, I hope this is useful to you.

AUGUST 6, 2016, COLUMBIA, MISSOURI

We were on the eighth show of a twenty-city tour, and the van had become sort of a biome. We heeded warnings that there weren't many gas stations for the seven-hour trek from Minneapolis to Columbia and stopped for gas at a rest stop outside of Des Moines. We'd learned to keep such stops brief. When you're a bunch of shaggy brown dudes on tour, leaving the van can be a grab bag. Our only other stop was when signs on the interstate announced we were in Iowa, and all the cornfields in the state had gathered to receive us.

The only things that really change at rest stops are the slogans on the bumper stickers. On the East Coast, they're pretty much all sports related. As you leave the coasts, they get more and more gun related. I remember trying not to chew fast food with my mouth open, reading bumper stickers like IF YOU CAN READ THIS YOU'RE IN RANGE or TERRORIST HUNTING PERMIT.

Back in the van, the ride felt dreamlike. I was nodding off in the back and getting woken up periodically by turbulent winds. I remember looking out the window into the vast flatness around us and feeling exposed. The landscape was disorientingly flat. No matter where I woke up, the view was the same. I rode in a permanent state of not feeling like I was going anywhere.

We arrived at the venue to find comfort of sorts in a BLACK LIVES MATTER sticker on the door.

We sound-checked and hung out with Soft Sculpture, a local seven-piece goth-experimental project. Their guitarist, Emma, had booked us.

The place was empty (and didn't really ever fill up), but I never had high hopes for Missouri. It was cool hanging out with Soft Sculpture. The headlining band...not so much. The way each member walked in the door made it clear they weren't happy to be there.

When the show started, Soft Sculpture and the Kominas were, more or less, the only nonwhite faces in the room, and the crowd was small enough for me to notice the faces in it. We were self-conscious when we played—I could tell. But the drums were really loud in that small venue, which is really important to me. When I feel the vibrations of the kick in my skull, it's like a fix.

It takes me to a place where I stop thinking about the instrument in my hands; the bass guitar feels more like a piece of wood with wires in it.

It's the beauty of playing basements and small venues, away from the self-indulgent monitor mixes.

I kept turning my back to the small audience to make eye contact with Karna. I never know when he's going to run into the audience or jump off the kit and say something profound in the mic. Sunny sang a few more songs, and a small consort of superfans had requests, so we took them. We were just over a week into the tour, and there were moments that still needed tightening up. We got through it, though.

As Karna began unscrewing the nut to remove his cymbals, I could tell something was off. He waited until we had broken down our equipment before putting one fingerless gloved hand on my shoulder.

"Let's go for a smoke," he said. He wasn't interested in watching the headliner. Outside, he turned to me and said, "That band's singer was complaining about cutting their set short for that Muslim band, dude."

I paced outside for a bit, not wanting to be inside while they were playing.

In the parking lot later, we walked by them as they loaded up their rental. I was still unpacking what they had said. We were that Muslim band. It brought up bad memories of the band's early days, when no one knew who we were so headlines would refer to us as a "Muslim band." We got in the van, followed Emma's car to a punk house, and tried not to think about it.

* * *

The path from the front door into the house was obstructed by a couch that reeked of cat piss. It was like the occupants were trying to stockpile empty cans and bottles of beer. We greeted a white couple who were on a mattress, smoking weed and watching cartoons. Two more sofas were in there, which the more sensible among us claimed right away.

I lay down on the cat-piss couch, which I must have subconsciously decided to punish myself with, and rode out my remaining insomnia.

The highs and lows of that tour were very severe for me. It was our first long tour of the USA in a while, and this particular one was a slog because we had lost touch with so many contacts in the middle of the country. We didn't know what we were walking into from show to show. We played for hundreds in New York City on that tour. And to a total of four people in Detroit.

On that cat-piss couch, I kept wondering what exactly I was doing with my life, what my goal actually was. When the band started out, it was a way of connecting with other quirky brown kids as much as it was about finally writing the kinds of songs we couldn't when we were the only brown kids in bands filled with white kids. At the recent New York show, the audience was mostly desi with other POC. A brown high schooler wearing a rad patched-up denim vest came to our show with her mom. After we played that show, I learned her name was Suha. She said we were "cute, not really punk punk. More like Green Day. You could be popular."

I lay there, laughing, thinking about this, and trying not to inhale too much cat piss.

AUGUST 14, 2016, OLYMPIA, WASHINGTON

The promoter for the gig in Olympia said we could get paid more if we participated in a panel that was taking place a few hours before the gig. On the drive up, we tried to figure out what we were going to say. We ended up talking a lot about our early days and reflecting on our relationship with the media.

We were unprepared for the media attention we got when we first started playing out. The *Boston Globe* came to our second show ever. We were all highly opinionated punk kids, naively giving interviews about the Iraq War or the whiteness of punk. Often the early stories that would get published about us were from writers trying to make their own points about Islam, immigrants, and assimilation.

Between 2007 and 2009 we gave plenty of standoffish interviews with people who tried to peg us as some sort of exception to a rule. *Wow, they're not terrorists.* We were trying to get our gig flyers out there and our music reviewed, and instead we were doing a lot of "Oh, you were expecting ISIS?"

We played punk spaces, but no punk magazines wanted to write about us. Some professors wrote about us from a distance, but they never entered the mosh. The brown kids who loved us, who ended up becoming journalists later, were still kids then. When we started, we wanted to be an angry sound. We became a footnote for some journalists' "Look at these Muslims assimilating" narrative, and we unraveled.

Shahjehan once said that a lot of the words that come so natural to us now (like "microaggressions" or "gaslighting") weren't used that widely back when we started. The press we've gotten in the past few years is way less hazardous to our health. But sometimes I'm worried about the damage that's already been done. I'm scared of what I may symbolize to people who don't know me. I received a link recently to someone's Instagram account: it was a picture of my face tattooed on their white, pasty arm. I wanted to ask why, but I just ignored it and scrolled down.

Olympia turned out to be cuter and smaller than I expected, in contrast to all the hard-core bands that have come out of it. It's a granola vacation spot, and our show happened to overlap with an international metalfest. Just a few hundred metalheads were enough to overrun a small town like that. Headbangers, man. Everywhere you looked there were people in leather jackets, vests, with indecipherable logos. Sunny asked me to put on some music, so we decided to blast them with Beyoncé to see if they'd sing along. They didn't.

The panel went down at a large coffee shop full of laptops and white people. We met a cool Iranian punk kid who went by the name Hell. She brought a friend with her to our show and they moshed furiously. The pit that opened at the basement we played in was so sick. It was a mix of kids, way more diverse than I would have guessed based on the people outside. It made me feel good, like we were some kind of flash point in a small town like this.

Then a bunch of lanky white guys began taking up space in the mosh pit, and Sunny had to say, "Bros, fall back," in the mic. They refused, so we stopped playing, shouting, "Bros, fall back," until they finally did.

"Yo, those dudes were in G.L.O.S.S. shirts," Karna said as he got up from behind his kit and the rest of us were loading our stuff out.

"No shit," I said, surprised.

G.L.O.S.S., or Girls Living Outside Society's Shit, was a sick trans feminist hard-core band from Olympia that broke apart as soon as they began to get traction. I never saw them live, but all four of us were big fans. Unlike us, they strictly adhered to a hard-core punk sound, their unrelenting aggression paired with messages about taking space back and rage against misogyny made their purpose pretty clear. Seeing a bunch of lanky white dudes in their shirts take up space in the pit was disheartening. The last line of G.L.O.S.S.'s breakup statement really resonated with me: "Being in the mainstream media, where total strangers have a say in something we've created for other queer people, is exhausting." They were a band for a certain audience, and once they became bigger, their fan base started to include those guys. Their decision to break up on the verge of some kind of band-career breakthrough made complete sense to me.

AUGUST 29, 2016, NASHVILLE AND MEMPHIS, TENNESSEE

The trees along the highway in Tennessee are a shade of green too intense to describe. Asad Faruqi, a documentary filmmaker from Karachi, came along to chronicle the southern leg of our tour. He said the green was like nothing he'd ever seen.

We had booked the gigs in Tennessee when the tour was halfway done because we realized we should take a break from driving and find a way to stay somewhere cheap.

The last-minute show we got in Memphis was in a dive bar, and just as we loaded in, the sound guy walked up to us and told us, "There's no bands booked tonight. It's only an open-mic night." Shahj quickly began texting the promoter and handling it. I walked to the back of the bar and pulled my notebook out of my pocket.

Sunny and Asad were filming funny videos nearby. I overheard some random guy say to them in a laughing tone, "I like to keep a watch around the neighborhood, and if you see something, say something."

He smiled a really wide, melty smile.

When the band finally got sorted to play, we decided to play our song of the same name. We played a bunch of our most pointed songs, like "Pigs Are Haram," "Sharia Law in the USA," "Tahrir Square Dance," to a bar full of random white people in Memphis. It was really weird. It was nice to yell those words at them.

I ended up crashing with a friend of the promoter. He had two options for sleeping places: his small living room, which was where he kept his extensive mannequin collection, or the hammock hanging on the balcony. I chose the hammock.

The next day our show was in Nashville. All of us were explosively tense with each other. The promoter said that the show was at a house party near the city, but we must have driven for maybe twenty miles, passing nothing but trees and tiny ranch houses set on vast plots of private land.

People were littered all around the single-story ranch house when we pulled up. Dozens of drunk and fucked up white kids lingered around. By this point, Karna and I had made a little game out of counting the white people with dreadlocks; I think we broke our record that night. As we lugged our gear to the living room, we guessed no one was going to actually come inside and watch us.

We were right. We were maybe two songs in when a few people filtered in. It wasn't a lot, but fifteen is better than five. We had to interrupt the show again, mid-song, because some guys were getting too rowdy and obstructive for everyone else.

"We're not going to continue playing if you guys are going to be assholes," Sunny said.

One of the guys started saying "No" defiantly back at us and pulled a drumstick out of his backpack and began waving it in our faces like he was a conductor. We paid him no mind. I put a little more air time in my next jump when we started the song over, and watched him sulk into a corner of the room.

We were almost done with the last chorus when that same guy walked past Sunny and right up to me, waving his stupid drumstick. He walked up to Karna too. His eyes looked completely dead. I wanted so badly to stop playing and hit him, but I knew it was too risky to open up that can of worms in some random house in Tennessee where we were the only nonwhite faces for miles.

A guy who looks like me can't go through America like Henry Rollins, fighting whenever provoked. It would be fatal. Brown punks get to do other things. In a recent interview, Rollins said he started traveling and making documentaries because "you can't get to Morocco with just rock 'n' roll." We got to go to Casablanca once, with just rock 'n' roll, and played one of the biggest festivals there.

AUGUST 3, 2017, NEW YORK CITY

We were preparing to hit the road again a month after Ramadan. I had just moved to a somewhat remote rural area in Central Massachusetts, where there isn't any cell reception, and I felt profoundly isolated. My wife, Sidrah, who lives in Toronto, still hadn't gotten her visa, even though we've been married since 2014. I was desperately trying to get my head clear. I spent five weeks writing a lot, biking around my suburb, and trying to avoid thinking about suicide.

I managed to curb a lot of my vices post-Ramadan, but my real vice at that time was anger. I was constantly angry. I fed it by reading things I knew would make me angry. I'd read a piece by Tasbeeh Herwees criticizing *The Big Sick,* and to some extent *Master of None,* for the way they adhere to the Americanized = good, traditional = bad narrative in their own way. She rightly pointed out how so many Muslim American guys incorporate shedding religion, eating pork, and becoming a "secular" Muslim in their narratives as a rite of passage. And it's so easy for us. A big inspiration behind wanting to be in a band was looking up to my cousins Amna and Zainab, who had a riot grrrl band with their friends in Saginaw called the Suburban Nodnicks. Every lyric was a statement. I never got to see them play—I was living in Lahore at the time—but they brought me their one and only cassette when they came to the city for a visit, before they broke up the band and went to college.

I was probably fourteen at the time, and I didn't really know punk music, so that tape sounded like something I'd never heard.

Going on tour or taking the band more seriously wasn't even a thought for them. They probably personally couldn't justify spending that much time on something that seemed so...indulgent. I had so much more leeway, comparatively, to disappear on my family and do my own thing. I'd reckoned with the ways it was easy to be unserious, but leading up to the 2017 tour, it was time to rediscover the intent behind my work again. Punk is supposed to be more than just "a way to blow off steam" or "recreational." I started treating it more like a gift.

I stopped smoking cigarettes, drinking, and smoking weed (which

I couldn't keep up), and I got a lot further than I did when I quit for health reasons alone. For the next tour, I felt like I needed to go against the grain and play the bars completely sober. I remember poring through some of the letters and emails I've gotten over the years from kids discovering the Kominas. We don't have a very "normie" fan base. When our fans come to watch a show, I look out at them watching us, but I can tell some of them are looking inward. We do something—we underline that it's okay to be this fucking weird, and that respectability is a giant hoax. Our fans' love of us is really personal; even if it's a connection they imagine, it's real.

All of my thoughts seemed gravely serious at the time. I kept having flashbacks to the worst moments of 2016 and dreading how I would react if the same shit that happened in Memphis happened in Nuremberg or Manchester.

In preparation for the tour, I did things I hadn't done since my teenage days, like stitch up a punk vest, bleach denim, and tie-dye shirts in really dark colors. I biked around a lot and was making it a point to talk to Sidrah as often as I could. There was always some small issue with her spouse visa, like documents not being printed on the correct card stock, or being printed on the wrong size of paper, which forced us to ask for new documents, forever holding up the process. I felt really self-destructive at times. I tried not to talk too much to myself, but I didn't know how to talk to anyone else. I began to realize how warped I was inside, and I started fearing that if I ever drank again, I would hurt myself.

My bandmates and I live in separate cities, and we barely have time to get accustomed to each other before we get done with rehearsals and leave for a tour. But our first show of the tour, at the Museum of

Modern Art, went really well. Then we had to get ready to leave for Norway the very next day.

AUGUST 4, 2017, HORTEN, NORWAY

I felt like I was losing control in the back of the black cab on the way to the airport. I was scared about what could go wrong.

There was an absurdly long line to check in for our flight. I remember pulling my hoodie up nice and tight, trying not to accidentally make eye contact with anyone. Somehow I couldn't properly explain my pain to my friends. I tried to do so with Shahjehan and it blew up in my face.

"We're all making sacrifices to do this," he said. "You sound ungrateful."

I don't know what was happening to us that year, but everyone was feeling defensive. I tried to bring it up again on the flight, but our conversation got heated. I ran out of words.

When we got to Horten, I had about an hour to sleep and another to eat with the guys. I quickly drew on my Kajal moments before walking onto the stage to play "Sharia Law in the USA" in front of hundreds of drunk punks at Kanalrock. Sunny trolled the audience with this incredible line: "So you think we all look the same, huh?" he said. People laughed. "We think *you* all look the same." People got awkwardly silent. Then we launched into a song from our very first album, *Ayesha*.

We have a few fans out in Norway. Not as many Pakistanis come out to our shows in Horten as they do in Oslo, but Horten can afford to bring us across the Atlantic, which helps us tour Europe in the first place.

That morning before we flew to Stockholm, I went for a long walk along the canal as the sun rose. I sat by the banks of a fjord and resolved to come back with Sid one day.

I remember the first time the band played Horten years ago. We jumped in a fjord the first chance we got. It felt like the first and last time we'd ever make it there. Sitting just then, with my feet in the water, I couldn't believe we had made it back.

I didn't feel anxiety again until we were at the airport in Oslo. We've had bad luck flying out of Norway before. There was the time we got to the gate with our instruments and were asked to reboard and go through security again. Shahjehan said security took him aside and put their hands in his drawers. I was trying to take my mind off that memory while we waited to board the plane to Sweden. It was then that I was finally able to explain to Shahjehan how low I had been feeling. He hugged me, and we boarded the plane.

OCTOBER 26, 2017, CHICAGO, ILLINOIS

A radio DJ had recently asked us, "Are you guys actually friends? We've been hanging out with you for a week, and you're so careful with your words to each other, you don't seem very close."

From the beginning of August to the end of October we had been touring continuously, save for a short break. We were haggard. That night would be the seventh show of a tour opening for the band Sinkane. The last two nights of shows, Toronto and Chicago, were back-to-back and an eight-hour drive apart. It had been nice to spend a night with Sidrah and, honestly, so brief it felt surreal.

I'm pretty familiar with crossing back into the USA from Canada, and I know that Customs and Border office at Detroit is filled with bastards. They have always given me trouble. The last time I crossed through there, in 2013, I was detained for four hours. I had been coming back from visiting Sid, and I got asked to leave the bus for questioning. They held me in a secondary screening room overnight while the bus left without me.

It could go shitty, but I was hoping it wouldn't. When we were asked to leave the car and walk into the waiting area, I began to prepare myself emotionally. Me, Karna, Sunny, and Shahjehan all sat down next to each other in the customs office, and the officer called us up one by one, instead of as a group.

One thing I learned from being in this situation is that you never know whether you're being called in for a quick question or if you're being properly detained until you've been sitting and waiting around for over an hour.

Before the officer called me up, I had made up a strategy to be very dull.

"What do you do for work?"

"I'm a social media manager for a Public Radio show, like a journalist."

"Social media manager? What is that, Facebook? Is that really journalism?"

Ah, a power trip, I thought.

I described in dull terms what my average day at the office looks like: "We start every day at the office with an 8:30 morning meeting," I told him. And, "I have to double-check my facts just like the other journalists."

He eventually asked me to sit down, but without handing me my passport. A subtle sign that this was going to take longer.

His interview with Shahjehan went on for a little too long, and when Shahjehan returned to his seat he quickly took his glasses off and began rubbing his temples.

He kept repeating, "This is not good. This is not good, man. I think I fucked up."

Sweat began to bead up on his forehead.

"What happens if they ask me about what Imran's doing?" he said, referencing an ex–band member who had left to become a social media manager for an Islamic university in California.

He was freaked out.

"You tell them Imran left to become a social media marketer for a university," I told him quietly, though I don't think it reassured him. I tried to remind him, "Dude, it's not a crime to work at an Islamic university."

The words didn't seem to mean anything to him, though. He was talking like he was going to be arrested.

"The guy pulled up a bunch of Google Image searches of us," he said, his voice shaking, "and got to the one of us using an American flag as a welcome mat, and was like 'Is this some kind of joke?'"

Shahj got called up again, and this time two officers were talking to him. Karna quietly asked me what was up, and we both tried to have a conversation in hushed tones about Shahjehan freaking out but realized we were only going to look more suspicious, so we sat in agonized silence.

In the meantime, Shahjehan sat back down between us, and Sunny was called up.

One officer who had been behind the counter asked Shahjehan if they could speak outside, which seemed weird as hell, but it's not like he had a choice in the matter.

It had been about ten minutes when Shahjehan returned and the dickhead customs officer at the desk handed us back our passports. It had been nearly three hours. Not the longest it's taken me, but not the shortest either.

"He asked if we're an antifa band," Shahjehan said as we loaded back into the van. "'Would you consider your band antifa?'" he mimicked in a dopey tone.

When we had gotten about a mile from the customs office, we pulled over into a rest area to smoke a cigarette and process what had just happened. Within seconds we were fighting with each other. We started nit-picking each other's "performance" at the border and what the best way to deal with the situation was.

"Dude, you should just answer yes-or-no style," Karna said to me.

"I've been stopped so many times, once you get detained, there's no way they're going to let you go until they take a few notes on you," I replied.

"It's not some game," said Karna.

I didn't have a response then, and to be fair, none of the guys have to travel between Canada and the USA as much as I do.

Once, I was crossing back to the States through Niagara Falls, after visiting family. My parents were driving and we were waiting in the middle of a long line of cars to present our passports. An officer walked up to our car, knocked on my window, and asked for my passport, before opening my door and ordering me to get out. I was handcuffed as soon as I stepped outside the vehicle. That agent shoved me awkwardly past the long line of waiting cars into the immigration office and sat me down in a dark secondary screening room. They asked me some pretty routine questions, like if I was traveling with any firearms or what the purpose of my trip was, but I stammered, handcuffed and sweating, fearful that something absurd would happen to me. Just like Shahj had been. At one point, the guy who had handcuffed me said something like "Why are you getting nervous? You watch too many movies."

As he uncuffed me, I wanted to be like, *Dude, uh, maybe* you *watch too many movies.*

Eventually they let me out—it wasn't long, maybe a few minutes, but it felt like forever. I was reunited with my parents in the waiting area, but they did not give back my passport. They kept me waiting for an hour, until I was summoned to a much nicer room in the building, one with a glass table. There, a redheaded Homeland Security agent asked me, "How Muslim are you? Like on a scale of one to ten?"

This was without knowing anything about me. When this guy found out I was in a punk band, he randomly hit me with "How do you feel about CBGB's closing down?"

Sometimes they just want to fuck with your head a bit. If you're a person of color coming to the USA for a visit or tour, it's best not to come via road. Buy a flight.

Back in the van, we started to calm down.

"They asked me where my dad was from," said Shahjehan. He said an officer had wanted to buy one of our "Pigs Are Haram" stickers.

That gave me the shivers. It was definitely going in some file on us.

He continued to recount what happened. "After paying me five for the sticker, he asked me if he was haram."

"What did you say, dude?"

"I said, 'I don't know you, man,'" he said.

I don't think I have ever loved my bandmates more than I did for the rest of that drive back.

We made sound check, and all the sound guys and staff at the club had heard what had happened and wanted to be kind to us. Loving, even.

When the show finally began, the place got pretty packed with the jam band/hippie crowd we had gotten used to while playing with Sinkane. It's funny to think of those experiences happening on the same day. We ended up playing for two, three hundred people that night, and Karna even got behind the mic and told the story about what had happened to us. We put on an intense show.

At that point we just needed the release. We played that night for each other. Who gives a fuck about what anyone thinks.

Dispatches from the Language Wars

Daniel José Older

> For the translator, who stands astride two
> cultures, possesses two different sensibilities,
> and assumes a double identity, a translation is a
> journey of self-discovery.
>
> —Husain Haddawy, *The Arabian Nights*

1.

When I was young, I used to try to come up with the most ridiculous, untranslatable words in English and ask my mom what they would mean in Spanish. She would give her best guess, and I'd say, "No, that's not it. Try again." Then, inevitably, she would roll her eyes, scrunch up her face, repeat the same word with a Spanish accent, "búger" (No, not moco!) or "esquísh," and go back to frying potato pancakes or grading papers. Despite the performance of irritation, her eyes always revealed a pool of laughter and, somewhere just beyond that, the faintest trace of pure sadness. It was well hidden, that sadness, but somehow still palpable to little me, and still, after all these years, clear through the foggy lens of memory.

The reason for the sadness was that these occasional moments of mischief were the only times in my childhood when I showed any interest in my mom's native language. From some early moment, I simply decided, without question, not to waste valuable playing time trying to learn Spanish. My parents would gently coax me toward it, include it in our daily household banter, and I always sailed through middle-school courses, but that's as far as I would let it go. Until I was twenty-one, I refused to actually commit to the language in any way beyond filling in textbook blanks and awkward telephone calls to Miami relatives. I remember staring blankly at my own middle name, unsure where the accent went.

But there is more to this story.

A multicultural child is born in the United States, and beneath all the warm smiles and congratulations, a gladiator arena unfolds itself within which the wider world will watch the epic blood sport of identity play out. Sometimes there are winners and losers; no one ever gets out unscathed. To which side will the child tend? What negative and positive attributes will manifest across this clean slate? Xenophobia, however deeply buried in promises of One Happy World and One Happy Family, begins to churn. The fear can be expressed subtly, in hints and allusions, in bad jokes at gatherings, facial expressions. Or it can be outright: "Don't speak that Spanish here."

As I write this, thousands of kids are being ripped away from their parents in the hypermilitarized US-Mexico borderlands. Hate crimes surge as America's long-running white supremacist wet dream comes even more brutally to life each passing day. The institutional annihilation of voting rights, cultural studies, and any semblance of racial justice has become the norm once again. Deportation squads target innocent passersby for the simple act of speaking Spanish.

This sudden upswing is of course only a symptom. The underlying illness that state-sanctioned hate crimes spring from has always been there, stretches back through our history in the form of violent cultural erasure. The abject, petulant refusal by those responsible to confront the ragged legacy they still benefit from has allowed it to fester so long and explode into what it is today.

The United States has no official language, but over and over, language plays a central role in discussions about our national cultural identity. With words, laws, and petty insults, the various encampments struggle over language like missionaries and martyrs at the gates of a holy city.

This country holds the third largest Latin American population in the world. Not all Latinx people in the US speak Spanish. Some speak only English, some Portuguese, and plenty speak one of the thousands of Latin American indigenous languages. For many of us, though, even those of us who tried to reject it as kids, Spanish forms a key part of our memories and identities. Whether as a language of oppression or resistance, it has formed a part of how we understand the world.

And when in our young lives do we begin to internalize what the whole world is yelling at the top of its lungs? When do those messages creep past our parents' cautious encouragement and seep into some part deep inside? When did I give up on Spanish? At some point, very early on, I must've looked out at the world, looked into my television set, looked to the non-Spanish-speaking people around me with the question: Is Spanish something I need in life—is it a necessary part of me? And the answer came back a resounding no, tempered only by plain indifference.

It was almost two decades before I was able to look back and hear the quiet yeses that had been whispered in my ear all along. To her credit, my mom knew enough not to try to force it on me, that if I was going to come around at all, I would have to do it by myself. I dug into my memories, catalogued the disapproving stares, the subtle hints, the blatant threats. Then I stepped back to take it all in. And because the fallout from the language wars reaches far deeper than the headlines, burrows like a parasite through the branches of our family trees and into our very hearts, what I looked back on was a lifetime spent allowing one part of myself to devour another. I had internalized the same bigotry I cringed at in the newspapers, and I had turned it against myself.

When I did realize that Spanish was a part of me, it didn't strike me like a thunderbolt from heaven. The truth didn't come in one definitive stormy moment on a mountaintop but over the course of many, many nights, in the slowly gathering clouds. Simply put: I got sick of simplifying myself. After one too many bad jokes about being half this and half that, one too many little boxes to shade in with number-two pencils, one too many halfhearted shrugs and mumbled explanations, I slowly, finally decided to put my foot down and make some sense of myself.

For the first twenty years of my life, Spanish had always crept around the outer borders of my world. I couldn't take back all the years of miscommunication with my own family members, but I could make sure that it would never happen again.

I went home. Took a summer and spoke only Spanish with my mom. Hammered down the nuances of grammar that I'd fought off years earlier. Discovered the joyful poetry of the subjunctive, that strange future-maybe tense that doesn't quite have an English equivalent. Where once I had cringed, I found a long-lost home hearing the extra *e* native Spanish speakers toss lovingly in front of words that begin with an *s*.

When you translate, something is always lost and something else gained. These are the immeasurable units of language, the tumbling impossibility of meaning stretched over the equally impossible borderlines of culture and perception. In English, we are born, passively. It happens to us. In Spanish, nacemos: we actively enter into this world. "Consúltalo con la almohada," the Argentine journalist Marcos says to his bullfighter girlfriend in Pedro Almodóvar's 2002 film *Hable con Ella. Talk it over with your pillow.* "Sleep on it," the subtitle lazily translates, and I think: *I guess...*

Of course, we are always translating. Expression in any form becomes a clumsy kind of grasping—and it's only heightened when the options increase, as with the great tapestry of words and expressions that Spanglish has become. Perhaps that's why we talk so much with our hands. Squeezing reality into the box of language becomes an ongoing wrestling match with a laughing, unquantifiable angel. And, as with Jacob, it is the struggle that forges us into who we are; it is where we learn our own name.

2.

Nowadays, whenever I ask my mom about a tricky word in Spanish, she lugs out her great big *Diccionario Etimológico* and reads to me, as from a storybook, the long path of the word through history. The ancient Indo-Aryans divided their armies into four divisions: the foot soldiers, horsemen, elephant riders, and war carriages. They carved representations of each into figurines they dispatched across a game board, and so a combination of the Sanskrit words meaning "four" and "bodies" came down through Arabic to become the Spanish word for chess, "ajedrez." "Sarcófago," from the Greek words for "flesh" and "eat," refers to the stone used to build the ancient coffins, which the Greeks believed would devour the corpses inside.

Jorge Luis Borges said that language is an aesthetic medium, just like painting or writing, that each word is a poem. And since each word arrives with its bags packed full of several centuries of secrets and insinuations, we see that the poem is an epic one, the story of a journey. The story tumbles on like *The Arabian Nights,* a living mythology, revealing and concealing itself endlessly and always growing. Here and now are only temporary resting places in the life of any word, which will inevitably continue its path long after we're dust, telling our stories alongside all the stories before ours. With each new meaning, each tiny tinkering and misplaced letter, another moment of humanity becomes etched into our daily lives.

Take the Latin word "pupa," meaning a "doll" or "young girl." From this one word, from the tender concept of a small child, grows a whole library of meanings. Botanist Carl Linnaeus used the word to describe one period in the life of a butterfly or a moth, when it's wrapped in the chrysalis. "Pupilla," the diminutive form of "pupa," came to mean "student," which went on, via Old French, to become the English "pupil." And because when we look into each other's eyes we see tiny, flickering images of ourselves, the ancient Romans also used the word to refer to those dark pools within the iris. Another morphology of "pupa" wandered down through the ages to make the word "puppet." So the eyes become small stages across which we watch our own image dance, and so the children of a community became, as the old saying goes, reflections of their elders.

Through translation and its accompanying deep dive into the roots of words, we arrive at a deeper understanding of our own language.

Just as the story of Persephone's abduction explains why spring turns to fall, as the expulsion from Eden describes the birth of shame, and the theory of evolution traces the origins of humanity, so the history of words illuminates the long saga of our perception of reality. How close any of these stories comes to really explaining what they speak of is irrelevant. The truth is in the telling. Today's Big Bang Theory will be tomorrow's Creation Myth. What matters is what the stories tell us about ourselves, the makers of myth, the translators of reality.

And what the epic myth of language tells me is that the United States has never been a monolingual country and it never will be. The ghosts of a thousand other languages haunt the houses of each word we speak. Forged in the fires of oppression and resistance, we are and always have been a nation of complex identities, slowly gathering clouds, epic poems, and power plays, and so the question of national identity isn't up for debate. It was answered many, many years ago, and the answer continues to echo down, day after day, across the entire country. The echo will never stop ringing, not because of high fertility rates or illegal entries but because no Act of Congress, no state of heightened alert, no amount of border control or bigotry, will ever be able to stop our children from recognizing the faint traces of pure sadness that linger in our eyes when we try to describe the meaning of a word that has no translation.

Juana Azurduy Versus Christopher Columbus

Two Antagonistic Logics for the Building of Argentina

Adrián and Sebastián Villar Rojas
Translated by Jane Brodie

I.

In 2010, during the bicentennial of Argentine independence, the center-left government of Cristina Fernández de Kirchner decided—in an act of historic reparation—to remove the statue of Christopher Columbus outside the presidential palace in Buenos Aires.

The replacement statue of Juana Azurduy, a Bolivian woman, would honor the forgotten heroes of the wars of independence.

An Italian-born conquistador—a white European male and symbol of the Spanish Crown—was, then, replaced by an enormous image of a Bolivian mestiza, a patriotic woman warrior of South American independence.

In 2015, Mauricio Macri, the leader of a nascent right-wing, pro-market political force, was elected president after twelve years of Kirchnerist administrations, first under Néstor Kirchner (2003–2007) and then under Cristina Fernández de Kirchner (2007–2015). The monument to Juana Azurduy was immediately removed.

Few acts performed by governments epitomize as patently as these removals how one system of ideas and ideals can be replaced by another.

How do these systems take root, and what inflections make change possible? Does the origin of one of them lie in the fifteenth century, when the Ottoman Empire drove Europeans to search for an alternative to the Silk Road, which for centuries had enabled commercial exchange between Europe and Asia? Might the origin of the other lie in 1992, during the debates in the Spanish-speaking world on the occasion of the five-hundredth anniversary of the "Discovery of America" (1492), when the official—white, European—version of events was scrutinized by critical revisionism?

Old words, like "discovery" and "cultural encounter," were utterly discredited as new ones, like "conquest" and even "genocide," were used. At the center of the declining Eurocentric narrative was Christopher Columbus. In Latin America, he was knocked out by a powerful, perhaps unexpected, blow: an alternative story told by the defeated, the descendants of the millions of native victims who were now demanding truth and justice, and the right to their land and identity.

II.

In 2005, a group of Bolivian people from the Aymara native community performed a ritual in front of a skeleton of one of their ancestors on display in a glass case in the La Plata Museum of natural history in Argentina. Their action triggered an investigation by La Plata University Research Group in Social Anthropology (GUIAS is the acronym in Spanish), a group formed in 2006 specifically to follow the case.[*] Among

---

[*]   "The GUIAS Collective is a self-summoned organization of the Natural Sciences and Museum Faculty of La Plata National University. Our founding goal is to

the macabre things GUIAS discovered in the museum before being kicked out were archaeological archives containing over ten thousand bones belonging to at least two thousand unidentified human bodies, presumably members of massacred native communities. They discovered as well hundred-year-old documentary photographs of Mapuche and Tehuelche prisoners in vexing situations. Some of the people in the images were completely naked, others in native costume, and still others in Western clothing. Some of the photographs show prisoners performing forced labor in sugarcane plantations and refineries.

In 1886, Francisco Pascasio Moreno (1852–1919), a prominent explorer and the founding director of the La Plata Museum, convinced the Argentine government to hand over Mapuche and Tehuelche individuals who had been taken prisoner during the Conquest of the Desert, a series of military campaigns waged between 1878 and 1885 to expand the national government's dominion over the Pampa and Patagonia, currently central and southern Argentina. To that end, the Conquest of the Desert brought the extermination of the native communities who still controlled those lands. The Mapuche and Tehuelche groups were held captive on the museum's premises, enslaved, photographed, used as models for dioramas, and exhibited as "living fossils"—the term Darwin used to describe the hunter-gatherer population that remained in the southern extreme of the Americas. When one of them would die—often in strange

address the claims made by the Original Peoples to not display and to restore to their communities all of the human remains that are part of 'archaeological collections,' especially the 10,000 human remains found in the La Plata Museum. In pursuit of this goal, we have been working since 2006 on the identification of these remains for later restitution." GUIAS blog, http://colectivoguias.blogspot.com/2013/02/prisioneros-de-la-ciencia.html.

circumstances never investigated by the police—their flesh would be removed and their skeleton displayed in the museum's cases as part of its archaeological collection. Several skulls of Mapuche and Tehuelche people were sent as gifts to museums of natural history in Paris and in London. Obsession with collecting the skulls of "savage peoples" in order to measure, compare, classify, and exhibit them was a distinctive feature of nascent modern sciences like anthropology and archaeology—both fueled by the mid-nineteenth-century neo-colonial rediscovery of the world. Along with the many megafauna fossils also shipped to Europe, this vast collection of skulls donated by Moreno and by other eminent evolutionists, like Florentino Ameghino (1854–1911), was why Argentina and its "naturalists" gained such prestige in the most highly regarded academic circles in Europe.

In the wake of independence in the 1800s, Argentina looked to Europe for guidance as it attempted to forge a national identity. England was a model of "progress" and France of "culture." Under the influence of both of those admired nations, the Buenos Aires elite strove to build a modern state based on the West's "best" and "most advanced" ideas. Buenos Aires was eager to become the Paris of Latin America, and that required establishing strong ties with every field of human knowledge: the country's "wise men" must be proven up to its ambitious project of progress.

Still in the hands of the rebellious Mapuche, Tehuelche, and Ranquel peoples, the Pampa and Patagonia had to be conquered not only for economic and political reasons but also for the sake of modern science. The bodies of the white man's enemies would be an important piece of booty, something to be taken full advantage of by those "wise men" struggling to gain a place for Argentina in the most prestigious cultural, academic, and scientific networks in the West.

III.

The second industrial revolution, in the 1870s, was also—indeed, above all—a transport revolution. It began with the global expansion of motors, first steam and later internal combustion. Fleeing hunger and war, millions of human beings boarded ships fueled by coal and steam in the ports of Europe heading for the Americas.

Thus began the second great wave of migration to the "new continent," this one much bigger and faster than the first. Steam-powered ships did not depend on sea currents and winds. They were autonomous, reliable, and frequent. With the use of metal alloys, wood, and industrial lacquer, their tonnage grew exponentially. Commercial transport, a huge new business, was born on a grand scale, and with it, the mass movement of people by land and sea.

Trains and steam-powered boats were heralded as symbols of progress and civilization. In the novel *Around the World in Eighty Days,* published in 1873, Jules Verne speaks of the virtual shrinking of the world, rendered controllable in space and time.

In just a few decades, tens of millions of Europeans came to the Americas by ship in pursuit of a better life. Compared to previous centuries, the numbers were overwhelming, with masses leaving ports in Hamburg, London, and the Mediterranean, as well as France, Belgium, Netherlands, and Denmark, heading toward North, Central, and South America. Others migrated across the Pacific (large numbers of Chinese arrived in Peru). Over the course of just a handful of years in the late nineteenth and early twentieth centuries, a current of human displacement rooted in capitalism, opportunity, starvation, and war took place on a scale greater than the one witnessed by three entire centuries of exploration.

IV.

"To govern is to populate," said Juan Bautista Alberdi (1810–1884), one of the most influential liberal intellectuals and political thinkers in Argentine history. In his 1852 book *Bases,* he laid the foundation of the country's constitution. For Alberdi, immigration was a privileged source of "progress and civilization," but mostly it was the only means to build a sovereign nation in a territory the Buenos Aires elites considered unpopulated and inhospitable to civilized society. They believed that large swathes of wild land were still in the hands of small pockets of "savage" hunter-gatherers.

Like Domingo Faustino Sarmiento (1811–1888), the other great liberal thinker from the second half of the nineteenth century, Alberdi envisioned welcoming the "surplus population" of the United Kingdom, Germany, the Scandinavian countries, Switzerland, and Northern Europe in general on the coasts of the River Plate.

Both Alberdi and Sarmiento stressed the importance of encouraging settlements of what they called "industrious, civilized, and free Northern European workers," especially Anglo-Saxons. They believed those migrants would bring with them the know-how of Great Britain's industrial revolution, Protestantism's stoic faith in material progress, and love of freedom and mutual respect.

Alberdi in particular did not seek to exclude anybody but—in an early case of cultural eugenics—to encourage the "desired" type of immigration and to distribute it all over the nation's territory, thus avoiding concentration in big port cities: "To govern is to populate, but to populate can also be to infest, to brutalize, to enslave. The difference lies in whether the transplanted population is civilized or primitive, poor, corrupt.... But no foreigner, no matter how vile he may be, should be

excluded. If exclusion of the vile is permitted, the exclusion of the vir-
tuous will follow as a matter of course. In freedom of migration, as
in freedom of the press, license means legality.... Northern Europeans
will naturally go to North America. After all, the north in both worlds
is, it would appear, the realm of freedom and industry. South America,
though, must give up the illusion of receiving immigrants capable of ed-
ucating it in freedom, peace, and industry, unless it is able, by artificial
means, to attract them.... The art of populating is, above all else, the art
of distributing the population."* Between 1880 and 1914, the Argentine
government, heeding Alberdi's advice, opened agencies all over Europe
to encourage the idea of emigrating to the new promised land. "Come
to Argentina," they urged, "where there is an abundance of jobs and
food, and productive land you can easily own." Despite government
efforts, the largest wave of immigrants to South America did not come
from Protestant Northern Europe but from its Catholic south, mainly
from Spain and Italy. Furthermore, the dream of a settlement of Northern European farmers—in Sarmiento's view, the Swiss family farm was
the ideal production unit—that would defend the hinterland against the
"uncivilized Indian" would soon collide with the powerful interests of
the large Criollo landowners reluctant to share ownership of the fertile
Humid Pampas with "foreign rabble." There, most of the few settlements of that sort were scattered over the provinces of Santa Fe, Cór-
doba, Entre Ríos, Corrientes, and Misiones—that is, up north from the
hardcore region of the Buenos Aires large landowners. A rural middle
class of farmers—which both Sarmiento and Alberdi, looking to the
United States, had envisioned as leading the way to healthy economic

---

*   J. B. Alberdi, *Bases: y puntos de partida para la organización política de la República
Argentina* (Buenos Aires: Talleres Gráficos Argentinos de L. J. Rosso, 1914).

and social development—did come to exist, but it was tiny. Far from what they wanted, and akin to what they had warned against, great port cities would be the final destination of most of the millions of immigrants: sooner or later the immigrants realized that land ownership was almost as unlikely in Argentina as it had been in their native countries— large estates would ultimately win out.

V.

"Let's water with the Indians' blood the roots of the tree that will be planted by the Anglo-Saxon laborers," wrote Sarmiento soon after being elected president in 1867. The frenzy to spill native blood and replace it with European blood in what would be, along with the genocidal campaigns waged in North America and Australia, one of the most ferocious—and successful—biopolitical projects known to modernity was reined in until infighting between Criollo elites from the different provinces of the former Viceroyalty of the River Plate could be worked out. Once united, they could conquer the internal frontier together.

This unification of the huinka (in Mapuche language, "white people") would not be easy.

England demanded food for their industrial workers from countries with agricultural potential, such as Argentina and New Zealand, and that led to further expansion of the hinterland, which had been paralyzed by decades of disputes between caudillos— charismatic local rulers of the inland provinces—and the landowning and commercial bourgeoisie of the rich province of Buenos Aires and its homonymous capital city.

Some hard questions had to be asked: Who would rule the future nation, and how would they rule it? What kind of political system would best be able to balance power between the central authorities and the provincial states? Who would finance this nation-state? And, most important, who would have control of the customs taxes collected in the Buenos Aires port, the only way goods traded with European metropolises could get in and out of the country and the largest source of income for the entire nation? These were some of the critical questions answered with bullets during the sixty years it took for a unified nation to emerge. It was during the second industrial revolution, the one that took place in North America and Europe from 1870 to 1914, that agriculture became Argentina's way into the concert of modern (far) Western nations.* The economic integration of the country as a massive food provider was key to political unification.

Huge new ships allowed millions of tons of cereal grains and refrigerated beef to be shipped internationally. The destination for the vast majority of those agricultural goods was Great Britain, which in exchange provided Argentina, and other colonial and neocolonial allies, with industrial products manufactured in Manchester, Liverpool, and London. The first worldwide division of labor was born. The current dialectical interaction between industrialized and raw-material-producing nations took shape during this period, the age of the imperialist expansion of capital.

Mass agricultural production for export demanded and impelled

---

*   French historiographer Alain Rouquié, a specialist in Latin American military history, has used this prefix—"far"-Western nations—to refer to the peripheral, dependent capitalist countries that were born from the Western colonies of the European powers, except for the case of the US, and that now constitute a distant second or third ring within the concept of Western countries. It is useful for grasping the geopolitical situation of South America.

the fast organization of a nation-state whose identity centered around Buenos Aires and its Western idea of civilization. It had little if anything to do with the large masses of land that held millions of pounds sterling worth of agriculture and livestock. That land was still largely inhabited by native peoples. The impending massacre seemed inevitable.

VI.

The identity of Argentina was being formed by future citizens getting off boats hailing from Spain, Italy, France, Ireland, Wales, Scotland, Russia, Poland, Ukraine, Belarus, Prussia, Austro-Hungary, Turkey, Syria, Lebanon, and elsewhere. Recent arrivals were housed for a few weeks by the Argentine immigration authorities at the Immigrant Hotel, just a few hundred meters from the Buenos Aires port. Between 1880 and 1914, more than four million human beings arrived on the coast of Argentina from Europe and the Ottoman Empire, adding to a population that, in 1862, had hovered around one million. In a few years' time, those immigrants' Argentine-born children would speak the Spanish particular to the River Plate; in schools, they would be instructed in the identity of a nation with anthem, flag, and official history. Total integration and acculturation through elementary school was a major goal of the young republic, which was determined to make "civilized Argentine citizens" out of millions of foreigners from around the world who spoke dozens of languages and dialects. An entire Foucauldian set of biopolitical and disciplinary institutions—from museums to jails, from hospitals to universities— was built during these years. Meanwhile, General Julio Argentino Roca (1843–1914) planned and carried out a sort of "final solution" to what was called the "indigenous question." From 1878 to 1885, he led what, pursuant to revision, is currently understood to be the first Argentine genocide: the Conquest of the Desert.

Hundreds of years before the Argentine republic was even envisioned, a population—around sixty thousand people in the 1870s—inhabited their own territories according to their own laws and customs: *Wallmapu* is the Mapuche term for their ancient lands (in English, "surrounding territory"), which encompassed what are now the central and southern regions of Chile and Argentina. It is estimated that the Argentine government massacred at least twenty thousand human beings; thousands of others were driven out by boat or in forced marches to concentration camps in different parts of the country (the infamous island Martín García, for instance, held a maximum-security military prison where countless Mapuche died of hunger, disease, abuse, and isolation). Thousands of others were reduced to servitude, becoming domestic workers in cities or performing industrial labor in the sugar refineries of Tucumán province.

In 1879, the Argentine newspaper *El Nacional* published a chronicle of the procedure: "After traveling mostly on foot, the Indians and their families arrive as prisoners. The desperate wailing is relentless as children are taken away from their mothers and given to white families as slaves. Neither the children's screams and howls nor the mothers' pleas, arms held to the heavens, is heeded. The Indian men cover their faces or stare at the ground in resignation, their wives pressing their children to their bosom."*

---

*   *El Nacional*, December 31, 1879, originally cited in Osvaldo Bayer, "Desmonumentar," May 16, 2010, *Página/12*, https://www.pagina12.com.ar/diario/contratapa/13-145745-2010-05-16.html.

Jorge Julio López, a retired Peronist bricklayer who had been kid-napped and missing from 1977 to 1979 during the last military-civil dictatorship in Argentina (1976–1983), described a scene similar to the one in the 1879 *El Nacional* chronicle in his testimony during the 2006 trial of Miguel Etchecolatz, an organizer of state terrorism during the so-called Dirty War: "Then they bring out Patricia [Dell'Orto], who was screaming, 'Don't kill me, don't kill me, take me to prison but don't kill me. I want to bring up my little girl, my daughter.' And, if her body is ever found, you will see that it bears the wound of a gunshot that came in here [pointing to his forehead] and out here [pointing to the back of his head]. Afterwards, they brought out her husband, Ambrosio De Marco, who was lying on the floor because of the torture. Two or three of them dragged him out and then shot him. Mark my words, if their remains are ever found, you'll see that both have bullet holes in the head." A couple of hours after giving this 2006 key testimony against Etchecolatz, who would be sentenced to life imprisonment, López was kidnapped and disappeared—this time forever—presumably by police-men who still followed Etchecolatz's orders.

As López—and hundreds of other survivors—dared to testify, the Argentine armed forces, this time organized into "task groups" trained in torture by French specialists who had fought the National Liberation Army (FLN is the acronym in French) in Algeria, engaged in 1976 in a second genocide virtually one century after the first. They once again ignored the screams of the victims—those kidnapped by the military and police were mostly Peronist activists, politicians, and union delegates—who were taken to the more than three hundred fifty clandestine detention centers located throughout the country.

Both the "savage Indian" of the nineteenth century and the Peronists of the twentieth were constructed as the evil Other lurking within the national frontiers. For the Buenos Aires oligarchy, that Other had to be put down if the sacred values of Western civilization were to prevail.

VII.

In order to denounce how science has been used, at the La Plata Museum in particular, to violate the human rights of native communities, GUIAS held an exhibition called *Prisoners of Science*. It featured hundreds of photographs found in the institution's basement, photographs that point to the pseudoscientific and derogatory logic central to the practice of appropriating the bodies and lives of a group of human beings for the almost sole purpose of constructing a discourse of racial inferiority that would legitimize the theft of their lands. The exhibition opened in the Patagonian city of San Carlos de Bariloche; at the center of its main square is an equestrian monument to General Julio Argentino Roca. The general in the statue stares out at the conquered horizon over the lake that paradoxically bears the name of a Mapuche lonko (in English, "chief"), Nahuel Huapi. *Prisoners of Science* culminated symbolically when exhibited at the Haroldo Conti Cultural Center, a space for memory and human rights located on the premises of the former Navy School of Mechanics (ESMA is the acronym in Spanish), one of the largest clandestine detention centers during the last civic-military dictatorship. More than five thousand people were held in captivity at the ESMA and later thrown into the sea in "death flights." Due to the ideological matrix at stake, the interests represented, the military resources mobilized, and the extermination techniques used, the two genocides are, in GUIAS's view, virtually the same. Both involved forced disappearance, appropriation of children, execution, suppression of identity,

physical and psychological torture, and other techniques. As the collective itself explains in the text that accompanied the exhibition: "In the
specific case of the museum in La Plata, . . . science would articulate and
enact a discourse geared to demonstrating the inferiority of the original
populations to the white man and his 'civilization,' an ideological position held to be scientifically true and, therefore, grounds for 'sentenc-
ing' that population to extinction. . . . Several factors have converged to
enable the current historical reparation and struggle for justice for the
victims of both Argentine genocides, perhaps the most important one
being thirty years of continuous democracy [1983–2013]. It is thanks in
part to an unprecedented period of democratic governments that native communities have been able to reconstruct their identity, and to
engage in struggle and to voice demands. They will continue fighting
for the restitution of their ancestors' remains."

A crucial component of the new situation described in the text
is the reopening, in 2005, of the criminal cases of those responsible
for state terrorism from 1976 to 1983, cases against figures like
Etchecolatz—a result of the demand for justice by human rights organizations such as Mothers and Grandmothers of Plaza de Mayo, and
Sons and Daughters for Identity and Justice Against Oblivion and Silence (HIJOS is the acronym in Spanish), among many others.

The work performed by GUIAS has complemented the work of
the Argentine Forensic Anthropology Group, formed in the 1980s.
That group has overseen the identification of the skeletal remains of
those detained and disappeared by state terrorism, remains found in
mass graves or in individual graves but under false identities. From
the perspective of the search for memory, truth, and historical reparation, the La Plata Museum can now be reread as itself a mass grave:
only a tiny portion of the more than ten thousand bits of human

remains (bones, organs, skin, scalp, limbs) were correlated to an individual body and duly identified when "archived" at the institution at the end of the nineteenth and early twentieth centuries.

While in countries like Greece and Egypt the ground hides archaeological riches, the ruins of temples and pyramids, in Argentina the soil bears vast deposits of dinosaur fossils—the Argentinosaurus, found in Patagonia, is the largest known prehistoric animal anywhere on earth—and, some geological layers higher, countless graves and tombs with bones of the Others: the victims of two genocides that, though a century apart, were remarkably alike in terms of goals and interests, and even procedures.

That soil—its surface still, and not by chance, the productive basis of a deindustrialized and dependent country—has a great deal to tell us about ourselves and about our drive to disappearance. In an iconic song composed in 1983, the year democracy was restored in Argentina after the "Years of Lead," Charly García, an outstanding figure in Argentine music, gathered all the bones and fossils hidden under the soil of history and memory in his song "Los dinosaurios" ("Dinosaurs"). The chorus references how the neighbor, the radio singers, the guys in the newspaper or in the streets, may or may not disappear...but dinosaurs... they will disappear. The "dinosaurs" were—as those listening to the song immediately understood—the old and ailing military men.

VIII.

Amid the names of the many military officers that are now also the names of streets and avenues in every city in Latin America, the name of one woman stands out: Juana Azurduy (1780–1862).

Born in Toroca, Potosí, Viceroyalty of the River Plate, she was a patriot who fought in the Spanish American wars of independence (1808–1833) for emancipation from the Spanish Crown. After dying indigent and forgotten, her legacy was restored one hundred fifty years later thanks to progressive governments in Argentina and Bolivia in the early twenty-first century.

She was a symbol of everything that had been suppressed and denied by the nineteenth-century liberal elites who envisioned Argentina as a neocolonial country based on mass European immigration. Behind the shift were Evo Morales, the first Aymaran president of Bolivia and a figure supported by an increasingly powerful indigenous movement, and Cristina Fernández de Kirchner, the first woman elected president of Argentina, who was a leftist Peronist activist during her youth in the seventies and, at the time, the leader of a progressive social and political coalition. Both leaders decided to pay homage to a woman whose biography represented—in a way the traditional forefathers could not (that is, from a new gender and Amerindian perspective)— the struggle of Latin American peoples. That fight for autonomy and sovereignty was being waged once again in the region during the years surrounding the Argentine bicentennial (2010).

Juana Azurduy was of mixed race. Her father was a rich European landowner and her mother was an Amerindian woman from Chuquisaca. She spoke Spanish as well as Quechua. A rebel, she was, at the age of sixteen, expelled from the convent where she was studying to be a nun, and at twenty-five, she married Manuel Ascencio Padilla, with whom she joined the Revolutionary Army in 1809, at the age of twenty-nine. After a series of military defeats during which they lost all their property, Azurduy and Padilla—"the warrior lovers," as they were known at the time—turned to guerrilla warfare against the royalists. For her bravery, Juana was awarded the rank of lieutenant colonel. In 1816, she was wounded in battle and captured; her husband was killed trying to rescue her. She survived and—then a widow with six children—continued fighting for the cause of independence. In 1825, General Simón Bolívar, known as the Liberator, visited her. Upon seeing the dreadful conditions she was living in, he assigned her a pension and declared, "This country should not be called Bolivia in my honor; it should be called Padilla or Azurduy, because it was them who made it free."[*]

The monument to Juana would replace the one that, in 1910, on the occasion of the centennial of independence, was given to the Argentine Republic by the Italian community; though they had mostly landed less than a decade earlier, hundreds of thousands of Italian immigrants already enjoyed a respectable place in society. The carvings on the plinth under the statue of Christopher Columbus made reference to progress, reason, science, and civilization. He was the hero those "good immigrants" had chosen to express their gratitude for their new home in America.

It was not until 2014 that the statue of Columbus was replaced by the one of Juana. Notwithstanding, that change in symbols uniquely captured the drama of two antagonistic political and social projects that have been fighting each other throughout the nation's two-hundred-year history. Indeed, that struggle lies deep within Argentine society: Do we see ourselves as Europeans in the Americas, serving Western interests unconnected to our Latin American neighbors? Or

---

[*]   Rogelio Alaniz, *Hombres y mujeres en tiempos de revolución: De Vértiz a Rosas (Men and Women in Times of Revolution: From Vértiz to Rosas)*, Santa Fe, Argentina: The Littoral National University, 131.

are we committed to searching for those Others we have denied in order to pursue our own ethnic plurality, and to found a new relationship to radical Otherness and thus to the ethically and culturally plural nation we actually are? Will we, along with those Latin America neighbors, build what we might call the "greater motherland," a land more inclusive, fair, and free, on the principle of our common native and mixed-race roots? Or will we and our Latin America neighbors set ourselves to build bilateral, individualistic relations with our present and past Western metropolis, on the basis—especially in the case of Argentina—of the denial of that plurality and in favor of our white European ascendants?

As a mixed-race woman and a guerrilla combatant who gave up everything for her revolutionary ideals, Juana is a good example of how far we must be willing to go, of how much we must be willing to lose, but also of how much we have to gain if we dare to jump into the abyss of political emancipation(s).[*]

---

[*] Emancipation, as formulated since the Enlightenment (only one true path: Western reason, of which orthodox Marxism is an inheritor), should give place to its plural, detotalized, twenty-first-century version: emancipation(s), the possibility of building a progressive political unity matching a myriad of diverse struggles for full citizenship and recognition (race, gender, sexuality, class, etc.)—defined by Ernesto Laclau and Chantal Mouffe as the construction of a collective political subject, a universal singularity, an empty signifier only valid in a certain place and time, unique, topographically determined, and always temporary, departing from democratic demands and open identities willing to go beyond neoliberal multiculturalism, culturally "cool" but politically impotent. See Laclau and Mouffe, *Hegemony and Socialist Strategy*, London: Verso, 1985; and Laclau, *Emancipation(s)*, London: Verso, 1996.

No Es Suficiente

Dani Fernandez

One of my favorite scenes in HBO's *Insecure* happens in the very first episode. Issa, an African American twenty-nine-year-old woman, who teaches at an after-school youth program, is speaking before a class of students. At the end of her speech, a young girl raises her hand and asks, "Why do you sound white?"

I know how that goes.

People tell me I sound white. People say my father sounds white. I always figured that helped him close business deals on the phone. I would watch as my father slipped back into his Mexican accent around his family and then bounced over to sounding "white" around his business colleagues. Even when I was little, I understood the privilege that comes with sounding white. People trust you.

White people trust you.

But you know what you sound like when you're a Mexican who sounds white? Pocho. You sound like you sold out.

I was reminded of this feeling when I was on a panel about Latinx superheroes at a comic convention, which is ironic because we never really had many Latinx superheroes in comics. At least not mainstream ones. Whenever someone asks me who my hero was growing up, I say Selena. She was my Wonder Woman. Who also showed me how good my boobs could look bedazzled.

Other than that, I mainly looked up to white superheroes. They were the standard for what a hero should act, be, and look like.

At this particular panel, a woman raised her hand and told the room she was spanked by her abuela when she and her siblings spoke Spanish in the house. English was the prize. Learning it was not optional. It was the one thing we needed to survive, to fit in. Not Spanish. At least not for my family, and not for hers either.

My father didn't teach my brothers and me Spanish. If we wanted to learn, it was something we had to pursue on our own. That involved VHS tapes of a big green Snuffleupagus-lookin' monster named Muzzy. If you haven't learned Spanish from a dollar-store Super Mario villain, treat yourself.

Today, knowing Spanish is a plus. "Do you speak Spanish?" is a crucial question asked in auditions, on college applications, and in job interviews.

My father worked in marketing and advertising. I imagine that when you're a Mexican man in the '70s and '80s trying to represent famous US brands, having a Spanish accent is not actually a plus. Remember, this was long before the days of the Budweiser Lime-A-Rita. So I doubt they thought brown businessmen knew white middle America the way they do. It was only as an adult that I understood this and why my father learned Spanish from his Mexican parents and we didn't. The elders in my family often spoke Spanish when they didn't want my cousins and me to know what they were talking about.

Throughout the house, I would often sing the songs my father played, without ever fully knowing what they meant.

* * *

Meanwhile, I excelled in English. If you ask my mother about what I was like as a child, she tells *everyone* the same thing, that "you could always catch her curled up with an apple and a good book!" I'm thirty and she still tells men I date this. Growing up, I was so obsessed with my English classes that I even took on my older brother's assigned reading of *The Lion, the Witch, and the Wardrobe* and wrote part of his paper for him.

In elementary school, my class slowly started to learn Spanish, and given my last name, skin color, and heritage, everyone assumed I already knew.

I should have.

Why didn't I?

My brothers and I went to a predominately white private Catholic school that my parents couldn't afford but still felt compelled to send us to. That's how important it was to them. I don't know if that was their religious side or the need to appear successful, or both.

There were multiple years when my brothers and I shared a single bedroom. One of those years was in my tía Yolanda's house, where my parents, my brothers and I, and my aunt and my uncle all lived together. Imagine being a young woman growing underarm and pubic hair being stuck in a room when your brothers are *also* growing underarm and pubic hair. We would take turns with who got to sleep in the real bed and who had to sleep on the blow-up mattress on the floor. If you were to get me drunk, I'd confess to you that I secretly cherished that time we had, living close together. Especially now that we all live in different cities and have partners and lives.

My brothers and I hated private school. I would come home

almost *every single day* crying. There was a white girl in my class, Emily, who used to tease me for my last name.

"Fernandez? Your dad is my gardener."

I remember I turned to her and said, "My dad works in advertising."

School, specifically, made me hate so much of myself. I developed curves *very early* on while most of the girls were tiny, white, and blond. A boy in my middle school PE class convinced several other boys, including the one I had a crush on, to call me "Shrek." That damn movie is still triggering to me to this day. I had a thick athletic build, full lips, and a lion's mane of brown hair that my mother would sometimes spend an hour trying to detangle. My parents repeatedly told me that with my genes I would never be skinny. That all the women in my family had curves. I used to weep about it.

I'll show you, I thought, as I developed an eating disorder. By the time I was sixteen, I was anorexic. Some days I would eat nothing but a single orange. I would cut it in sections and have a section for breakfast, a section for lunch, and so on. By seventeen, I was both anorexic and bulimic. If I ate, I threw it up. It would be years before I started dating men who liked my body the way it was and subscribed to the belief that "thicc thighs save lives."

Because I went to school in predominately white areas, I never had my heritage questioned. I was clearly not white, and given the states I grew up in (California and Texas), everyone just assumed I was Mexican. In fact my ethnicity was always already bubbled in on my standardized tests, while other kids got to select what they identified as. This didn't bother me; I just remember noticing it. Not until I moved to Los Angeles and started auditioning for roles did I hear from white agents that I wasn't actually "Mexican enough."

What? I thought. *You're telling me my brothers and I were teased for not being white enough and now we're not Mexican enough?*

Once, a casting director told me I wasn't acting "Latina enough," and I asked if he wanted me to do the lines in Spanish, and he said, "No, just act more Latina." Which likely to him meant being loud and having an attitude and a quick temper. Which I certainly have, but not *all* Latinas have. Some are quiet and soft-spoken, and it doesn't make them any *less* Latina. I know several of my African American friends have been told in auditions that they need to "black it up" or be "blacker," as if this white casting director even knows what "being black" means.

The first year I did stand-up, I told jokes about all this stuff, about not being Mexican enough to white people. This set of jokes normally got a ton of laughs, mainly from white people. And when I was new in Hollywood, I thought, *This is good. People are laughing!* But they weren't laughing *with* me. And I noticed sometimes when I would do this routine, some of the Latinx people in the audience weren't laughing at all. I realized that was my fault. Because there are plenty of Mexican comics who can make fun of their families and childhood without it feeling like they are punching down. And yet it started to feel like that was exactly what this part of my routine was. I was young and insecure and needed to be accepted, and I felt my family was an easy target. I think I tried to justify this by the fact that I was teased for being Mexican in school, and I might as well use my Mexicanness to make people laugh! But it was the same people laughing each time: white people.

I stopped doing those jokes.

I remember being on another panel at a comic convention and a young Latina woman in the audience raised her hand and said she was working on a project and received feedback that one of her characters needed to be "more Mexican." What does that mean? Should their skin color be a certain shade? Should they speak only Spanish? Is the extent of their mother's medicine cabinet Vicks VapoRub? This is something that I and many of my colleagues have debated. What does it mean to be "more Mexican?" How can you group an entire people all together as the same? When a white person suggests something be "more Mexican" or "more Latino," I often ask them to *show* me what they mean, 'cause odds are it's stereotypical as hell. It's what they *think* a Latinx person is.

I have noticed a certain *thing* going on with white writers in Hollywood. In an effort to capitalize on what casting directors and agents call "the diversity trend" (it's not a trend, by the way…we are not temporary), television writers often make one or possibly two of their main characters people of color, without actually being connected to our communities. It's one thing to select a few brown faces for a project. It's another to have a project actually written by brown writers, meaning the brown faces are more than just wallpaper.

In a study done by the dean of social sciences at UCLA that looked at 234 original series across 18 platforms (including digital) for the 2016–2017 television season, only 14 percent of writers were from a minority group.[*] I also know my Latinx friends would love it if casting directors stopped assuming all Latinx people are Mexican. We don't

---

[*] Tracy Jan, "How White TV Writers Decide the Stories Hollywood Tells America," *Washington Post*, November 6, 2017.

all sound and look the same! We don't all know each other either. We're not all on some secret Hollywood Latinx group text message chain...that you know of.

This disconnect between white writers and their brown characters was particularly eye-opening in a screenwriting class I took in Hollywood. Reading the scripts of several other writers, I realized they saw Mexicans *only* as poor laborers. And that was it. The entirety of who we are as a people often came down to poor, brown people who speak broken English. Which we know to them means uneducated. It doesn't matter what other language you speak or how many languages you may know. If you can't speak English, to white Americans you are uneducated. It never seems to cross these people's minds just how diverse Mexico actually is. It has university professors, anime enthusiasts, engineers, chefs, celebrities, comic book artists, politicians, athletes, YouTubers, screenwriters, spoiled teens ignoring their parents to play on their iPhones, and Fall Out Boy concerts. Yes, Mexican people listen to millennial pop-punk bands and every single other genre of music. Yes, Mexicans can be laborers. They are some of the most skilled, hardest-working people in the world. But laborers are not all they are. Why do white people have such a narrow view of us?

Two years ago I received a script for a role in which I would play a Mexican maid to two white men. I remember noting that the *one* Latina in the script was serving white people.

I have heard from people in the community who say, "Well, my mom is a maid. What's wrong with that?"

Nothing. Nothing is wrong with having a service job. In fact many of us have had service jobs in our lives. If you want to talk about a stereotype, I was a nanny to several white families for many years. But I have seen Mexican actors limited to those roles in television and film again and again. I want us to have the diversity of roles that white actors are allowed to have. That's what I want. That's my problem with this. That we are still so singularly viewed. And before you try to come at me with the "Well, Latinos are taking our acting jobs in Hollywood" argument, please know that we still make up only 5.8 percent of all speaking roles in television and film.

5.8 percent.

I was recently involved in a scandal when I shared audio that had been sent to me by a fellow student at my acting studio who caught the owner of our studio telling a struggling white actress in class to dye her hair, change her name to Rosa Ramirez, and start passing herself off as Latina in order to get more roles.

"Just the fact that your name is Rosa Ramirez is gonna get you a meeting…So you might try it…Go to the head-shot shop and tell them you're Latin. Wear something fucking red. Wear some fucking sparkly earrings. Change your goddamned name, and let's just do an experiment."

That's what white people think our culture is. Just some hat to try on! And if it doesn't work, they can toss it and try on another.

Also, we don't all wear red! I prefer purple.

There was a huge backlash from that audio clip, and even worse than the coach's words on tape were those trying to justify them afterward.

"That's an actor's job. To pretend to be another person."

An astronaut is a hat you can try on, Becky, not someone's ethnicity. Not lying about your entire identity so you can steal a role from a Latina who is still one of the most underrepresented people in Hollywood. Over the course of this year alone I screenshot and shared with my friends several Facebook posts from white actresses asking for suggestions for more ethnic last names, saying their agents think pretending to be another ethnicity will help them get more roles. This is disgusting. I want to reiterate that this is a current and growing problem in my industry. This doesn't fix the studios' diversity problem. It contributes to it.

Throughout the history of cinema, we have been so limited in representation that when we finally get to move toward a few less stereotypical roles, they want to snatch those away too. They have spent their lives taking representation for granted; why would they want to change things now? Maybe, just maybe, if they were better at their jobs they wouldn't have to steal someone else's ethnicity in an industry already run by people who share theirs.

"But, Dani, what about when your dad sounded white on the phone to close business deals? Or Asian actors who have changed their names to sound white to fit in?" Yes, those are things people of color *had to do* in order to survive racism in a country set up to benefit white people. That is *still* the way this industry is set up, but it is slowly, very slowly, changing. I have been able to use some of my influence to get my extremely qualified and talented friends of color hired at studios. Now when I have to turn down a hosting gig, I recommend three or four other women of color to take my place so the studio can't possibly have an excuse to replace me with a white guy.

So at the end of the day, who gets to determine if I am Latina enough? Or if *you* are "enough" of your ethnicity? Even though it was a joke in the show, in real life, educated women like Issa Rae shouldn't be told they "sound white." Because white people shouldn't get to own sounding educated. Or American. For some reason, sounding "American" means sounding white, despite the fact that the US is a country made up of immigrants. There are Asian Americans, African Americans, Native Americans, Mexican Americans, etc., who can all sound "American." I want to make this clear: Yes, there is a privilege to sounding American in America. But it doesn't erase your heritage and skin color. It doesn't erase your experience, your ancestors, or the struggles that come with being a person of color in this country. Sounding American shouldn't mean you sound white. Because white people are not the only ones who get to claim this country. Despite what anyone may tell you, this country is also ours.

Skittles

Fatima Farheen Mirza

This image says it all. Let's end the politically correct agenda that doesn't put America First. #Trump2016

If I had a bowl of Skittles and I told you that just three would kill you, would you take a handful? This is our Syrian refugee problem.

—Donald Trump Jr., September 2016

After living in the Bay Area since my father first immigrated there in 1985, my family moved in 2016 to a suburb of Dallas, Texas. By then, my youngest brother, Mahdi, was the only child still living at home.

"Will you talk to Mahdi?" Baba would call and ask me. "Cheer him up? He seems depressed."

My other brothers and I would joke that while we had bloomed late, Mahdi had been born cool, but after moving to Texas, he had become withdrawn, muted. We were annoyed our parents had not thought it through: of course moving Mahdi to classrooms where he was suddenly the only kid of color, and to a neighborhood where TRUMP signs sprouted weekly on rough lawns, would have an effect.

When I tried to pry from Mahdi what he was going through at school, he'd only respond, "Just tell me how to explain to them that they're being racist."

We'd practice hypothetical arguments over the phone—logically, emotionally, statistically. Sometimes Mahdi shared what was said to him that he'd frozen in response to. How a classmate tapped him, asked him if his middle name was Mohammed, and when Mahdi said, "Yes. How did you know?" the classmate told him, "I'm keeping an eye on Mohammeds."

We imagined responses for next time, serious at first, and then biting, and eventually just funny, until we were both laughing. Each time we were about to hang up, Mahdi would ask me to not tell Mumma or Baba. I thought they should know, but he'd insist so strongly, I had no choice but to listen.

When Trump first proposed a Muslim ban, my grandmother lowered her voice and told me, "Keep your passport on you. They've made their intentions clear. We have to be ready to leave at any instant."

She was a worrier, and I'd often reassure her the world was not as dangerous as she imagined it. To be told to carry my passport was far more extreme than being told not to venture out alone at night, but even as I told her she was worrying unnecessarily, somewhere, lurking in my heart, I didn't know: the line between conceivable and inconceivable was blurring. That year, I began to experience what I thought of as a kind of vertigo: feeling stunned as the world shifted around me before settling into a new concrete reality. By 2018, the sensation was familiar, and the Muslim ban was couched as a travel ban, done in the name of national security, but we were there, watching, when he first said it: "a total and complete shutdown of Muslims entering the United States."

What surprised me, watching the news, was how little I was *actually* surprised by the hateful content. As though I'd always sensed it, unspoken unless I confronted it in men on airplanes, asking me if I was one of the good ones after learning my name. I was surprised too by how casually, how openly, and without shame he spoke, and how without shame his platform was received: how they cheered, celebrated, as though he was not just emboldening them but also liberating them.

My parents, though appalled, did not echo my grandmother's apprehension. When my brothers and I voiced our own fears, they'd tell us the line we had grown up hearing, any time we walked away from an anti-Muslim interaction: "Don't worry. He's just one man." And then, as though to convince us, or themselves, "There are checks in place. This is not legal."

One afternoon, when I was still in high school, Mahdi came home from soccer practice, his backpack slung over his shoulder, and found me sitting before the television screen. There had been a terrorist attack and I'd been watching the same footage loop for hours.

"Please don't tell me they're Muslims" was the first and only thing he said. I was startled by his tone—so angry, so disgusted, that it seemed for a moment as though he too hated Muslims.

I remember turning to look at him. He was only ten. I said nothing, but my expression must have given it away. Mahdi looked as though he were about to cry and also as though he were just tired of it, tired in the way we all were—experiencing with each attack that blend of horror and shock but also the knowledge of what it would bring. Mahdi threw his backpack down and raced up the stairs, slammed his door shut, and did not emerge again for hours, an unrelenting rhythm of a tennis ball hitting against his bedroom wall.

In Texas years later, Mahdi confessed he'd started telling his classmates he was Catholic. For some reason we laughed at this, even as something in my chest softened. It was then that the image of my brother as a boy returned to me, how he had thrown his backpack down, just sick of it. How I had not begun to wonder then what I wonder now: what the accumulating effect of all of this will be, in ways so slight and untraceable I can return to each of these scattered moments and still never know how they have formed and marred our daily experience in this world, and the sense of our place in it.

During the two years my family lived in Texas, my mother never admitted to feeling unwelcome or unhappy. Instead, she'd insist that life anywhere was life, the sky anywhere was the sky. But sometimes I'd catch her trailing off when she spoke of our neighbors, a note of disappointment in her voice: "We brought them pies when we first moved in, we wave at them every time we walk by, but nothing, no warmth."

So when the doorbell rang almost a year after their move, Mumma was surprised to open it to the young daughter of our thin-lipped and straight-faced neighbors. By then, the news was constantly playing in the background of our home, and each campaign update was more disheartening than the last—give them IDs, register them in a database, heighten surveillance in Muslim neighborhoods. Whenever

I visited, I'd turn it off, tell my parents it wasn't good for Mahdi to hear the same messages looping.

"This is for your family," the girl said, extending a bag of candy.

Later, Mumma would tell me she felt relieved, as though she were exhaling. As though she had not realized she had been holding her breath, waiting for a gesture like it—and confessing her reaction proved to me the existence of the thoughts she guarded us from. For a moment, Mumma thought our neighbors were conveying that they knew they had been unwelcoming but now would be different, that although the atmosphere was thick with an ugliness impossible to ignore, it would not affect what existed between them, neighbor to neighbor.

"Thank you," Mumma said, and the girl ran off. Then Mumma looked closer: it was not a gift bag but a ziplock plastic bag, unadorned and filled only with Skittles.

Mumma left the plastic bag of Skittles on the counter, and even though she spoke of it as harmless, as only slightly and possibly unsettling, she repeated the incident to each of us, and then to each of her siblings. My brothers and I were angry. We wanted our parents to either confront the neighbors or report it. To us, it was irrefutably threatening, and sickening that the neighbors had sent their daughter, a young girl. The incident came just days after Donald Trump Jr. had compared Syrian refugees to a bowl of poisonous Skittles.

"It is just candy," Baba said, refusing to budge and forbidding me from writing about it. "This kind of thinking is not good for you. We will not be making a big deal out of nothing."

Mumma was equally determined: "We will give them the benefit of the doubt, and if we do say anything, it will be 'Thank you for the candy'—we will continue to show them by example that we are normal people."

I was tired of it all: not just fearing for my family's safety; not just the image that started to haunt me right before I fell asleep, of my mother in her hijab, alone in a dark parking lot; not just comforting Mahdi after his classmates shoved him, calling him ISIS; not just the flicker in the back of my mind that wondered what future we, as a country, were laying the groundwork for, one so precariously balanced it could be as simple as a match struck against a box to light a flame, and when the flame came, in what way, exactly, would we experience its burn? I was tired, most impossibly, of my parents' refusal to admit how tiring it was at all, of their insistence that all was well, that we had not been wronged—which was another way of saying: We do not deserve better than this. That this is the way of being treated, spoken to, and spoken about that we have resigned ourselves to. And what pained me as their daughter was a lingering thought: *Is not our belief in how we should be treated a reflection of how we see ourselves?*

The Skittles, still in the plastic bag, sat untouched on our kitchen table. Mumma, despite having voiced her initial relief, was now silent. It was as though once she saw how the incident unnerved us, she decided to swallow her own shock and convinced herself it had been harmless.

"Mumma," I finally said, trying to reach her true self, "if you really believe it wasn't malicious, then why don't you eat them?"

"I'm not going to eat them."

"Then let us eat them."

Mumma stood from the couch, lifted the bag of Skittles, and emptied them all into the trash.

* * *

It's an anger I've known since I was a girl, one that revolves like a spinning needle. First, my anger points to the one who is racist. We are
reentering the country, watching as the border control officer is rude
to my mother, watching him make fun of her, tell her how we pronounce things in America. Mumma is looking down, Baba too. They
are apologizing to him, then repeating themselves. Or I'm a teenager,
driving with Mumma in a parking lot, when she hits the brakes because a man has just stepped out. "I'm sorry," Mumma tells him,
lowering the window. "Are you all right?" "What," the man begins to
shout, "are you going to bomb me next, lady?" And Mumma stam-
mers apologies as he continues to yell. If these incidents are directed
at me, I am free to respond emotionally. If directed at my brothers, I
am defensive, protective. But come near my mother and the anger is
so particular and unbounded that I snap, tell the border officer that in
America we pronounce things how we like, and we are led to another
room, or I shout back at the man in the parking lot, having never even
known I could string together curse words so creatively and angrily
against a stranger. During the drive home, or seated in the window-
less airport room as we wait to be questioned again, I am the one
who is lectured, told how my stupidity will get us all in deep trouble.
Later, when my parents see how hurt I still am, they soften to me, and
I am comforted. "It's all right, Fatima. He's just one man. His hate is
his burden to bear."

But once we are home and safe, the needle turns to point at my
parents instead, and I ask them: Why did you look down, why did
you not argue back, why did you apologize to him? The man in
the parking lot, the man at border control, the man in security, the
neighbor who does not wave back, all these changeable men who

approach my Mumma and Baba with an unchanging conception of them. Why did you not demand, as I try to demand, how we deserve to be treated?

Is this very demanding born from a space in me that I can fill with anger or hurt or a sense of injustice, one that exists easily in me but reluctantly in Mumma and Baba, because I have grown up thinking of myself as an American and have known nothing else? Is the very sense of entitlement my protests stem from the same entitlement I resent in others, who wield theirs to say, "This is who our country is for, and by asserting its exclusivity, this is how we will make it great again"?

Every few months, while I lived in Iowa, Baba would call me and ask if I could write a novel about a white family instead. It was a familiar pattern: each time my brothers and I applied to colleges, we argued with Baba about our personal essays. He did not want us to write about our identity at all. Not how it had shaped us or what it had taught us—perhaps hoping that if we did not admit to difficulty, it would not be difficult for us. "You won't get in," he'd tell us, frustration in his voice, but also some fear. "They will read your applications and throw them away."

In Iowa I'd remind Baba for the hundredth time that this was the family I was writing about. He'd sigh, tell me he was worried for my future, worried no one would read it. I'd respond with conviction, partly knowing that if I was firm in my stance, if I refused to falter, he'd have no choice but to be convinced, or at least to relent until he felt compelled to ask me again. I was not writing for readers, I told him, but for these characters, this family, to do justice to their lives.

I was not offended. I was hardly even disappointed in Baba's lack of belief in the novel, knowing it was rooted in a desire to protect me. Still, what saddened me was what it revealed about my father's belief in his own life, the undercurrent beneath his doubts that said, *Who will care about me? About a family like mine?*

My father had consumed the stories of others and the flattening narrative framed by the media for so long that I sometimes wonder if, when he lowers his gaze as the border control officer turns aggressive, there is a part of my father that has believed what the world has said about him. That it was not made for him. That in choosing to move here, he reached for more than he was originally allotted, and though he has worked to form a beautiful life, though he has lived here longer than he has lived elsewhere, he is still borrowing his place, walking through the world the way a man who knows he is borrowing does: gently, as though what he has built can be taken away. But if he does not draw attention to his difficulties, if he ensures the survival of his children by teaching them to do the same, then he can get by, carry on, continue creating the life he has wanted for himself, for his children.

After hearing the election results, I called my brothers and asked them to please not go out that night—a line I never thought I'd speak, having rolled my eyes for years when hearing it from my grandmother.

"I can't go to school tomorrow," Mahdi told me. "I just can't do it."

I told him I'd pretend to be Mumma and would call in sick for him, and he could go to the movies instead. We would not tell Mumma or Baba. Each of us was in shock. That night, the vertigo hit so strongly, it would be months before my mind settled to the shift, and I knew:

what was possible or impossible to expect in one's lifetime was so delicate, and so easily undone. Each time I closed my eyes, my mind crowded with headlines and chants from the campaign I had not even realized I'd absorbed. For years we had been told it was just one man, not tied to anything greater. Yet just one man takes a stage and addresses a nation, and the next day my brother is shoved in the hallway of his high school. And just one man tweets a photo likening refugees to a bowl of poisonous Skittles, and that very week Skittles are delivered to my mother.

My brothers and I were born here because our father, at twenty-two, decided to follow a boyhood dream. I wonder if it is because we had no choice in moving here that it is easy for us to criticize. Perhaps for my parents it is far more frightening, when doing so would also be to question their own choices, and to admit to feeling unsafe or unwelcome would also be to wonder if they should have moved here at all. Each question, each doubt, if followed, like pulling a thread that could unravel the foundation they built their lives upon.

That night, when I spoke to each of my brothers, my voice was even, controlled. I was calm, wanting to comfort them. But when I finally called Baba, something in me broke, as though I was still a girl who needed her father, as though I would always be.

"Don't cry," Baba said to me. "Don't let this change you."

I'd spent years wondering why my parents were the way they were. Wondering, after each anti-Muslim interaction, if Baba's reaction was because he had accepted these to be the conditions of his life. But that night, his voice was calm so that I could be free to experience and express my own bewilderment. He was protecting me from his reaction, as Mumma had, in changing how she spoke of the Skittles incident. A protection no different from Mahdi asking me to not speak of what happened to him in the hallways of his high school, and when I pressed him for a reason why he was being so stubborn, he finally said it was so Mumma and Baba would not have to feel bad about deciding to move.

On the phone, Baba continued, "I will not let this change me, Fatima, change how I think. I will not resign my fate to feeling unwelcome here. I will still wave at my neighbors."

Return to Macondo

Susanne Ramírez de Arellano

> Big is the Empire we battle, but bigger is our
> right to be free.
> —Pedro Albizu Campos, leader of the Puerto
> Rican abolitionist movement

The plane glides low above the water and hugs the coast and its silvery ribbon of waves. I look out the window as we make the approach toward Luis Muñoz Marín Airport. The arrival never lessens my anticipation; it's a bittersweet fragrance of mango and old love letters. I spy the rooftops among the mangrove swamps and the palm trees. I always imagine that if I stretch out just a bit—I can lay myself down in their green lushness. I can feel the heat, even inside this air-conditioned steel.

As we land, the passengers, mostly the sons and daughters of Borinquen returning home (and tourists dressed in tropical horror), applaud like mad. It is a loud, euphoric, I-am-finally-fucking-home applause. Like convicts being released after decades in solitary confinement. By the way, Borinquen is our real name.

This euphoria would never happen on a Virgin Atlantic plane

landing at Heathrow, much less arriving in San Salvador in the midst of a civil war.

I am Puerto Rican, born and raised in the Palestine of the Caribbean. It's an island that has been passed around for centuries by colonizing powers, like the dregs of war, or one of those busty Victorian prostitutes on the BBC. You know the ones I mean. The ones you would never see in Downton Abbey having tea with Lady Mary Crawley.

Many people associate Puerto Rico with Macondo, that mythical village imagined by the great Colombian novelist Gabriel García Márquez—a pottage of colonialism, banana plantations, pirates, and revolutions.

My Puerto Rico is one of tastes and smells. I grew up cloistered with coconut kisses, guava and cheese pastries, tuberoses, and my aunts. Do you remember those mango trees just to the left of the front porch of Titi Margot's house? The Reinita birds—"Little Queen" in Spanish—perched daintily on the laden branches, content to sing all day long, as the mangoes fell heavily down to the ground. *Plop, plop, thump.*

I undressed them one by one while keeping a rhythm in my aunt's favorite rocking chair. Slow and quiet—like a mantra—back and forth, peel, back and forth, peel. The fruit was soft to the touch, and the shape of a woman about to give birth. The honeyed smell hung in the air as it was torn open—one bite transformed a mango into your madeleine cake forever, the juice sticking your fingers together like glue.

My other special place to sit was under a tamarind tree, its branches spread out until they almost touched the river below. Sitting under its shade, I would crack the hard, brown skin of the tamarind and bite down—a rush of lemon, apricot, and date.

At four o'clock in the afternoon—"merienda" hour—my aunt,

when she wasn't knitting or reading cowboy novels, would strain coffee in a sock and serve it in a big cup with mallorcas, sweet breads shaped like a snail's shell that tasted of buttery egg, crowned with powdered sugar.

I'd pick them up ever so slowly so as not a grain of sugar was lost. Rice would be steaming on the stove and the beans soaking in salt water in a bowl on the counter, next to a platter of green bananas pickled in onion and garlic.

And at night, a beautiful gold and lapis lazuli statue of the Virgin Mary, with a silver crown on her head, safe from little hands under a crystal dome, stood guard on my nightstand. As long as she was there, all was right with the world. But I still had Yemaya, the African goddess of the sea and the moon, tucked under the bed to ensure more than just divine intervention. You can never have too much luck.

This is home. This is the center of all things, the core of me. An island with a deep-seated pride and a sometimes unimaginable magical reality, made even more phantasmagorical by our colonial history. A place where time flows, stops, and reverses and anything is possible. When I say "anything," I mean *anything*—because in Puerto Rico the dead go to meet their maker dressed as Green Lantern or El Che. They also vote.

And what is the natural soundtrack to all of this? Our national pastime: politics. Endless debates on politics and the island's status: is she or isn't she a colony, a state (of the United States) in waiting, or—that love that dare not speak its name—independent. Round and round, the debates go, in the living room, at family gatherings, on the radio, and on television—morning, noon, and night.

In political terms, Puerto Rico is not a circus, because it can't afford the tent. It sits stewing in a colonial limbo, hanging on a thread, eaten by men with money bags.

But this is not the Puerto Rico you read about in the United States of America. Not at all. We are, in the words of its fearless leader, a shithole nation.

We are billed as lazy, second-class citizens from an island in the middle of a huge ocean. A bit of "This is mine 'cause I won it in a crap shoot with those Spaniards, although what the fuck do I do with it?" Where you go in your imperial splendor (and that hair—it looks like a feral cat on his head) to throw bog rolls at people who have lost everything and where Wall Street is the United Fruit Company of its time.

My Puerto Rico sits in jarring contrast to the one portrayed in *West Side Story* by Rita Moreno, complete with exaggerated accent and swirling skirts, as she sings "America"—while the Sharks dance like mad urban urchins in the background.

Let's stop here for just a bit of history to put it into context. Not much, just enough so you can see how fucking complicated this colonial thing is.

Puerto Rico was force fed four centuries of colonialism courtesy of the Spanish Crown and then shitkicked into modernity by the spit-shined boot of America. First sepias, then red, white, and blue were scratched on our national soul—in an attempt to forever alter the daguerreotype.

It was 1898, and General Nelson Miles of the US Army impaled us with the Stars and Stripes, telling the island's inhabitants that the United States had arrived "to bring you protection, not only to your-selves but to your property, to promote your prosperity...and to give...the advantages and blessings of enlightened civilization." Sure, especially to protect your property. The last time Puerto Rico was free and enlightened, the Taino were in charge.

The Americans called the invasion their Manifest Destiny. Something like a God-given right to take what wasn't theirs. How that differs from imperialism, I will never know.

I never bought into the American Dream. It was a visceral reaction. This dream always had the rank smell of bullshit to me. I didn't believe it, no matter what new toothpaste or amazing trip to the moon they were selling. Maybe it's because I grew up in the shadow of the Cuban Revolution, Vietnam, Cerro Maravilla, and Martin Luther King Jr.—shit that would give you a sharp sense of the ridiculous.

Growing up with all of this around me made me a rebellious and opinionated colonial subject, one who devoured Pablo Neruda and *El Principito* and read the revolutionary writings of the Spanish poet Miguel Hernandez.

As they say at home, "Yo nunca me comí el cuento" (I never ate the story), that fable of the Land of Milk and Honey. It was too sugary and cloying, like the ending of a bad Hollywood movie. I could not see myself as a US citizen—and a lesser one at that. I knew somewhere there was a catch, but it was hard to discern where among all the convoluted explanations and justifications. I carried a US passport, but I was called an immigrant. I couldn't vote in their elections, so therefore I had no representation, yet we fought their wars. Who can forget Al Pacino in *Scent of a Woman*—"Ah, Puerto Ricans, they make the best infantry men."

I was expected to turn myself inside out, forget where I came from, and pledge allegiance to a flag that was not mine. But the Cubans had shown us that we could stand up, that we could be something more than just second class, more than "spics" in a movie, more than "savages" the Americans just had to civilize.

My father thought I was a Communist, referring to me as an air-conditioned socialist. To Don Lorenzo Ramírez de Arellano, the two were the same thing, and America was Mecca.

"Te voy a mandar a cortar caña en Cuba con los Guccis puestos," he would say—I am going to send you to Cuba to cut cane wearing your Guccis. Because being sent to cut cane in Cuba in expensive footwear was the worst thing that could ever happen to a human being, especially a privileged Puerto Rican like me.

But I knew something was rotting in the Potomac. There was something off, discordant, not right. The beginning of my career as a journalist would provide the concrete evidence I was looking for, that truth buried inside the colonial explanations of my ancestors.

I arrived in El Salvador to cover the end of the civil war. Young and inexperienced, Salvador would teach me how to be a journalist. It would teach me fear—the cold sweat trickling down your back kind. Leaden drops of dread in a country that Washington heralded as a democracy.

Walking through the arrival gate at the airport, the heat hit me like a punch in the face. A fine mist wallpapered the air and stuck to everything—my clothes, hair, and face—and went right up my nose, making it hard to breathe.

Looking for my ride, I passed poster after poster of children with crutches or prosthetic limbs, victims of land mines supplied to the Salvadoran military by Uncle Sam. *This way to hell, but watch your step.*

How to describe the savagery that was El Salvador at that time, where the music of the day was gunfire and helicopter blades, slicing through death and heat? Where life was the cheapest I had ever seen it?

We were traveling to cover an exhumation, which would give me my first eyeball contact with brutality in this Central American nation since accepting the job of El Salvador bureau chief for the wire service United Press International. It took place in a town outside the capital San Salvador. The story was this: ten people had been executed in an attack. The FMLN, the Salvadoran guerrillas, claimed that the military had done it, that they had rounded them all up, tied them together, opened fire, and lobbed hand grenades at them. The military claimed that the rebels had done it, in much the same way. The dead had been interred for more than one week. Much like a Fellini film, the exhumation was being done by two of the town drunks, bottles in hand as they dug the bodies out.

Out of the blue, a Francis Ford Coppola–esque vision caught my eye. He was dressed all in black, classic Ray-Bans shading his eyes, unshaven, a lit cigarette dangling from his mouth. His T-shirt read simply NAM. He was sitting on the side of a dirt road next to a makeshift bodega, a case of beer by his feet. Shouting and spraying spittle into a walkie-talkie, he directed the chopper traffic that was ferrying Salvadoran soldiers attacking a town close by. The dead and the soon to be dead.

I asked what he thought of the war. He smiled.

In a voice best suited to Lieutenant Colonel Bill Kilgore, he said: "Ah, best little war in town."

I half expected him to follow it up with "You smell that? Napalm, son. Nothing in the world smells like that." The gringos fucking love that smell. It validates them.

Fresh from their Vietnam acid trip, the United States felt it had the right to intervene in El Salvador. It financed and orchestrated the destruction of its civilian population, arming a right-wing government in its fight against Marxist guerrillas—to torch what it saw as a Communist contagion in the region. (God forbid, no more Cubas, no more Fidel Castros.)

More than 75,000 civilians died at the hands of government forces during twelve years of war, one fought via a diplomacy by death squads. The Americans taught the Salvadoran army how to kill like the Vietcong.

Today, despite the carnage, not much has changed in El Salvador. It is still one of the most homicidal places on earth. In 2015, 324,000 Salvadorans were displaced by crime and violence. Most Americans couldn't find El Salvador on a map and couldn't care less that Washington is the reason Salvadorans are fleeing to the United States in the first place. These Salvadorans are mostly women and children who risk everything to escape death at the hands of violent "maras"—modern-day death squads, born out of that little guerra and trained on the streets of Los Angeles that now visit terror on their own people.

Immigration is retribution; it's payback for the killing fields of Washington. But the legacy of that little war is now small children held in cages in detention centers in Texas. The separation of families. As Trump moves to end immigration protection and build a wall to keep out what Uncle Sam wrought, 200,000 Salvadorans may be forced to leave the United States.

After my work in El Salvador, I got the Holy Grail, an opportunity to work with a US network, one of the most powerful and influential at the time. They hired me straight after my stint at the little war; they said they loved my work in El Salvador.

I had to sign a bunch of papers, tick a number of boxes (you know how Americans love boxes). There was one for African American, another for White, yet another for Hispanic, and then there was Other. Shit. I was Puerto Rican, so that was Hispanic; I was White, so that was not Hispanic—and Other? No, I didn't think I was Other—although my background would suggest otherwise.

"What do I tick?" I asked the lovely man who was to be my boss.

"Oh, that's easy," he said with a crooked smile. "You are a twofer. You just sign here and here."

A twofer, I thought. What the fuck is that—a disease? Or does this shit come with magical powers?

"No, you tick Hispanic and then Female. We get two for one in you—a real complete package."

Bloody fantastic, the colonial schizophrenia of Macondo with which I grew up followed me everywhere. Thanks, García Márquez.

A colony sells its soul slowly, in increments, over time. Our past is relegated to oblivion, and we're told (in my case, by the nuns) that the island had no history. But I never believed what the nuns taught. How could anyone take gospel from women dressed as penguins in the Caribbean sun?

Recently, Hurricane Maria demonstrated what the US thinks of Puerto Rico. Around 3,000 people died as a result of this catastrophic event—an American tragedy, supposedly.

As the late, great Anthony Bourdain wrote, "It has been six weeks since the hurricane, and 70 percent of Puerto Rico's 3.4 million American citizens are still without power. About 25 percent are without fresh drinking water—people are drinking from streams and other contaminated sources. They are burning their dead. This is, of course, unthinkable. And grotesque. It is also true."*

But did the White House give a shit? Not a toss. Why? Because Puerto Rico is a colony and its citizens are mostly brown people—the "mass of mongrels...hostile to Christianity," in the words of a US senator at the time of the conquest, those invisible men and women of Ralph Ellison.

Again, Bourdain (a Good Gringo in my book) wrote with eloquence and a keen understanding: "How American is Puerto Rico? How American do they want to be?

"And how does the rest of America feel about Puerto Rico? How much responsibility are Americans willing to take for their aspirations, their well-being, their basic rights as humans, as citizens? The answer to that last question appears to be: not much."**

Even before Maria, we were in the crapper. Puerto Rico was already $73 billion in debt and bankrupt. Hurricane Maria made the situation worse. A record number of people have since left the island. Puerto Rico, once the US showcase in the Caribbean, is now a colonial embarrassment.

After Maria, all the pain and humiliation that cut a deep groove through the years molded into anger with a purpose, a sharper focus. It was a coconut of anger, designed to split open and reveal the truth when you threw it to the ground.

Colonialism has fucked us up. It feels like forced prostitution, a gulag of the soul. We're left confused, like we landed in an

---

* Anthony Bourdain, "Bourdain's Field Notes: Puerto Rico," November 1, 2017, https://explorepartsunknown.com/puerto-rico/bourdains-field-notes-puerto-rico.

** Ibid.

alternate universe where we're not us but what someone else determined we are.

And this is exactly why I hate *West Side Story*, and in particular the song "America," in which the refrain, sung by Anita (played by Rita Moreno in dark makeup and with a cartoonish accent that Moreno later said made no sense at all), insists that Puerto Rico is an island that should sink into the ocean, and that we would all "like to be in America" because "everything is free in America."

My riposte? The truth, as sung by Bernardo (played by Greek American George Chakiris, also in brownface): "Life can be bright in America, if you can fight in America, if you are white in America." Now, that is more like the reality as it stands today.

America is now a place, as the Rufus Wainwright song goes, that has already been burnt down, a place that has already been disgraced. The world, who loved you well, is now tired of you, America.

But for Puerto Ricans who have an opinion and demand a say in their future, this is the Golden Ticket. For it seems that at this juncture the United States no longer needs the adornments of a colony. In fact, Puerto Rico, waterlogged, broke, and in the dark, is now seen by the White House as fit for a fire sale.

This is the time and place where it all should end. We must admit to ourselves—once and for all—that we are the masters of our own destiny. "Redemption," "freedom" . . . these are words you can taste, as sweet as a mango. It is when people lose everything that they truly know their worth.

Above all, we are an island nation with a desire to be free of this colonial bullshit. Oh, that I live to see our self-determination. And may we always remain a bit like Macondo.

244 Million

Mona Chalabi

Get a pair of scissors and cut out the page on the right. The piece of paper you're holding now represents all 244 million migrants in the world today.*

Let's find out more about them.

1. Fold the piece of paper in half along the middle line. Now you can see 51 percent of the paper. That represents the 51 percent of all international migrants that end up in high-income countries that are part of the Organisation for Economic Co-operation and Development. The rest move to other rich countries that aren't part of that club (20 percent), middle-income countries (another 25 percent), or low-income countries (4 percent).

2. Unfold the piece of paper, and fold the two top corners inward along the outermost lines. Now you can see about 78 percent of the paper. That represents the percentage of all migrants that are age twenty-five and older.

3. Fold the paper inward again along the next lines. Now you can see about 54 percent of the paper. Imagine that just 54 percent of those migrants send money back home. That would equal $309,218,110,000 (if that's hard to read, the number is $309 billion). People working abroad often send money to their friends and families, but up to 20 percent of their hard-earned cash can vanish in transfer fees charged by big companies.

4. Fold the paper away from you along the middle and then fold it along the last lines. Now you can see about 11 percent of the paper. Out of everyone who has migrated, 12 percent, about 30 million, are refugees or stateless people.**

Now you have an airplane. How far can you fly?

---

* All of these statistics are from the United Nations Population Fund's 2015 data. Even more people would migrate if they could.

** We know that those two groups overlap, but there aren't good, up-to-date statistics on how many refugees are stateless and how many stateless people are refugees.

How to Center Your Own Story

Jade Chang

A month after my novel was published, we lost the election. I was in the midst of a book tour when it happened, spending an extra day in Austin before driving to a bookstore in Dallas. I'd made an early departure from an election viewing party the previous night and woke up on a borrowed futon to a gray and drizzly sky, scared that the world had changed.

Was everything going to be different? Was this the beginning of the end? Were we about to enter a time of internment camps and exclusion acts and even more racist policing? All fall I'd felt a heaving, an unraveling at the edges, an impending, upending *something,* and now it really seemed like the worst would actually happen.

I packed up and got into my rental car, maps prepped for the three-hour drive. On the road, everything felt ominous. Was the guy in that truck keeping pace with me on purpose? What about the one who zoomed past, honking? I sped into the fast lane, ready to outrun them all, when I realized that I didn't have enough gas to get to Dallas. I slid back across the highway, gunning for the next exit. Oh great. Waco. A town that exists in the American imagination as a land of extremist white supremacists. Unfair? Probably. At least they'd definitely have a gas station.

I pulled into the first one, relieved that no one else was there. I popped open the lid, unscrewed the gas cap, and tried to pay at the pump.

CARD UNREADABLE. Dammit. I'd have to go inside.

Across the lot, the store gleamed bright and new and frightening. Anyone could be in there. And maybe now they'd feel limitless, emboldened, like they could do anything to me. But I couldn't get to Dallas without gas, so I swallowed that unfamiliar fear, pushed open the door, and stepped into the freezing-cold sugar-and-coffee smell that marks every American convenience store.

You know that moment, early in a relationship, when you both realize that you actually like each other? And you smile and smile at each other because you both feel seen and loved and unaccountably relieved? That's what happened when I stepped into the store. I looked at the man behind the counter and he looked at me with the same worried eyes, and in our shared relief we both smiled at each other so hard that you'd swear we were soul mates.

"Hi," he said. "Crazy day! Strange day! Nice to see you!"

I nodded more vigorously than I'd ever nodded before, and we smiled again.

Phew! our eyes said. *It's you!*

Do I even need to tell you that we were both brownish? We were.

I paid for my gas and headed toward the door, waving, feeling warm and relieved. But as I walked back out into the strange gray world, as I jammed the pump into my rented car and watched the numbers tick forward, my anger rose too. Why *should* I feel so relieved? Our laws hadn't changed, the structure of our republic hadn't changed, our president was still black. Yes, there were people who might feel more license to attack or discount me, but they had always existed, had always acted, and always would. I drove, mad at my own fear, at the way it threw me off-kilter and made America into someone else's country.

I'd written an entire novel that insisted on the centrality of my characters to the story of America. A novel that refused to engage with the idea of the immigrant or person of color as an outsider. The family at the heart of my book is not immune from failures of confidence, but all of the family members are point-of-view characters in their own lives. Their understanding of their place in the world is not based on someone else's definition. They never doubt the legitimacy of their own gaze. They center their own stories. None of this was an accident. Art is always a political act.

So it was confusing that I could create an entire fictional world that did not waver from that stance yet still have difficulty maintaining it for myself in this real and imperfect world.

When my editor first told me the publication date for *The Wangs vs. the World* I worried that it would be hard to launch a book in the weeks leading up to a presidential election. Friends reassured me, insisting that the race would already be virtually decided by then, that news outlets would be hungry for something else to talk about.

We all know what happened instead. But it turned out that being on a book tour in the days after November 8 was an unexpected benediction. Everyone I encountered was raw and open and eager to talk, eager to gather together and question their assumptions about the country. The topsy-turvy uncertainty of the 2008 financial crash had initially pushed me to write this novel, and now I was talking about it in another upside-down era. A decade ago the sense that anything could happen had been exciting. Now it was frightening. But maybe that fear was a useful reminder to stay vigilant.

There's a sign that's been popping up at recent protests: IF HILLARY HAD WON, WE'D ALL BE AT BRUNCH RIGHT NOW. I mean, sure. Who wouldn't almost always rather be eating waffles? (Except me. I hate brunch, but that's a topic for another protest.) But there's an uncomfortable truth that hides behind the blithe jokiness of the sign: who laughs easily at it and who doesn't. For the people choosing to make and carry those signs, that *is* their truth. They're centering hard. And for those who know they're not part of a "we" for whom a Hillary win would have meant a problem-free life, it reads as willful cluelessness. Do I think that the people carrying these signs should be condemned? I don't really care. For me, this misguided brunch statement is more a reminder to make your own sign, and raise it high.

Whether or not you're a writer, centering your own story is a vital act. There's a widely accepted concept in psychology called narrative theory, which is essentially the idea that storytelling is so basic to humans that we have to be able to tell a coherent story of our own lives in order to form a healthy sense of self. No one else can tell that story for us or to us.

And if you do happen to be a writer or an artist or a filmmaker or really anyone who puts a story out into the world in these chaotic days, centering that story is a claiming of power. So how do you stand easy in that power? I don't think there's ever a final, definitive answer to that question. But here are a few shifts in thinking that have helped me.

STEP 1: ALWAYS REMEMBER THIS—JOY IS A REBELLION.

Eventually I made it to that bookstore in Dallas, where I very nearly ended up doing the proverbial reading for a single attendee. But later that week, the weirdest thing: a literary panel that felt electric. The room pulsed with the energy of a hundred people searching for an answer or a joke or a hand to hold, for a reason to be together in that place, in that moment. Although my fellow authors—storyteller Tara Clancy and comedian Negin Farsad—were amazing, I wasn't vain enough to think the power in the room was because of us. No, it was because everyone who had hoped for a different outcome to the election was flailing, and it felt better to flail among others. Also helpful was the panel's prophetic title, "If We're Not Laughing, We're Crying."

One of the strange gifts of a public panel is that sometimes, when you have to answer a question immediately and in front of an audience, you find yourself articulating something you've thought around the edges of but haven't yet managed to pinpoint. On that day it became clear that the first step to centering your own story is the decision to live unapologetically. Because when you are daily faced with reminders that there are people in public office who want to negate your existence, living unapologetically is an act of defiance. It's not everything. It's not a solution. But it's a completely worthwhile act. And if living unapologetically is a rebellion, then joy itself is a rebellion.

Because here's the best thing: joy scares people. It scares people because it's rooted in desire. And desire is about knowing yourself. Here's the other thing that's rooted in desire: anger. Anger is not necessarily corrosive. Anger can be glorious, a purifying flame that burns away comfortable lies and acts as an engine of change. Anger is also a freeing of desire.

The idea of centering your own story can seem nebulous. What is your story, anyway? My focus is always on the two poles of our selves, joy and anger. There are so many ways to figure out who you really are. One of the best is to be honest with yourself about what you really want. When you are, you will know and own your joy and your anger.

STEP 2: LET THE SPECIFIC BECOME THE UNIVERSAL.

"*I* liked it; I'm just not sure that *other* people will get it."

Ah, the familiar refrain of gatekeepers everywhere, operating on the fear/hope/conviction that there is only one form of universal story and anyone who's not like them can't possibly be telling it. Really, though, the more specific a moment is, the more it becomes relatable to a wide range of people.

The strange paradox of America is that everyone wants to be an outsider. It's one of our favorite myths about ourselves, along with the American Dream and American ingenuity and, probably, some still-messed-up version of manifest destiny. Maybe it's a deep-seated Christ complex—the outsider as savior, the outsider as the one who changes the world. But if everyone's an outsider, then there is no inside, there is no mainstream. There is no ordinary. No normal. We are all a collection of highly specific histories.

I don't believe in characters that are "just like any other person, except that they happen to be Chinese!" White characters don't "just happen" to be white. Their whiteness may be unexamined, but they are purposefully white. Each one comes from a specific place and has a specific family experience. We are born in specificity.

If a movie needs to have two women with names talking to each other about anything other than men in order to pass the Bechdel test, you'd think that a POC version would be two people of color with names talking to each other about anything other than race, but I disagree. What I'd propose instead is two people of color with names actually talking to each other *about* race or culture in a way that is wholly for themselves, that does not contain an apology or an explanation for anyone else's benefit. That's what we want more of. That's what will resonate. And, yeah, call it the Chang test.

Shows like *Insecure* and *Atlanta* have built their audiences on those moments. So does the new show *Vida,* about two Latinx sisters who return to a Boyle Heights struggling with gentrification.

These shows reflect the real-life conversations we have every day. Recently, I was struck by an episode of the surprisingly heartfelt reboot of *Queer Eye for the Straight Guy.* At one point the subject, Neal, who is Indian, stands in front of his dowry suitcase with Tan France, the show's fashion expert, who is Pakistani and Muslim. The two of them discuss the riches in the suitcase jokingly, with full knowledge of what it means to their families, and as the audience, we feel the subtext of that moment, even if we don't come from a country with widespread modern-day dowry practices. It was exciting to see on a show that has such mainstream aspirations. Immediately, though, Tan appears in a talking-head intercut to explain things. (Their chances of passing the Chang test ruined!) I like imagining this dialogue between the two of them in a movie or TV show, without commentary, something frivolous and fun and so very universal.

STEP 3: KNOW THIS—YOU ARE NOT A SUPPLICANT.

> We are beginning to understand that the world
> is always being made fresh and never finished;
> that activism can be the journey rather than the
> arrival.
>
> —Grace Lee Boggs

Consciously and unconsciously, with both the very best and the very worst of intentions, people will try to make you feel like a supplicant. Like your place in the world is conditional, contingent on your willingness to perform an accepted role or dole out gift bags of gratitude. They're wrong. And sometimes remembering that, and reminding them of that, is activism enough.

A month after the election, I did an interview with a literary magazine. It was a written Q&A, and the last question was, in part, "Is America done with us?" The only response I could give: "How can America be done with us when we are America?"

At another event around that same time, a woman about my age, white, dressed like the coolest ceramics teacher at your 1970s high school, waited until the last book was signed and pulled me aside, a look of concern on her face. "I wanted to ask you something," she said. "Or I guess I wanted to express some solidarity. It must be so difficult right now to write and talk to people when you're just an outsider. But I want you to know that I'm glad you're here." There's an easy answer to all of that, which is just "Thank you. I'm happy to be here." That's what you say when you don't want to make the nice people feel bad for being nice to you, and then you go home and dissect the moment with all of your friends. But it wasn't niceness. It was a subtle assertion of power, and I'm tired of pretending that I don't see those. I thanked her for coming, and for buying a book, and then I suggested that, just for herself, she think about why she used the phrase "just an outsider."

There's an essay by Saeed Jones called "Portrait of the Artist as an Ungrateful Black Writer" that has been on my mind since it first came out in 2015. In it Saeed writes about the nauseating balance between feeling desperately grateful to be allowed into the proverbial room and feeling resentful that his gratefulness is expected. He also references James Baldwin's observation, "I walk into a room and everyone there is terribly proud of himself because I managed to get to the room."

Here's the thing. I don't feel like a grateful first-generation immigrant. I don't feel like I owe my existence to any person or institution's beneficence. I don't feel conditional; I feel like a fact.

STEP 4: ~~NEVER COMPLAIN.~~ NEVER EXPLAIN.

There are three main kinds of questions that people ask at a reading or an interview.

The first is purely informational: "How did you get an agent?" "What was it like working with an editor?" "What kind of research did you do?"

The second is to establish a connection: "My family lost their fortune too! Did yours?" "I had a terrible, sexy boyfriend that I couldn't shake for ages too! Did you?"

And the third is to reclaim power.

At a recent event a woman turned to me and said, "Well. I have a question about your book."

"Yes?"

"Why wasn't it set in San Marino?"

She smiled at me, waiting.

For a moment I was completely confused. I mean, okay, why *wasn't* it set in San Marino? Or Anchorage or Long Beach or Saint Louis? I don't know. Because I wanted to set it in Bel-Air? And then I realized what she was trying to signal.

"Oh," I said, "you mean because there are so many Chinese people in San Marino?"

"Yes! Exactly! That's where all the wealthy Chinese people are! They're not in Beverly Hills. I lived in Santa Monica. I know!"

"And yet that's where my characters live. In Bel-Air."

"But they really should be in San Marino, shouldn't they?"

One family must be all families. This Chinese family that I literally made up in my mind cannot behave in a way that disrupts her understanding of the universe. She lives in places like Santa Monica and Beverly Hills. They do not.

It's not always literary redlining. I've also been asked, repeatedly, to explain whether I am more Chinese or more American. When I've sidestepped the question, I've been presented with possible percentage distributions. "Like, do you feel fifty-fifty? Or more forty-sixty? Probably sixty percent American, forty percent Chinese, right?"

Justifying the existence of my characters does not interest me as a project. Justifying my own existence interests me even less. Here's my calculus: the more secure someone is in their own personhood, the less likely they are to ask me to define mine. Identifying these insistent requests for explanations and refusing to engage with the ones that are more about the questioner's need to preserve their own worldview is a big step toward centering your own story.

I've also been asked to give my opinion on how each of my characters does or does not conform to Asian stereotypes. I'm not interested in trotting out stereotypes when I've done so much work to dive into specifics, but sometimes even an outright refusal isn't enough. There was one particularly dogged questioner who kept coming back to the topic until I finally said that I would comment if she would tell me exactly what stereotypes she wanted me to comment on. "Oh no," she said, shocked. "I can't do that! *You* have to name them. *I* can't name them. That would be racist." I suggested that trying to force me to name and explain demeaning stereotypes was in itself a racist act. And then, yes, she cried.

Naming things really makes a difference. I thought about microaggressions all the time before I had a name for the phenomenon. Once I did, once they could be reliably tagged, they also felt like something that could be dealt with effectively. "Mansplaining." "Rape culture." All of those terms help clarify the intention of an act or a situation, and that's the kind of explaining I can get behind. But refusing to name a thing carries its own form of power.

STEP 5: CREATE YOUR OWN CURRENCY.

There's a form of currency from immigrants and people of color that publishers, producers, and audiences have long recognized: pain. Whether it's the larger pain of being a refugee or an enslaved person, or the smaller-scale pain of not fitting in, for a long time these were the only stories that got told. Or, rather, the only stories that got sold. Things are slowly changing. We're creating new forms of currency in which our joy is as valuable as our suffering.

Last week I was at a gathering of women, a sort of talking circle put together by Anjulie, a songwriter friend. There were more than a dozen of us, almost all working in entertainment, and the discussion that day focused mostly on the politics of getting paid.

Near the end of the afternoon another songwriter, Eden xo Malakouti, told us that she'd recently been given a piece of advice by a well-known actress: "When you come into an industry and you bring something new and fresh, when you bring a different point of view, people will pick you up and consume you like a ripe, succulent, juicy piece of fruit. They'll just suck everything out of you. They'll lick up every drop, and then they'll think they're done with you. They'll try to crumple you up and discard you like a peel and core. But what they don't know, what they don't know and what you have to remember, is that you're not the fruit... you're the tree." You're the tree! It's an excellent philosophy for life.

During those right-after-the-election days, I was still in New York and was asked to go on a radio show to address the question "In this new, post-election reality, has the role of the novel, and the novelist, changed?" The other guests were Alexander Chee and Imbolo Mbue, both novelists I had already met and loved. The host asked us how we handled writing and publishing "if you do not fit into the mainstream, especially in these post-election times." Alexander replied that as a gay, Korean American writer he had no literary forebears and had never fit into the mainstream. From the beginning, he said, "I had to become the thing I was looking for." He created his own currency, and finally, finally, people who see *him* as a literary forebear are arriving to spend it.

After that show Alexander and I went to lunch at a fancy pub around the corner. We splashed out a bit—champagne and oysters. I'd been on the road for weeks, eating confusing meals, and every fizzy sip of champagne exploded in my head like the best little fireworks. We talked about luck in all its different forms, and as we talked the platter of oysters came, nestled in crushed ice, each one plump in its shell. And then, because fact is always stranger than fiction, he dressed one, tipped it into his mouth, chewed gently, then, with a sure smile, reached between his lips and pulled out a pearl.

All I'm saying is this: Be the star of your own life.

Acknowledgements

Chimene:

Thanks to Bea Galilee, Nika Lineva, and Yemisi Brookes for your endless loving support. Thank you to Natalie Matos for always keeping the dialogue going. To Aydin Canel for reminding me always of the Turk that I am. Thank you to Priya Minhas for your fearless cheerleading and hard work. For Cara Barry and Jessica Fagin, for always. To Helen Woodfield, Rysz Lewandowski, Leanne Stelmaszczyk, Edith Bergfors, Vanessa Farinha, Mark Hedden, Emilie Peyre Smith, Louis Mustill, and Arron Smith for your constant presence throughout my life. To Rosie Knight, Musa Okwonga, and Inua Ellams. To Sabrina Mahfouz and Anthony Anaxagorou. To Gavin James Bower, Niven Govinden, Stuart Evers, Lisa Baker, Suze Azzopardi, and Solly. To the British *Good Immigrant* Family. To Zerrin and Recep Şehitoğlu for absolutely everything. To the Turkish Cypriot community here, there, and everywhere. To Nikesh for being family.

Nikesh:

I never imagined the original *Good Immigrant* book would have the impact it did, and so I am indebted to all the original contributors and people who supported our crowdfunding campaign, who wrote about, tweeted about, and talked about the book. I am indebted to everyone who trolled their racist uncle with a copy on his birthday. Thank you to all contributors and guest editors of *The Good Journal,* to Niki, Salma, and Arzu at The Good Literary Agency, and to everyone at Unbound. Thank you to Katie, Sunnie, and Coco. To my family and to Mimi and Bobby. Thank you to Nii and Niven and Salena for starting me off, and to my family—Chimene, Inua, Rosie, and Musa—for keeping me going. And to my sisters, Nishma, Leena, Krupa, Kavita, Priya, Reshma, Meera, Mira, Amee, Raksha, and Shalini.

Save libraries.

I miss you, Mum, so very much. Every single day.

Both:

Thank you to every single one of our contributors for your hard work, honesty, and brilliant essays. This book exists because of you. Thank you.

Thanks to Julia Kingsford, everyone at Unbound, and Darren, Daniel, Sarah, Ming, Vera, Salena, Sabrina, L, Leo, Musa, Inua, Riz, Vinay, Bim, Reni, Coco, Kieran, Nish, and Himesh for being with this project from the start.

Thank you to Sharmaine Lovegrove at Dialogue Books and Jean Garnett (Little, Brown US) for believing in us and giving us a platform to carry on the conversation, and for being careful and generous editors. Thank you to Karen Landry and Alexandra Hoopes, and everyone at Little, Brown US and Little, Brown UK. Thank you to Jane Brodie for translating Adrian and Sebastian's piece and to Susanne Ramírez de Arellano for translation support. Thank you to Bumble Ward. Thank you to Hari Kondabolu.

Thank you to *Catapult,* who originally published Porochista's piece; to *Racked,* who originally published Jenny's piece; and to *Medium,* who originally published Teju's piece.

Thank you to immigrants, children of immigrants, relatives of immigrants, friends of immigrants, employers of immigrants, and anyone who made a journey from there to here and opened the world up in the process. This is for you.

About the Authors

Fatimah Asghar is the creator of the Emmy-nominated web series *Brown Girls*, now in development for HBO. She is the author of *If They Come for Us* (One World/Random House, 2018) and a recipient of a 2017 Ruth Lilly and Dorothy Sargent Rosenberg Poetry Fellowship. In 2017 she was listed on the Forbes 30 Under 30 list.

Mona Chalabi is a journalist who translates data into written pieces, illustrations, audio, and film. She and her work have appeared in the *Guardian*, the *New York Times*, and *FiveThirtyEight*, as well as on shows from the BBC (*Is Britain Racist?*), National Geographic (Neil deGrasse Tyson's *Star Talk*), and Netflix (*The Fix*). She is one-half of the team that created the Emmy-nominated video series *Vagina Dispatches*, and her illustrations, which depict everything from immigrant detention to balding patterns, have been commended by the Royal Statistical Society. She's a second-generation UK immigrant and a first-generation US immigrant.

Jade Chang is the author of *The Wangs vs. the World* (Houghton Mifflin Harcourt, 2016), which has been named a *New York Times* Editors' Choice as well as a Best Book of the Year by Amazon, BuzzFeed, *Elle*, and NPR, and was awarded the VCU Cabell First Novelist prize. The novel will be published in twelve countries, and NPR said this: "Her book is unrelentingly fun, but it is also raw and profane—a story of fierce pride, fierce anger, and even fiercer love."

Alexander Chee is the bestselling author of the novels *Edinburgh* and *The Queen of the Night,* and the essay collection *How to Write an Auto-biographical Novel.* His essays and stories have appeared in the *New York Times Book Review, T Magazine, Tin House, Guernica,* and *Best American Essays 2016,* among others. He is an associate professor of English and creative writing at Dartmouth College.

Teju Cole is a novelist, essayist, and photographer. He has been honored with the PEN/Hemingway Award, the Windham-Campbell Prize from Yale University, the Internationaler Literaturpreis, the Rosenthal Family Foundation Award of the American Academy of Arts and Letters, and a Guggenheim Fellowship, among others. His most recent book is *Blind Spot.*

Yann Demange is a director and producer known for his award-winning films *'71* and *White Boy Rick,* as well as the acclaimed television series *Dead Set* and *Top Boy.* He won Best Director at the British Independent Film Awards for *'71,* which was nominated by BAFTA for Outstanding Debut. He has directed commercials for Nike and music videos for Plan B, among others.

Nicole Dennis-Benn is a Lambda Literary Award winner and a finalist for the 2016 John Leonard Prize National Book Critics Circle Award, the 2016 Center for Fiction First Novel Prize, and the 2017 Young Lions Fiction Award for her debut novel, *Here Comes the Sun*— a *New York Times* Notable Book of the Year and an NPR, Amazon, and Barnes & Noble Best Book of 2016. She's a recipient of the New York Foundation for the Arts Artist Fellowship for her forthcoming novel, *PATSY.* Her work has appeared in the *New York Times, Elle,*

Electric Literature, Ebony, and the *Feminist Wire.* She was born and raised in Kingston, Jamaica, and lives with her wife in Brooklyn, New York.

Jean Hannah Edelstein is a Brooklyn-based writer and the author of *This Really Isn't About You,* a memoir, published by Picador UK in 2017.

Dani Fernandez spent much of her youth bouncing between Southern California and Texas, and her after-school hours writing nerdy fan fiction. She has written on shows for New Form, Fullscreen, Epic Meal Time, and various humor sites and has hosted for channels including Nerdist, Skybound, HowStuffWorks, Mental Floss, Geek & Sundry, and Hyper RPG. She has performed at The Comedy Store's *Roast Battle, The Fictional Roast* at Meltdown, *Tournament of Nerds* at the Upright Citizens Brigade, and Cracked.com Live. She has been a panelist at San Diego Comic Con, LA Comic Con, and WonderCon, discussing the importance of Latinx representation in comic books and film.

Rahawa Haile is an Eritrean American writer. *In Open Country,* her memoir about thru-hiking the Appalachian Trail, explores what it means to move through America and the world as a black woman (forthcoming from Harper). Find her on Twitter @RahawaHaile.

Maeve Higgins is a writer and comedian who has performed all over the world, including in her native Ireland, Melbourne, and Erbil. Now based in New York, she cohosts Neil deGrasse Tyson's *Star Talk* on National Geographic and is a contributing writer for the *New York Times.* Her latest collection of essays, titled *Maeve in America,* was published by Penguin in 2018.

Porochista Khakpour was born in Tehran and raised in the Los Angeles area. She is the author of *Sons and Other Flammable Objects* (a *New York Times* Editors' Choice); *The Last Illusion* (a 2014 Best Book of the Year, according to NPR, Kirkus, BuzzFeed, *Electric Literature*, and many more); and *Sick: A Memoir*. Among her many fellowships is a National Endowment for the Arts award. Her nonfiction has appeared in the *New York Times*, the *Los Angeles Times*, *Elle*, *Slate*, *Salon*, and *Bookforum*, among other publications. She lives in Harlem, New York City.

Krutika Mallikarjuna is a features editor and entertainment journalist who writes at the intersection of pop culture and identity. You can find her bylines at BuzzFeed, *Teen Vogue*, Shondaland, *TV Guide*, and Inverse. Her best writing, however, is undoubtedly found in drunk live-tweet form @krutika.

Priya Minhas is a writer and producer from London. Her writing explores South Asian immigrant identity and how it intersects with pop culture and womanhood. It has been featured in BuzzFeed, *Burnt Roti*, and *Kajal Magazine*, among others. She is currently based in New York, where she produces original content at Vevo and is working on her first collection of essays.

Fatima Farheen Mirza is the author of *A Place for Us*. She is a graduate of the Iowa Writers' Workshop, where she was a Teaching-Writing Fellow and a recipient of a MacDowell Colony fellowship and the Michener-Copernicus Fellowship.

Chigozie Obioma was born in Akure, Nigeria. His debut novel, *The Fishermen,* won the 2016 NAACP Image Award and was a finalist for the Man Booker Prize. His work has been translated into more than twenty-six languages and adapted for the stage. He currently teaches literature and creative writing at the University of Nebraska–Lincoln. His second novel, *An Orchestra of Minorities,* will be published in spring 2019 by Little, Brown and Company.

Daniel José Older is the *New York Times* bestselling author of the middle-grade historical fantasy series *Dactyl Hill Squad,* the *Bone Street Rumba* urban fantasy series, *Star Wars: Last Shot,* and the award-winning young-adult series *The Shadowshaper Cypher,* which won the International Latino Book Award and was shortlisted for the Kirkus Prize in Young Readers' Literature, the Andre Norton Award, the Locus Award, and the Mythopoeic Award, and named one of *Esquire*'s 80 Books Every Person Should Read.

Walé Oyéjidé, Esq., is a writer, designer, musician, and lawyer who combats bias with creative storytelling. As the founder of the brand Ikiré Jones, he employs fashion design as a vehicle to celebrate the perspectives of immigrants and other marginalized populations. Walé is a TEDGlobal Fellow, and he delivered a TED Talk about the utility of design as a subversive weapon against discrimination. His work appeared in the motion picture *Black Panther* and has been exhibited in group museum shows across the globe. He has also released a number of hip-hop/afrobeat albums as a producer and vocalist.

Susanne Ramírez de Arellano is an international journalist, a former news director for Univision Puerto Rico, and a former senior regional editor for Latin America for Associated Press Television who has expanded into other areas, including digital and transmedia storytelling. Ramírez de Arellano writes and comments on cultural, political, and gender issues with an expertise in Puerto Rico. She is a regular contributor to the *Guardian,* NBC Latino, Latino USA, Latino Rebels, and El Nuevo Día Puerto Rico, among other outlets.

Tejal Rao was born in London to parents from East Africa and India. She lives in New York and works as a reporter at the *New York Times* and a columnist at the *New York Times Magazine.* She was previously a restaurant critic and won the James Beard Foundation Award for restaurant criticism in 2013 and 2016.

Jim St. Germain is a public speaker, criminal justice advocate, and the cofounder of Preparing Leaders of Tomorrow, Inc. (PLOT), a nonprofit organization that provides mentoring to at-risk and formerly incarcerated youth. Jim has an associate degree in human services from the Borough of Manhattan Community College and a bachelor of arts degree in political science from John Jay College of Criminal Justice. He is on the board of the National Juvenile Defender Center and was appointed by President Barack Obama to the Coordinating Council on Juvenile Justice and Delinquency Prevention. He is the author of the award-winning memoir *A Stone of Hope* and a dedicated father to his son, Caleb.

Chimene Suleyman is a writer from London. She has written and spoken on race and identity for such publications as the *Guardian,* the

Independent, the *Pool,* the *Debrief,* the BBC, and many more. Her debut poetry collection, *Outside Looking On,* was a *Guardian* Best Book of 2014. She is an original contributor to *The Good Immigrant* (UK edition, 2016). She currently lives in New York.

Basim Usmani is a professional musician and freelance writer. His band, the Kominas, has been touring and releasing albums for ten years, and his writing has been featured in the *New York Times,* the *Guardian,* the *Boston Globe,* and BuzzFeed. Follow him and his band at @therealkominas and @basiroti on Twitter.

Adrián Villar Rojas is an internationally exhibited artist. He is the recipient of numerous awards, including the Sharjah Biennial Prize, the Zurich Art Prize, and the 9th Benesse Prize in the 54th Venice Biennale. He has had solo exhibitions at MOCA Los Angeles, the Metropolitan Museum of Art, and elsewhere. His group exhibitions have been at the 12th and 14th Istanbul Biennial, dOCUMENTA (13) in Kassel and Kabul (2012), and Argentina's National Pavilion at the 54th Venice Biennale, among other places. His 2013 film, *Lo Que el Fuego Me Trajo (What Fire Has Brought to Me),* was screened at the Locarno International Film Festival, and his 2017 film trilogy, *The Theater of Disappearance,* was screened at the 67th Berlin International Film Festival.

Sebastián Villar Rojas is a poet, writer, playwright, and theater director. He studied political science at the National University of Rosario and has a diploma in playwriting from the University of Buenos Aires. He has written, directed, and produced plays and published novels, short stories, poems, and essays in books, anthologies, magazines, and fanzines, winning local and national awards and scholarships. He has been collaborating with Adrián Villar Rojas since childhood.

Jenny Zhang is the author of the poetry collection *Dear Jenny, We Are All Find* and the story collection *Sour Heart,* which won the PEN/ Robert W. Bingham Prize and the *Los Angeles Times* Art Seidenbaum Award and was a finalist for the New York Public Library's Young Lions Fiction Award.

Bringing a book from manuscript to what you are reading is a team effort.

Dialogue Books would like to thank everyone at Little, Brown who helped to publish *The Good Immigrant USA* in the UK.

Editorial
Sharmaine Lovegrove
Simon Osunsade
Thalia Proctor

Contracts
Stephanie Cockburn

Sales
Sara Talbot
Rachael Hum
Viki Cheung
Barbara Ronan
Sinead White

Design
Helen Bergh
Nico Taylor

Production
Nick Ross
Narges Nojoumi
Mike Young

Publicity
Millie Seaward
Nazia Khatun

Marketing
Jonny Keyworth

Audio
Sarah Shrubb
Louise Newton